The Fall of Rome

The Fall of Rome

The Fall of the Roman Empire
Book Two

Nick Holmes

Puttenham
Press

Published by Puttenham Press Ltd
Copyright © 2023 Nick Holmes

ISBN 978-1-7397865-2-6

British Library Cataloguing in Publication Data.
A catalogue record for this book is available from the British Library.

Typeset in the United Kingdom by Indie-Go
https://www.indie-go.co.uk

For my children, William and Anna

History is little more than the register of the crimes, follies and misfortunes of mankind

— Edward Gibbon,
Author of *The History of the Decline and Fall of the Roman Empire*
(first published 1776)

We're on a highway to climate hell

— António Guterres,
Secretary-General of the United Nations
(COP 27, 7 November 2022)

Contents

Illustrations   xi

Maps   xiii

Introduction   xxv

Part I: Between Two Worlds

1   From City State to Superpower   1
2   The Crisis of the Third Century   11
3   Rome Reinvented   17
4   The Sons of Constantine   23
5   The Return of the Persians   29
6   Rebellion in the West   36

Part II: The Empire of Julian the Apostate

7   Julian in Gaul   47
8   The Battle of Strasbourg   54
9   Civil War   65
10   The Philosopher Emperor   70
11   War With Persia   76
12   The Spear of Destiny   83

Part III: The Road to Disaster

13   The Huns   97
14   Climate Change and Rome   105
15   Bursting a Blood Vessel   113
16   War With the Goths   124

17	The Battle of Adrianople	138
18	Making Matters Even Worse	149
19	Theodosius the Not So Great	158

Part IV: The Fall of the West

20	The Roman Empire Divided	169
21	Drifting to Disaster	181
22	Alaric's First Invasion of Italy	190
23	Stilicho's Finest Hour	196
24	All Gaul a Funeral Pyre	200
25	Stilicho's Fall	208
26	Alaric Triumphant	215
27	The Death of the Roman Army	222
28	The Sack of Rome	230
29	The Survival of the East	237
30	The End of Civilisation?	241

Conclusion	Was Climate Change Rome's Real Killer?	247

Find Out More About the Fall of the Roman Empire	253
The Roman Revolution	256
Acknowledgements	257
Roman Emperors (Augustus to Theodosius II)	258
Chronology of the Later Roman Empire	261
Further Reading	266
Notes	274
Index	279
About the Author	293

Illustrations

Photographs are from the Author's Collection unless stated otherwise.

Figure 1: Prima Porta statue of the emperor Augustus on display in the Vatican Museums.

Figure 2: Porphyry statue of four Roman emperors attached to the façade of Saint Mark's Basilica in Venice.

Figure 3: Head of the emperor Constantine from a colossal statue on display in the Capitoline Museums, Rome.

Figure 4: Gold solidus depicting the emperor Julian the Apostate (Classical Numismatic Group, Wikimedia Commons).

Figure 5: The Arch of Constantine in Rome.

Figure 6: Depiction of the Roman god, Sol Invictus, on the Arch of Constantine in Rome.

Figure 7: Ivory diptych thought to represent Stilicho, his wife Serena, and son Eucherius, on display in Monza Cathedral, near Milan (Monza Cathedral, Wikimedia Commons).

Figure 8: The Colosseum in Rome.

Figure 9: The Parthenon in Rome.

Figure 10: Interior of the Parthenon in Rome.

Figure 11: The Forum in Rome.

Figure 12: Part of the Aurelian Walls in Rome.

Figure 13: The Porta Latina Gate in Rome.

Figure 14: Tower in the Roman walls of Milan.

Figure 15: The Columns of San Lorenzo in Milan.

Figure 16: Mosaic depicting Christ in the Chapel of Saint Aquilino in Milan.

Maps

Map 1: Roman Empire in AD 337
Map 2: Julian's Persian Campaign, AD 363
Map 3: Origins of the Huns
Map 4: Hunnic Migration West
Map 5: Visigothic Invasions AD 376-410
Map 6: Barbarian Invasions AD 405-8
Map 7: Roman Empire in AD 410
Map 8: Ancient Rome
Map 9: Constantinople

Map 1

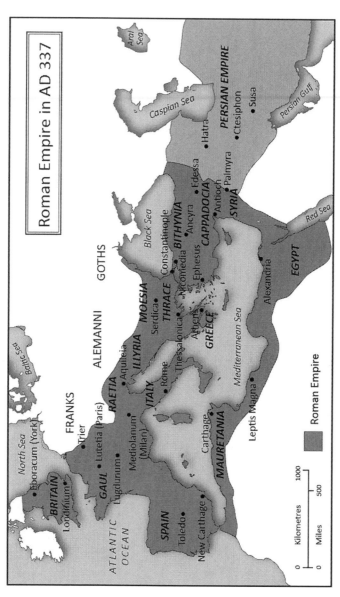

Roman Empire in AD 337

Roman Empire

Map 2

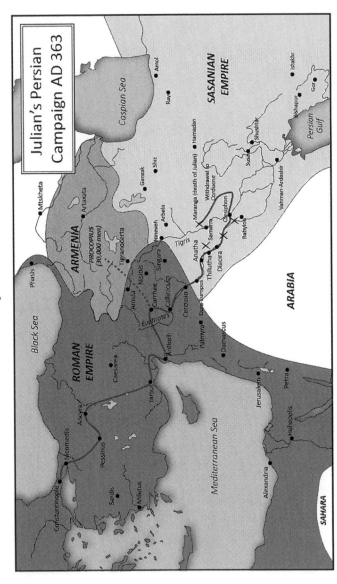

Map 3

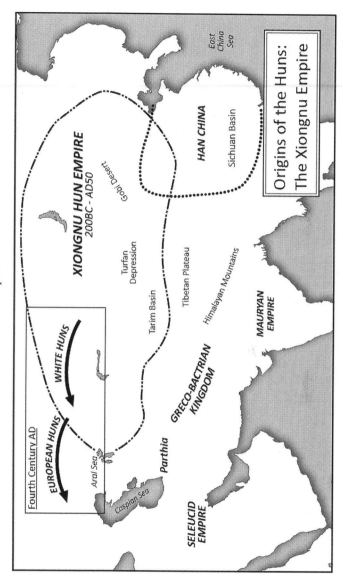

Origins of the Huns:
The Xiongnu Empire

XIONGNU HUN EMPIRE
200BC - AD50

HAN CHINA

East
China
Sea

Sichuan Basin

Gobi Desert

Turfan
Depression

Tarim Basin

Tibetan Plateau

Himalayan Mountains

MAURYAN
EMPIRE

WHITE HUNS

Fourth Century AD

EUROPEAN HUNS

GRECO-BACTRIAN
KINGDOM

Parthia

Aral Sea

Caspian Sea

SELEUCID
EMPIRE

Map 4

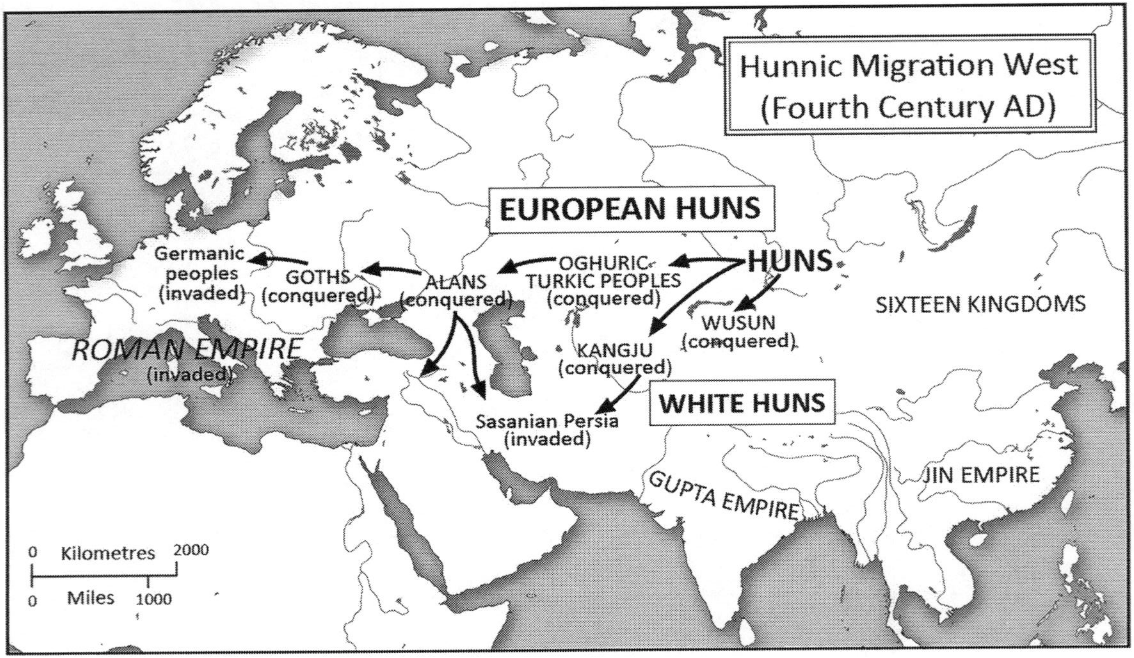

Hunnic Migration West (Fourth Century AD)

EUROPEAN HUNS

HUNS

WHITE HUNS

SIXTEEN KINGDOMS

JIN EMPIRE

GUPTA EMPIRE

WUSUN (conquered)

OGHURIC-TURKIC PEOPLES (conquered)

KANGJU (conquered)

Sasanian Persia (invaded)

ALANS (conquered)

GOTHS (conquered)

Germanic peoples (invaded)

ROMAN EMPIRE (invaded)

Kilometres   2000

0   1000

Miles

0

Map 5

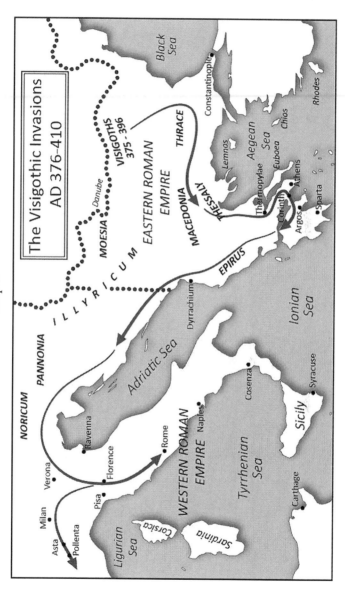

The Visigothic Invasions
AD 376–410

Map 6

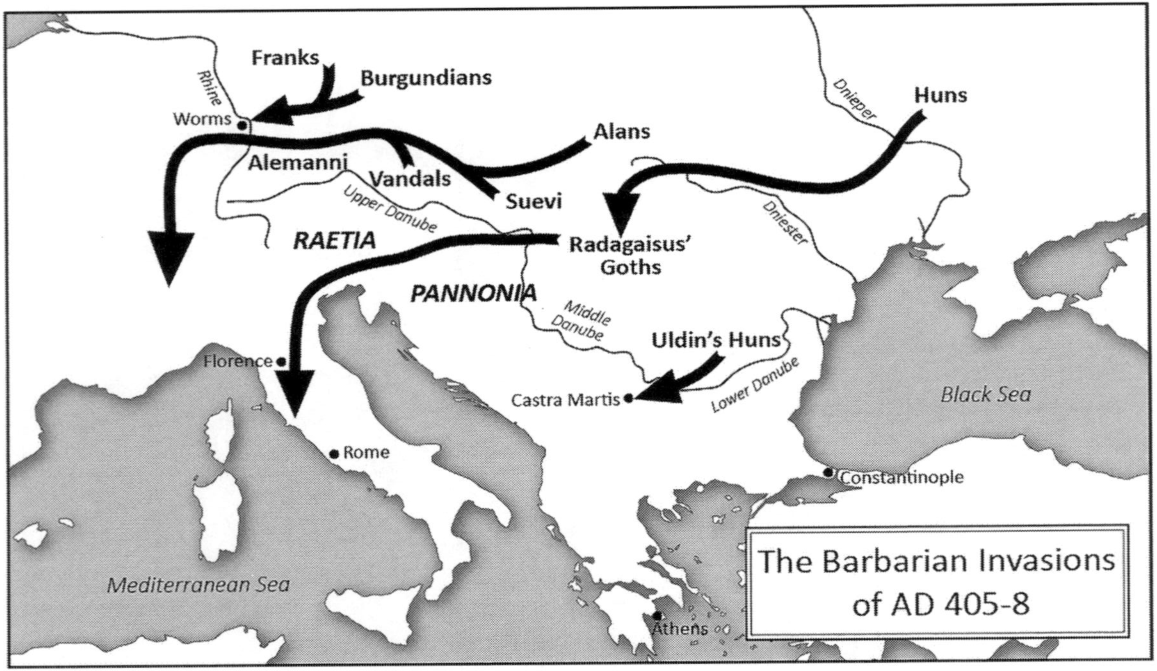

The Barbarian Invasions
of AD 405-8

Huns

Dnieper

Dniester

Alans

Suevi

Radagaisus'
Goths

Uldin's Huns

Lower Danube

Middle
Danube

Castra Martis

Black Sea

Constantinople

Athens

Burgundians

Franks

Alemanni

Vandals

Upper Danube

PANNONIA

RAETIA

Rhine

Worms

Florence

Rome

Mediterranean Sea

Map 7

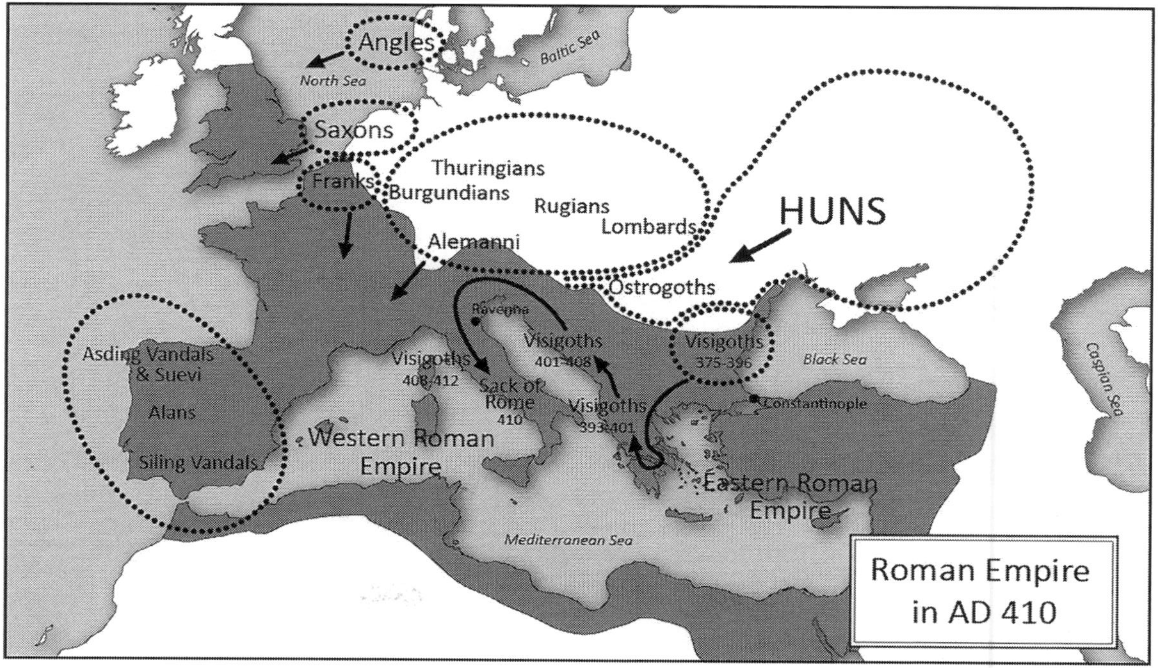
Angles
North Sea
Baltic Sea
Saxons
Franks
Thuringians
Burgundians
Rugians
Lombards
Alemanni
HUNS
Ostrogoths
Ravenna
Visigoths
401-408
Visigoths
375-396
Black Sea
Caspian Sea
Asding Vandals
& Suevi
Alans
Siling Vandals
Visigoths
408-412
Sack of
Rome
410
Visigoths
393-401
Constantinople
Western Roman
Empire
Eastern Roman
Empire
Mediterranean Sea
Roman Empire
in AD 410

Map 8

Ancient Rome

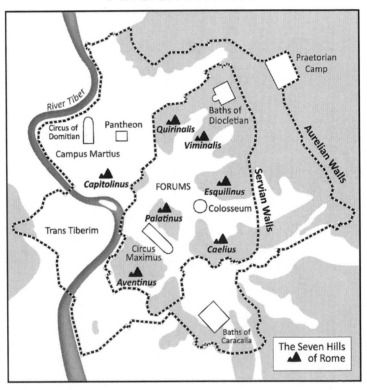

Praetorian Camp

River Tiber

Circus of Domitian

Pantheon

Baths of Diocletian

Quirinalis

Viminalis

Campus Martius

Aurelian Walls

Capitolinus

FORUMS

Esquilinus

Servian Walls

Colosseum

Palatinus

Trans Tiberim

Circus Maximus

Caelius

Aventinus

Baths of Caracalla

The Seven Hills of Rome

Map 9

Constantinople
330-413

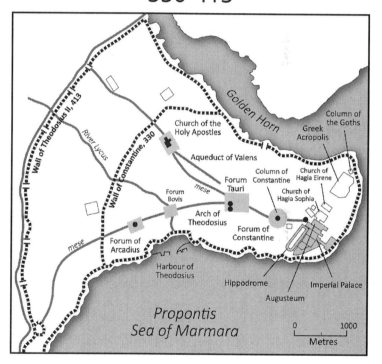

Introduction

Stinging, acrid smoke was billowing into the air.

Choking, Centurion Lampadius squinted through the heat haze. Behind him rose the noise of a vast Roman army. The blare of horns. The clatter of horses' hooves. The clang of iron. The tramp of nailed sandals.

The barbarians had set fire to the scorched August grass. Through the blinding wall of smoke, at the top of a steep slope, a huge line of Gothic wagons was spread out, like a fortified citadel.

The columns of Roman legionaries halted. Lampadius was a veteran of many wars. Experience had taught him the importance of preparation. But there was none today. The emperor Valens had rushed the eastern army into battle. He did not want to wait for Gratian's western legions. Even though they were just a day's march away, he wanted victory for himself. Lampadius cursed him. If only the emperor Julian had lived, things would have been different.

The Roman legionaries felt they were being cooked in their heavy armour. They were already tired and sweating from the eight-mile march to reach the Goths. Suddenly, as if from nowhere, the horizon was filled with Gothic horsemen. Valens had said they were out foraging. He had bet everything on a surprise attack against the Gothic camp. *What a fool he was*, Lampadius thought. He had been tricked. There was no surprise now.

Lampadius watched the Gothic infantry come out from behind the wagons to join their horsemen. The Romans now faced a huge Gothic host. Lampadius felt afraid. The same way he did when he first saw Persian war elephants. He knew that Roman discipline was the only thing that would save them. He called to his legionaries to form a *testudo*, or tortoise, formation. Shields were raised to ward off the arrows that fell from the sky. They advanced at a brisk pace to meet the Goths.

Both sides crashed into each other. The Romans were disciplined. The Goths were wild. Like savages, they flung themselves against the Roman shields. Roman swords jabbed at them, cutting off hands and arms, and stabbing into their sides. A Gothic warrior swung a great axe down on a legionary, splitting his head open. But the Roman line held firm. Lampadius rotated the legionaries from the back rows to the front in the way they had practised so many times on the parade ground. He hoped that discipline would keep the soldiers fighting. Eventually, the barbarians would tire and break away.

But not this time. The sun was moving west and still the Goths attacked. Blood made the ground slippery. The screams of the wounded were unnerving. *Where are the reserves?* wondered Lampadius. Something had gone wrong. The legion to his right was retreating. This was catastrophic. He called to the trumpeter to sound the order to change formation. But there were too many Goths crashing into them, swinging their long swords and sharp axes. His legionaries were breaking formation. He yelled to them to stand firm. But as he turned, he felt a Gothic spear pass clean through his breastplate and deep into his side.

*

The Battle of Adrianople was one of the worst defeats in the history of the Roman army. On that day, 9 August AD 378, the Goths annihilated the professional core of the eastern Roman army. Within hours, at least 20,000 legionaries and cavalrymen perished. 'No battle in our history except Cannae was such a massacre,' wrote Ammianus Marcellinus, our most trusted Roman chronicler of the fourth century.

It marked the beginning of the end of ancient Rome. Only 32 years later, in AD 410, some of the same Goths who fought at Adrianople would sack the city of Rome itself. And it was not just Rome that fell. By then, Germanic tribes had overrun most of the western half of the empire. So, how did this happen? How did ancient Rome, that had lasted for more than a thousand years, succumb in such a brief space of time?

The question has always puzzled historians and sparked intense debate. Almost every argument has been put forward from the rise of Christianity (as proposed by Edward Gibbon, the celebrated eighteenth-century historian, and author of the epic work, *The History of the Decline and Fall of the Roman Empire*), to lead poisoning (the Romans used lead piping for water) and even the enervating effects of having too many baths!

In this book, we look at new answers to the old questions. It follows on from the first in this series on the fall of the Roman Empire, called *The Roman Revolution*, which described Rome's survival through the 'crisis of the third century' and its adoption of Christianity. It unfolds a narrative of the years from the death of the emperor Constantine in AD 337, until the fall of the city of Rome itself in AD 410.

Our search examines the internal condition of the Roman Empire on the eve of the barbarian migrations. We will find an empire beset with internal religious conflict. This book questions whether the rise of Christianity was inevitable, as the consensus today still seems to think. We will focus on the empire of Julian the Apostate, and his attempt to turn the clock back and restore the pagan gods, as well as to re-emphasise Roman military might by conquering Persia. He nearly succeeded. His premature death removed the possibility of a very different outcome for the Roman Empire.

We will look at the late Roman army which, in the mid-fourth century, was still the largest and most effective military organisation on the planet, and try to answer the question why, by the beginning of the fifth century, it had collapsed so completely that it could not even defend the city of Rome itself?

We will look at the people in these years as much as the institutions they created or destroyed. Some of the most intriguing and colourful characters in history inhabited this time, from Constantine the Great, the grim general who found personal salvation in the teachings of Jesus Christ; to Julian the Apostate, the bearded young philosopher and soldier who rejected Christianity. From the Vandal commander,

Stilicho, devoted to his Roman wife, Serena, who valiantly tried to save Rome; to his nemesis, Alaric the Visigoth, the man who sacked the eternal city. And as Rome burned, the characters ranged from the sublime to the ridiculous, from Saint Augustine, who felt inspired to write *The City of God*, a cornerstone of Western thought, to the simple-minded emperor Honorius, who when told Rome was no more, thought this referred to his pet chicken called *Roma*.

The history of Rome, and especially its fall, has always fascinated both intellectuals and the popular imagination in the western world. From the writings of Voltaire and Gibbon in the eighteenth century to the film *Gladiator* today, an awareness of Rome's greatness and its decline forms an essential part of the western mentality. As one historian has said, '...deep within the European psyche lies an anxiety that, if ancient Rome could fall, so too can the proudest of modern civilisations.'[1] In particular, many writers have commented on the similarities between Rome and modern America. Two global superpowers, both confronted in their different ways with a rapidly changing world. One distinguished American writer has concluded that Rome can serve as 'either a grim cautionary tale or an inspirational call to action'.[2]

But the principal message of this book lies with a new subject seldom mentioned in Rome's history. This is the power of the natural environment over humanity. For the latest research suggests something entirely outside Rome's control precipitated its collapse. Just as the eruption of Mount Vesuvius in the first century AD suddenly destroyed the prosperous town of Pompeii, so a far greater environmental disaster on the Asian steppes 300 years later seems to have triggered a mass migration of peoples that overwhelmed Rome's defences.

Today, as human made climate change makes environmental disasters ever more likely, the story of Rome's fall has gained a new urgency.

Let us now listen to those voices from the past.

PART I

Between Two Worlds

1

From City State to Superpower

A sea of people in brightly coloured tunics broke into applause when he appeared.

The emperor Constantine led the procession on horseback from the public square known as the Philadelphion, down the broad road called the Mese towards his new forum. There in the centre of a great colonnaded circle was an immense column made of porphyry rock, over 150 feet high, higher even than Trajan's Column in Rome and as tall as the Colosseum.

This was the new forum of Constantine. The crowd followed the emperor and packed themselves into the open space within the forum's centre. There, they waited in silence. Ropes were slackly attached to a giant purple awning that covered a statue on top of the magnificent column. Suddenly, the ropes were pulled tight and a pulley system contrived to lift the awning away and reveal the statue it was hiding.

It was a gigantic figure cast in bronze. Holding a spear in one hand and a globe in the other, its head was adorned with a seven-point radiate crown. In fact, the statue was an ancient one of Apollo plundered from a Greek city on the Aegean coast. The head had then been replaced with one resembling Constantine's features and anointed with a radiate crown in the fashion of Roman emperors in the past.

The spectators gasped in awe. The statue had been polished so that it gleamed in the morning sun. It was said to be even larger than the legendary Colossus of Rhodes destroyed centuries before.

Constantine himself walked up onto a platform draped in purple. He wore gilded armour and a diadem of pearls and precious gems. He turned to the cheering people. They fell silent. Then he addressed them. He declared he would now dedicate this new city. Henceforth, it would no longer be called Byzantium but rather Constantinopolis, 'Constantine's city'. The date was 11 May AD 330. A historic date. The founding of New Rome.

But New Rome wasn't built in a day.

For a century after the founding of Constantinople, the Roman Empire was caught between two worlds. Between the dying vestiges of an ancient pagan empire centred on Rome, and a more vibrant Christian one growing in Constantinople. This book is about that time.

And to understand it, we must start with Old Rome and answer a question that is itself as old as the hills, one that forms the backdrop to world history.

How did Rome rise from a city state to a superpower?

To find the answer, we need to go back, over a thousand years before Constantine founded Constantinople, to a time when the Romans were just a small group of goatherds scrabbling to survive on a hill by the River Tiber.

The Romans themselves traditionally dated its founding

to 753 BC, by Romulus and Remus, the twins suckled by a she-wolf. This was a legend. Pure fiction. So, what really happened? Archaeological evidence points to the foundation of Rome in around 1000 BC, as a small settlement on the Palatine Hill. By around 500 BC, the goatherds had become something more than that. By then, they were occupying most of the seven of Rome's famous hills (see Map 8–Ancient Rome). The true origin of Rome lies with these hills, for they were suitable spots for primitive tribes to fortify. At first, the tribes fought each other. But then they joined together. Rome was born.

Roman writers, such as Virgil and Livy, would later say it was Roman fortitude that caused it to spread and dominate the whole of Italy. This is clearly wishful thinking. The truth is more likely that what initially propelled the Romans to greatness was their vulnerable geographical position. They were surrounded by enemies. To the north were the sophisticated Etruscans. To the south were the fierce Samnite tribes. Rome needed to survive. Necessity is the mother of invention. And if the early Romans learned how to do one thing well, it was diplomacy.

First, the tribes of the seven hills decided the only way to ensure their survival was to unite into a single political entity. With that done, they set about forming a network of 'allies', first as the Latin League of Italian towns, and then more widely across central Italy, so that by 265 BC, Rome had over 150 towns owing it allegiance in a sort of 'commonwealth'.

Again, it was political deftness that ensured Rome's early success. One thing the Latin League was very much *not* was an empire. Rome allowed its allies and even conquered towns considerable autonomy. Rome excelled at 'light touch' government and leadership. It required only military service from its allies and was ready to reward them with Roman citizenship or soft versions of it if they so wanted.

This subtle approach to government was in striking contrast to, say, the style of government of the Greek city states of the fifth century BC. For example, fifth-century Athens was so fiercely protective of its citizen status that it would not grant it to anyone born outside Athens. In contrast, Rome was not arrogant. It was happy to grant diluted citizenship to the members of the Latin League and an even more diluted version of citizenship to its *socii*, as its more distant Italian allies were called. This allowed it gradually to integrate most of central Italy into a Roman-dominated political entity. Turning these alliances into a Roman commonwealth of allied socii was the next logical step. But one thing we can be sure of – the early Romans had no plan for world domination. They would have been more surprised than anyone to hear that by extending their sphere of influence, they had taken the first step towards the creation of a future superpower.

So, what changed Rome from an Italian power to an international one? The answer was yet another conflict. Another fight for survival. And this time the threat lay outside Italy. It was with another city state. One located in North Africa. Carthage.

Carthage was one of the four 'superpowers' of the ancient world at this time, the other three being the successor states to Alexander the Great's vast empire: namely, the Antigonid kingdom of Macedonia; the Seleucid Empire based in the

Middle East; and the Ptolemaic Empire based in Egypt and the Levant. As such, Carthage represented by far the most powerful enemy Rome had ever faced.

During three separate wars, lasting some 80 years, from 264 to 146 BC, the Romans defeated and destroyed Carthage. However, it was a close-run thing. Rome nearly perished. Roman victory was immensely hard fought, with Hannibal inflicting some of the worst defeats ever suffered by the Roman army at the battles of Lake Trasimene and Cannae (217 and 216 BC) when he invaded Italy during the Second Punic War. But Rome prevailed for two main reasons: first, its superiority in manpower, derived from its control of a much larger population in Italy than Carthage possessed in North Africa. This meant it could absorb far higher casualty rates than the Carthaginians (which it needed to do given the military genius of Hannibal). Second, Rome proved to be far better at constructing a fleet than Carthage expected, leading to its victory in the First Punic War, and naval domination.

Roman victory over Carthage was the most important event in Rome's entire rise to power. Not only did it expand Roman territory into Africa and Spain, but it gave Rome complete mastery over the Western Mediterranean and a powerful navy matched only by that of Ptolemaic Egypt. Rome now came face to face with the remaining three 'great powers' of the ancient world.

However, in contrast to its hard-fought war with Carthage, victory over these was almost handed to Rome on a plate. The legions broke the power of the Greek states one by one. And they did it relatively easily. How?

One reason was the strength of the Roman army. The long war with Carthage transformed it. It caused the Romans to develop the most professional fighting machine ever seen in the ancient world. But an equally important ingredient was that, in contrast to its bitter power struggle with Carthage, Rome benefited from an unprecedented power vacuum that developed in the eastern Mediterranean in the second and first centuries BC. This was essentially because of the weakness of the Greek states – the Antigonid, Seleucid and Ptolemaic empires were all in decline.

It is worth pausing for a moment to consider just how fortunate Rome was in meeting the Greeks at exactly the right time in history. Counterfactual hypotheses can sometimes be too speculative to be useful, but the question of what might have happened had, for example, Rome encountered Alexander the Great a century earlier, is intriguing. Particularly since Alexander was contemplating a western expedition when he died at the early age of 33 (due it seems to heavy drinking at one of his riotous parties). If he had not died, Macedonian conquest of Italy would no doubt have been relatively easy at this time, and would presumably have eliminated Rome from the history books. But, as with so much in history, all we can say is that it did not work out that way. In short, the Romans got lucky.

With a hard-fought win over Carthage behind them, and an easy one over the Greeks, Rome's path to greatness now looked unstoppable. But then something went wrong. Rome became a victim of its own success.

The problem was corruption. And at the highest level. One of the most remarkable aspects of Rome's rise to power had been its republican constitution. In theory, Rome was actually a democracy. In reality, it was a republic controlled by an oligopoly of senators.[3] Nevertheless, the competition for power between the senators ensured it never became an autocracy. Astonishing though it may sound, for around 400 years, two consuls were elected to rule Rome for one year only.

But all this changed as Rome's newfound power led to an inflow of undreamed-of wealth and power into both Italy and the eternal city itself. This attracted a series of politicians to claim absolute power for themselves while disingenuously alleging that they were compelled to do this to save the republic. In this way, the story of the late republic has become one of history's most disturbing studies in the decline of constitutional government and the rise of tyranny. This decline began with Gaius Marius (157–86 BC), seven times Roman consul and widely regarded as the father of the Roman army. Marius broke the republic's rules by being made consul each year between 104 and 100 BC, although he did not openly abuse his power and even retired temporarily from public life in the 90s BC.

However, he was jealous of any rival, and this led to a disturbing civil war between him and another rising politician called Sulla. Marius and Sulla fell out so badly that Sulla felt compelled to march on Rome to safeguard his consulship. This action was the first nail in the republic's coffin, as it was unheard of for a Roman army to march on the sacred city. Sulla drove yet another nail in by forcing the senate to make him dictator. The next man to seize power and break the republic's constitution was Pompey. His command of most of the Roman army forced the senate to make him consul three times, again brazenly breaking the constitution. But, as the senate struggled to maintain its authority, a man who would become the most famous Roman of all challenged Pompey – Julius Caesar.

Like the others, Caesar said his mission was to save the republic. To cut a long story short, Caesar outfought his rivals and persuaded the senate to elect him 'dictator for life' (*dictator perpetuo*). According to him, this was of course only to keep the republic safe. However, he remained curiously unaware of the growing opposition to his rule in the senate. Some disaffected senators, led by Cassius and Brutus – former supporters of Caesar's rival, Pompey – hatched a plot to assassinate him on 15 March 44 BC, the famous Ides of March ('ides' referring to the seventy-fourth day of the Roman calendar).

Caesar's assassination and his supposed last words, *Et tu, Brute?* ('And you, Brutus?'), have been immortalised by William Shakespeare. On the floor of the senate house, he was stabbed to death. His death was a turning point, for it allowed one of the most remarkable politicians in history to seize power – Augustus, the 'grandfather of Europe', the man who created the Roman Empire and made it the model for so many European empires to come, from Charlemagne to Napoleon.

Augustus, who posterity calls the first Roman emperor, never actually called himself that. Indeed, his real name was Octavian. After Julius Caesar's death, he was one of the Second Triumvirate (the other two being Mark Antony and Lepidus) who ruled republican Rome. Civil war ensued, and it was when he defeated Mark Antony and Cleopatra at the battle of Actium in 31 BC, thereby restoring peace to the Roman world, that the grateful senate declared him Augustus, the 'illustrious one'.

Why was the senate happy to support Augustus but not

Julius Caesar? The answer was it had become tired of the brutal civil wars that stained the years of the late Republic. The senate, and the Roman people, were desperate to have peace. If Augustus could bring this, he had their support. Octavian was also the master of tactful diplomacy, unlike Caesar. He fashioned the empire as a republic, officially calling himself *princeps senatus*, or the 'first senator', and never dictator. He was the consummate politician. He always lived in simple accommodation on the Palatine Hill, as a model of austerity. The people loved him. The senate respected him. The accolades kept coming. He was given supreme command of the army as 'Imperator', literally commander, from which the term emperor is derived. He was given the title 'senior proconsul', meaning the head of all the governors of the Roman provinces. On his deathbed, the Roman writer, Suetonius, said his last words were, 'Have I played the part well?'

Critics of Augustus compare him with Hitler and Mussolini as an example of an autocrat condoned by a republican process. In contrast, his admirers emphasise that, unlike them, he bequeathed Europe 200 years of peace and prosperity – the *Pax Romana* (The Roman Peace) – the like of which had never existed before and which has never been seen since. It enabled the Roman Empire's extraordinarily diverse collection of races and cultures, ranging from the Britons and Gauls in the west to the Egyptians and Greeks in the east, to come together to be just one thing: Roman.

Augustus achieved this by establishing one of the biggest 'ideas' in history, indeed one that we still have today. The idea was that being Roman made you superior. One well-known politician[4] termed it 'The Dream of Rome'. Being Roman meant enjoying the benefits of peace and the rule of law and order. Augustus' stroke of genius was to offer this to diverse peoples across the empire. To participate, essentially all you had to do was to pay taxes. That was the Roman bargain. If you paid tax, you were entitled to receive the protection of the Roman army and the rule of Roman law.

Let us fast forward through Rome's glorious history in the first and second centuries AD. Although it suffered from the occasional short-lived 'mad' emperors like Caligula and Nero, for the most part the emperors were reasonably capable and effective. Hadrian, Trajan, the enlightened philosopher, Marcus Aurelius, and others ensured the 'Augustan constitution' was respected. In AD 212, the emperor Caracalla extended the concept of Romanness by introducing universal Roman citizenship for all free men in the empire (free women were given the same legal rights as Roman women). In reality, this was done to increase tax revenues by making all the empire's male inhabitants subject to inheritance tax, which Roman citizens had always had to pay. But it also reflected the increasingly cosmopolitan society of the empire and recognised that Italy was no longer as central as it had once been.

Augustus' concept of Romanness seemed to be flourishing. But all good things come to an end.

And for Rome that happened in the third century AD.

2

The Crisis of the Third Century

In the third century AD, Rome nearly fell.[5]

Germanic tribes crossed the Danube and the Rhine. The Persians took Antioch. Two emperors perished. Decius at the hands of the Goths and Valerian captured by the Persians. The empire burned. Where once the long straight roads of the empire had brought peace and prosperity, now they brought barbarian armies carrying terror, death and destruction.

The crisis of the third century was caused by the increasing strength of Rome's two main opponents – Persia and Germania.

Persia was not a new enemy of Rome but an ancient one with an illustrious past. In the sixth century BC, when Rome was only a small city state, the Achaemenid Persian Empire had been founded by Cyrus the Great. Within 100 years, it had become the largest empire on the planet, surpassing the Zhou Empire in China. But it met more than its match in Alexander the Great, who destroyed it in the 330s BC, spreading his rule as far east as India and Afghanistan.

In the aftermath of Alexander's conquest, Persia became part of the Seleucid Empire. Its sense of Persian identity faded until the Seleucids were overthrown by a more genuinely Persian dynasty called the Parthians. However, the Parthian Empire (247 BC–AD 224) was still culturally and economically the poor relation of the Hellenised Roman world. But then a dramatic change occurred. In the early third century, because of growing dissatisfaction among the Persian aristocracy with Parthia's pitiful performance against the Romans, a new Persian dynasty, the Sasanian, seized power promising to avenge Roman defeats.

A remarkable Persian *Shahanshah*, or king of kings, Ardashir rebuilt the Persian army, enlarging the regiments of heavy cavalry, which had always been its main strength. He bound the Persian nobility more firmly to his sway by appointing a network of his own newly ennobled supporters, he centralised taxation, and installed a new bureaucracy to collect increased revenues. A strong central Persian state was created and imbued with a new passion for the traditional Persian religion, Zoroastrianism.

This revitalised Persian empire erupted against the unsuspecting Romans in the AD 230s and 240s. Ardashir's son, Shapur I, a formidable soldier, led Persian armies to victory in Syria, capturing the frontier cities and even reaching Antioch, the Roman centre for its eastern empire. Roman armies were defeated, and in AD 260, the unthinkable happened. A massive Roman army was annihilated near Edessa and the emperor Valerian himself was captured. Shapur used him as a footstool to mount his horse before having him flayed, his body dyed purple and hung on display in the royal palace at Ctesiphon. Thereafter, Sasanian Persia remained a daunting enemy for Rome – the rival superpower on its eastern border.

Rome's other main opponent was Germania. At the time of the early Roman Empire, it covered a vast area, much bigger than modern Germany, stretching from the Rhine in the west to the Vistula in modern Poland in the east, and from the Baltic down to the Danube. However, although it was large, it was a poor and primitive land, inhabited by a huge number of small tribes perpetually at war with each other. As such, it posed little threat to the Romans. The only military success the Germans enjoyed against the Romans occurred in AD 9, when three Roman legions, under the command of Varus, were ambushed and slaughtered at the battle of the Teutoburg Forest. But this was the one and only example of German political coordination due to an extraordinary leader called Arminius, who briefly united some of the tribes. Afterwards, the Germans failed to exploit their victory, and remained politically disunited for most of the next two centuries.

This all changed in the third century. Even towards the end of the second century, in the reign of Marcus Aurelius (AD 161–80), there was a devastating invasion across the Danube by the Marcomanni and Quadi. The Roman army struggled to contain and then push back the barbarians. Then in the AD 250s, all hell was let loose. Between 254 and 258, the Rhine frontier was shattered and Gaul was invaded by the Franks, Alemanni and Marcomanni. These were proper invasions, not raids. At about the same time, Roman Pannonia (a territory stretching along the north Danube) was overrun by the Marcomanni, Quadi and Iazyges. The Marcomanni even reached Italy, advancing as far as Ravenna in 254. Meanwhile, the Alemanni descended into the Rhône Valley, which they occupied for three years and used as a base to raid the rest of Gaul. Another group of Alemanni crossed the Alps and advanced into northern Italy, where the emperor Gallienus defeated them near Milan in 260.

So, what had changed? How did the hitherto fierce, but largely ineffective, German tribes suddenly become so much more dangerous? During the second and third centuries, two changes conspired to make the Germans more formidable.

The first was the increasing militarisation of German society. Burial grounds show a greater focus on weaponry. Ironically, this was largely because of Roman influence. Having a wealthy and powerful neighbour, like Rome, caused German society to become more materialistic and hierarchical as sophisticated Roman products became sought-after status symbols. Roman weaponry was either purchased or stolen. Wearing Roman chain mail became a sign of superior social status. Tribal leaders needed to justify their status with prized Roman artefacts. The Germans had always had a warlike culture but, influenced by the excellence of the Roman army, some warriors became more like professional soldiers. Warrior elites developed either working for the Romans as auxiliaries or invading the empire.

This also led to consolidation. In the first and second centuries AD, a huge number of independent tribes (perhaps 300-plus) were scattered across Germania and had no intention of forming a united front against the Romans. But by the third century, they were more willing to cooperate, however loosely, to form new and larger tribal federations – such as those of the Alemanni and the Franks along the Rhine, and the Saxons on the North Sea coast. Indeed, the word Alemanni meant 'all men', signifying the union of many tribes into one.

But, despite the Persian and German onslaught, the empire survived. A new breed of soldier-emperors saved it. The emperor Aurelian, called *manu ad ferrum*, literally 'hand on sword' but perhaps better translated as 'man of steel', restored the army's iron discipline, and led the Romans to victory from Gaul to Syria. Aurelian must be counted as one of Rome's most important and successful emperors. He and his predecessor, Claudius Gothicus (so-called because of his victories over the Goths), came from humble peasant stock in Illyria. They broke with the tradition of emperors coming from senatorial families. They were soldiers who had worked their way up on merit. Chosen by the armies and not by the senate (although the senate was forced to endorse them after the event), they represented a revolution in Roman politics. The empire needed professional soldiers to save it, and these men did just that.

The empire became geared to total war. Aurelian built the walls that bear his name around Rome, which still stand today as one of the most impressive of all surviving Roman monuments. But they were also testimony to the empire's newfound vulnerability. For in the days of Augustus, it would have been unthinkable for Rome to need walls.

The history of the long wars fought by Aurelian to contain and then counter-attack the barbarians is the subject of the first book in this series. Named 'Restorer of the World' by the senate, Aurelian died unexpectedly and tragically in an army mutiny by some officers who had been misled into believing that they faced execution. The Roman world mourned his death but he had done enough to save the empire. He was succeeded by more soldier-emperors – Probus and Carus, in particular – who further strengthened the empire's defences.

The danger now was the unbridled power of the army, and the cost of maintaining a huge number of soldiers, which had effectively bankrupted the Roman state. Much of the empire, especially Gaul and the Balkans, had also been devastated by barbarian invasion and needed time and investment to recover. Rome had survived the crisis of the third century, but as the Duke of Wellington said of the battle of Waterloo, 'it was a damn close-run thing'. Now Rome needed to find a new purpose. It needed to be reinvented.

And Rome was lucky to find two emperors who did just that – Diocletian and Constantine.

3

Rome Reinvented

After the crisis of the third century, the classical Roman Empire lived on but in a new and intriguing form. This late Roman Empire, which remains strangely ignored compared to its classical predecessor, was perhaps even more fascinating.

In AD 284, a charismatic and tough soldier seized the imperial purple with the support of his army. His name was Diocletian, and his reign changed the empire as much as that of Augustus had done, 300 years before. To start with, he quelled the political infighting which had weakened the Roman state in the third century by establishing the *tetrarchy* – the rule of four emperors, each with their own quarter of the empire to defend against the barbarians. In his reign, he appointed two senior emperors, and two junior. While this worked well for him, it was only because he was an exceptionally inspirational leader and held in high regard, especially by his other three co-emperors.

Diocletian was not just a good soldier but he was also the best administrator Rome ever had. He set himself the task of ensuring the crisis of the third century was not repeated. To do this, he increased the size of the army and built extensive fortifications across the empire. This cost a fortune, and to finance it, he introduced a system of taxation and administration which was not equalled in its efficiency until the modern era.

Diocletian's reign was a golden age but his revolutionary political government relied on his charismatic personality. When he retired in 306, due to ill health – the only emperor ever to do this – power passed to a tetrarchy of emperors who fell out and fought each other for supreme authority. However, Rome's run of luck with its emperors continued, and the next proved to be another extraordinary leader. This was Constantine. By AD 324, he had secured sole control of the empire. He was another great soldier, statesman and, in the eyes of many – especially the Catholic Church – a great visionary, although it can also be argued that he created many of the problems Rome faced later, as we will discuss in future chapters.

Constantine has become synonymous with the idea of the rebirth of the late Roman Empire. Indeed, he is often called Constantine the Great. But many historians consider his achievements much more mixed than those of Diocletian, and his legendary status due to his conversion to Christianity. It was really Diocletian who created the solid foundations of New Rome, while Constantine implemented two monumental and better-remembered changes to the empire – its adoption of Christianity and the effective relocation of its capital to a great new city, Constantinople.

Like Diocletian, Constantine was a professional soldier, but he did not have the same unbridled respect from the army and his fellow tetrarchs that Diocletian enjoyed.

Having fought his way to the top of the Roman hierarchy, he felt less secure than Diocletian and looked for ways to assert his authority. However, in contrast to the more conservative Diocletian, he was a truly radical innovator. He was not afraid to challenge convention and was keen to make changes to the empire to strengthen his own authority and break with the past.

His adoption of Christianity and his foundation of Constantinople were both examples of this. Christianity was politically expedient since it conferred legitimacy on him as the protector of the Christian Church – the fastest-growing new religion in the empire. He could not have imagined the profound effect his actions would have. For he effectively invented the 'divine right of kings', a political philosophy that would dominate not just Rome and Byzantium but the whole of Western European political thought until the concept was challenged by the French Revolution of 1789.

His founding of Constantinople was essentially another example of political self-assertion. The city bore his name and, although the city of Rome was still by far the empire's largest city, with about a million inhabitants in AD 330, compared with only some 30,000 in Constantinople, he imbued it with a new senate and spectacular new buildings to rival those of Rome. While he paid respect to Rome and recognised the Roman senate as senior to that in Constantinople, he sidelined the city, which was also still mainly pagan, to suit his own purposes.

The radical changes wrought by Constantine to the government and religion of the empire were also clear reflections of a changing society. This was particularly true of religion. The crisis of the third century caused the classical empire to doubt itself. The rise of Christianity was a product of this. Having grown very slowly during the first and second century AD, suddenly in the third century, its numbers skyrocketed, from as few as 10,000 Christians in AD 100 to a million by AD 250, and to 30–40 million by AD 350, comprising around half the total Roman population. This extraordinary growth was fuelled by the fact that fourth-century Romans were disillusioned with their ancient gods, who had failed to defend the frontiers. Their temples were pulled down. Faith was now placed in a new god who, it was hoped, would prove more effective.

The Roman economy recovered after collapsing in the third century. Barbarian invasion and the need to pay the army had bankrupted the Roman state. This caused rampant inflation when the emperors debased the coinage to make a limited amount of gold go further. Constantine re-established a gold standard with the minting of the new gold coin called the 'solidus', which became the 'dollar' not just of the ancient world but of the later Byzantine state and even into the Middle Ages. With the frontiers and the coinage restored, trade resumed. Prosperity returned. The banking sector revived after its demise in the third century. Credit was again made available for commerce. The priest John Chrysostom has left us with vivid descriptions of the bankers at work in Antioch, lending money to merchants: 'The merchant who wants to get rich prepares a ship, hires sailors, summons a captain, and does all the other things necessary to set sail, and borrows money and tries the sea, and passes into foreign lands.'[6]

The introduction of universal Roman citizenship in AD 212 by the emperor Caracalla (done largely to increase tax revenues) had made the empire more cosmopolitan than ever before, and so long as you were a Roman citizen, the empire was no longer just a political system designed to enrich Italy, but a land of opportunity for all. Cities and towns recovered some of the life of luxury lost in the destruction of the third century. Great basilica-like churches were built as the temples fell into decay. These years were not as glorious as those of the Pax Romana but the Roman Empire was still the most powerful state in the world, surpassing the might of Han China, its closest rival, in the eyes of most historians.

The state displayed its power with monumental building projects. Constantinople became a magnificent new city, with its population growing at least tenfold within the space of a century, rising from around 30,000 in 330 to perhaps 300,000 inhabitants by 400. Developments in using concrete and brick enabled the construction of vast new buildings, such as the Baths of Diocletian in Rome, which even surpassed the gigantic baths built by Caracalla.[7] Maxentius began and Constantine completed the construction of a basilica in the Roman forum on such a colossal scale that even what little is left of it today dwarfs the other buildings.

Meanwhile, Roman art was also booming. Mosaics reached new heights of sophistication, as shown in the abundance of fourth-century examples uncovered in villas across the empire. For instance, the brilliance and beauty of the mosaics discovered in the Piazza Armerina villa in Sicily would have been widely replicated. In Britain, copious amounts of striking fourth-century mosaics are still being uncovered today. Mosaic art replaced Roman sculpture, which all but disappeared in the later third century. The changes in society did not end there. Gladiatorial combat was frowned upon by Christians and was abandoned in the late fourth century. Chariot racing took its place.

So, to fourth-century Romans the future looked good. However, despite the Roman recovery in the fourth century, the external world was far more threatening than it had been during the classical empire. Indeed, little did the Romans realise it but soon they would face a renewed barbarian onslaught, although this time with the addition of a terrifying new enemy, the steppe nomads called the Huns. Less than a hundred years after Constantine's death, the unthinkable happened – the sack of Rome in AD 410. But, as with most great events in history, the road to this was not straightforward. It contained a host of extraordinary people and events that conspired, against all expectations, to lead to the end of the western Roman Empire.

It is to this subject that we will now turn.

4

The Sons of Constantine

On 22 May AD 337, Constantine died just outside Diocletian's former capital of Nicomedia, in what is today western Turkey.

He is thought to have been about 65 years old, and had ruled as one of the tetrarchs (co-emperors) since AD 306, until he became sole emperor in AD 324. In his last days, he had been preparing a campaign against Rome's oldest and most dangerous foe, the Sasanian Persians, until soon after the Christian Feast of Easter, when he had fallen ill. He left the city of Constantinople, that he had founded 13 years before, and crossed the Bosphorus, aiming to reach the hot baths near the town of Helenopolis, dedicated to his beloved mother, Helena, hoping they might revive him. But when he was praying in a church his mother had built in honour of Lucian the Apostle, he felt worse and realised that death was approaching.

Although Constantine was a Christian, he had never been baptised, and now he hastily called his bishops to perform the rites that he had delayed for so long. His decision to delay baptism until shortly before his death may seem surprising for someone who appears to have been a committed Christian, but in fact it was a fairly common practice among fourth-century Romans, since baptism was regarded as the final chance to absolve oneself of all sin before entering the kingdom of heaven. Perhaps Constantine was also influenced by the knowledge that he had sinned many times during his turbulent life. For in truth, he was a ruthless soldier and politician, who had killed many of his rivals, and had even ordered the execution of one of his four sons, as well as his second wife, for reasons that have never been fully established but which may have stemmed from fear of rivalry with his son and the suspected infidelity of his wife.

As he approached death, while Constantine's baptism may have been uppermost in his own mind, in this regard he was alone. For the overriding question in the minds of everyone else was his succession. And the answer was something that has long baffled historians, just as much, it seems, as it did his contemporaries. Despite the fact that he had spent his life battling political rivals en route to securing sole control of the empire for himself, he chose to leave it in the hands of not just one emperor but five.

This pentarchy comprised his three sons and two of their relatives. His eldest son, also called Constantine, was to have Gaul, Spain and Britain, the same territories which Constantine himself had acquired in 306 when he had first become a tetrarch. His second son, Constantius, was to have the east, and his third, Constans, the central part of the empire with Italy and Illyria. Constantine also had a half-brother, called Dalmatius, who had always been a loyal supporter, and it was to his two sons that he also bequeathed more minor but important parts of the empire. One of them (Flavius Julius Dalmatius) was to have a part of Illyria while his younger brother, Hannibalianus, was given most of Anatolia.

Why did Constantine divide the empire into five parts? Perhaps the real motive was that by offering power to all his sons and relatives, he hoped to retain their loyalty during his own lifetime. If so, this reinforces the view, expressed by many of his contemporaries and later historians, that he was nothing more than a shallow ruler, interested in little other than his own well-being. For the truth was plain for all to see – Constantine's succession plan was an unhelpful division of power that was almost guaranteed to lead to internal dispute.

And that is exactly what happened.

Constantine's second son, Constantius, was the closest to Constantinople, and he rushed to the city to bury his father in the Church of the Holy Apostles, the magnificent church built by Constantine only a few years before as his intended mausoleum. But any intention to comply further with his father's wishes was abruptly curtailed. For a gruesome event occurred next, called 'the massacre of the princes', when all the dead emperor's relatives except for his three sons and three of his cousins were rounded up and executed. These included two of the five co-emperors chosen by Constantine, Dalmatius and Hannibalianus, as well as seven cousins.

What evidence we have points the accusing finger firmly at Constantius himself. However, it appears the massacre was also supported by some of the most influential army commanders in the empire, who particularly wanted to eliminate Dalmatius' two sons, since they were proven soldiers capable of attempting to seize control of the army. But, even if he was manipulated in this way, the ultimate responsibility must still lie with Constantius, and it is perhaps revealing that many years later, as he faced the prospect of his own death, he blamed his own inability to bear children as divine punishment for this crime of murder committed when he was only 21 years old.[8]

Once it was decided to proceed with the grisly executions, a pretext was needed. A story was conveniently invented that Dalmatius and Hannibalianus had poisoned Constantine, with the help of the seven cousins. Although we do not know the precise details of what happened, all these men were rounded up and executed. After this purge, the army commanders were happy to swear loyalty to the three of Constantine's sons, knowing that these young *Augusti* entirely depended on their support.

However, amidst the bloodshed, two relatives were spared, one of whom would play a critical role in future Roman history. This was the six-year-old Julian who, together with his 11-year-old brother Gallus, was deemed too young to pose a threat. Julian would later become one of the most celebrated of all Roman emperors, as Julian the Apostate, the man who tried to turn back the clock on Christianity and restore Rome's pagan traditions.

But let us return to our narrative. For a while, the three sons cooperated. They divided the empire roughly along the lines Constantine had originally indicated. Constantius II was the primary beneficiary of the purge, since he took over the lands belonging to Dalmatius' sons before they were executed, giving him full control of the east and Constantinople. The west was divided between his two brothers, with Constantine

II in charge of Gaul, Spain and Britain while Constans had Illyria, Italy and Africa.

However, this fraternal agreement was based on a precarious bargain since, as the eldest of the three brothers, Constantine II felt that he was owed the largest part of the empire, whereas the agreement clearly gave this to Constantius. Consequently, Constantine only accepted it provided he was made the guardian over the youngest brother, Constans, who was only 17 in 337, thereby effectively giving him the largest part of the empire.

Inevitably, this agreement became increasingly fraught as Constans grew older and neared the age of 21, when he would come of age and not require a guardian. Nervous about this, Constantine II struck first and demanded that Constans give him North Africa. Constans was initially intimidated by his brother and agreed to do this, although the request meant handing over Carthage, which was the breadbasket for Rome. Knowing that if Constantine II controlled Carthage, it would not be long before he demanded Italy as well, Constans decided to stand up for himself and refused to concede anything.

The tension between the two was now rising like heated mercury. In 340, Constans turned 21, and he broke with his bullying older brother and refused to acknowledge him as his guardian any longer. This was too much for Constantine II. The result was civil war. He invaded Italy in 340. However, what could have been a deeply damaging internal conflict was avoided when Constantine II was unexpectedly killed in an ambush outside Aquileia in northern Italy. As surprised as anyone by this, Constans emerged as the victor and assumed full control of the west. Now, the empire was divided between him and Constantius. Finally, and certainly by luck and not by judgement, Constantine the Great's absurd succession plan between five co-emperors had settled down to a much more manageable two.

Meanwhile, while his brothers had been boiling up for a full-scale civil war, Constantius II had been fully engaged fighting Rome's single greatest enemy: Persia. Sasanian Persia had been relatively quiet during both Diocletian's and Constantine the Great's reigns, but now it was re-emerging as the greatest threat to Rome's fourth-century prosperity. This change was brought about by the leadership of a remarkable Shahanshah, Shapur II, who would become the new scourge of the Romans.

5

The Return of the Persians

In modern Iran, there is a towering rock in the middle of the desert, on which are carved magnificent images from ancient Persian history. Given that written sources are frustratingly scarce, these rock carvings in the royal necropolis at Naqsh-e Rostam, near to Persepolis in the modern province of Fars, provide some of the best insights that we have into the long and bloody conflict between Rome and Persia in the third century AD. Particularly well recorded are the exploits of the greatest of the Sasanian Shahanshahs (king of kings), Shapur I, who is portrayed taking the emperor Valerian prisoner after his spectacular victory over the Romans at the battle of Edessa in AD 260.

But Shapur I's triumph was short lived. His army was defeated by Palmyra,[9] and after his death, Persia was weakened by a civil war with a breakaway province in the east known as the Kushano-Sasanian kingdom, which was fabulously wealthy,[10] according to Chinese sources, because of its domination of the silk roads. Diocletian completed Persian humiliation with the Peace of Nisibis in 299, which forced them to make considerable territorial concessions –

recognising the Tigris as the Roman/Persian frontier and ceding five satrapies west of the Tigris to Rome, besides agreeing to Roman control of Armenia and Georgia.

It looked as if the power of the Sasanians had been well and truly broken. But before long there emerged a new and very different Persia. And the reason was the accession of one of the greatest Persian Shahanshahs ever – Shapur II.

Just as his great-grandfather, Shapur I, had filled Roman hearts with fear in the third century, so Shapur II would do the same in the fourth. He was initially famous for coming to power when he was not even born. The story goes that a group of nobles conspired to murder, blind and imprison his three brothers when his father, Hormizd II, died in 309, so as to seize power for themselves. At the time, Shapur's mother was pregnant with Shapur, and the nobles – judging that they could control the child king when he was born – swore allegiance to the unborn child by placing the Sasanian crown on his mother's stomach. Whatever the truth about this, Shapur was born in 309 and survived the regency of those nobles who had so brutally dispossessed his brothers of their inheritance. We have no records of the political intrigues that must have existed during his childhood, but when he reached the age of 16, Shapur succeeded to his inheritance with no objections. The moment he was crowned, he displayed great self-possession and drive. He would spend the next 54 years, until his death in 379, in a whirlwind of activity that left Persia strengthened and Rome weakened.

The Sasanian Empire he inherited was a shadow of what it had been under his glorious namesake, Shapur I. Rome had humiliated it with the Peace of Nisibis in 299, and it had lost much of its eastern territory to the Kushano-Sasanian kingdom. If that was not bad enough, it had yet another enemy that was making inroads into the heart of the empire. These were the Arabs.

In the early fourth century, Arab tribes had invaded southern Iran and had taken control of the Sasanian province of Pars (modern-day Persian Fars) and the region around the Persian Gulf. Immediately on becoming Shahanshah in 325, Shapur II led an expedition against them which proved to be highly successful and particularly brutal. First, he pushed back a powerful Arab tribe called the Lyad from Pars and re-established Sasanian control on the eastern side of the Persian Gulf. He then led his army across the Gulf and invaded what is now eastern Saudi Arabia. He implemented a reign of terror, sacking the large Arab trading port of al-Khatt (modern Qatif), destroying other settlements, poisoning water wells and pushing the Arab tribes into the Al Hajar Mountains. The Arabs were so shocked by his brutal treatment of prisoners that he earned the nickname of 'he who pierces shoulders', in reference to his practice of piercing prisoners' shoulders in order to insert a rope and drag them in long lines across the desert.

He campaigned far and wide in the area that is now modern Saudi Arabia, even reaching Medina close to the Red Sea. Then having forced the Arab tribes back into the interior, he constructed a wall starting at al-Hira, which is today located in modern southern Iraq, and garrisoned strongpoints along the western side of the Persian Gulf. After this, stories of Shapur's cruelty passed into Arab folklore and the Arabs would not pose a major threat to the Sasanians until the age of the Islamic Arab conquests 300 years later.

By crushing the Arabs, Shapur had won his spurs and strengthened his position within Sasanian feudal politics. As evidence of this, he was not challenged by the Persian nobility throughout the rest of his reign. He could now turn to his greatest ambition: to defeat Rome.

Although the Peace of Nisibis had ensured 40 years of harmony between Rome and Persia, towards the end of Constantine's long reign tensions mounted between the two. This began when Shapur II's third brother, Hormizd, fled to Constantinople. Hormizd had originally been imprisoned by the same nobles who murdered and blinded his two other brothers in 309 before Shapur was born. However, in 323, Hormizd had escaped with his wife's help and presented himself to the emperor Constantine, who took a liking to this refugee and gave him a position in the Roman army and a small palace outside Constantinople. Not surprisingly, Hormizd became an enthusiastic Roman supporter, much to Shapur's annoyance, who regarded him as a potential threat to his own authority. When Shapur demanded his return, Constantine refused. Shapur resorted to bribery, sending Hormizd his wife, whose loyalty had facilitated his escape. But even though Shapur kept his side of the bargain and despatched his wife unharmed, Hormizd refused to move. Exasperated, Shapur felt Constantine had tricked him.

Another reason for the growing Roman/Persian tension was religion. While Christianity had been growing in the Roman Empire, Shapur had championed Zoroastrianism as the Sasanian state religion, and was therefore hostile to the growing Christian community in Persia. When Constantine became more overtly Christian in his later life, Shapur viewed the Persian Christians as potential traitors and persecuted them. This persecution escalated shortly before war broke out with Rome, since he imposed a double tax on his Christian subjects to pay for the forthcoming war. Confronted with this or conversion to Zoroastrianism, the bishop of the eastern Christian Church, Shemon Bar Sabbae, protested and was executed.

What Christians termed Shapur's 'great persecution' began in the 340s. This was fairly similar to Diocletian's great persecution nearly half a century before. Tens of thousands of Christians were martyred, including most of the senior clergy and both of Shemon Bar Sabbae's successors. However, while Diocletian's persecution was brought swiftly to an end, the Persian Christians were not so lucky and remained a persecuted minority for decades.

A third reason for the growing enmity between Rome and Persia was Constantine's own pride, according to the Roman chronicler, Ammianus Marcellinus. Ammianus says that one day a traveller from India arrived at Constantine's court bearing gifts for the emperor from the peoples of Asia in honour of the Roman emperor's great reputation. However, the traveller claimed the Persians had mistreated him and stolen many of his precious goods. Ammianus says that Constantine believed the man and wrote to Shapur demanding the return of his gifts. Not surprisingly, Shapur denied all knowledge of the affair, whereupon Ammianus says Constantine declared war on Persia, starting a conflict that would last for most of the fourth century, and from which Rome would emerge very much weaker.

Ammianus was a critic of Constantine's, and his account is almost certainly biased against him. However, it is probably true that Constantine suffered from a touch of arrogance towards the Persians, buoyed up by their poor track record against Rome in the last half century, together with his own sense of invincibility as he relished his sole rule of the empire. Whatever his true motives, it is clear that in his last years he was preparing for war with Persia.

However, when it came, the timing of this war was poor for the Romans, since it occurred shortly before Constantine's death in 337. Although, as Ammianus says, Constantine was the first to declare war, it was Shapur who struck first by invading Roman Armenia.

With Constantine's unexpected death, the conduct of the war immediately fell to the young Constantius, and, as his brothers Constantine II and Constans jostled for power in the west, the eastern Roman army found itself fully committed against the Persians. His younger brother, Constans, was particularly unhelpful and ensured that no Roman reinforcements arrived from the west to help. Constans commanded the elite Illyrian legions, which had formed the backbone of both Aurelian's and Diocletian's armies, and he kept these idle on the Danube while the eastern Roman army fought a bloody and bitter contest with the Persians. This was a mistake which Constantius later resolved to remedy when he secured sole control of the empire.

In fact, there was no winner in this first Roman-Persian war. Fought between 337 and 350, it was long, bloody and inconclusive. Although it was the largest Roman military engagement since Constantine the Great had defeated his rival Licinius in 324, we have virtually no meaningful detail about the campaigns. All that exists is a summary of the conflict saying that there were nine separate battles, the most significant of which was the battle of Singara (modern Sinjar in Iraq) in which Constantius was at first victorious and plundered the Persian camp, only to be defeated in a night attack that rendered the battle inconclusive. Shapur succeeded in occupying Roman Armenia but he failed to take the critically important fortress of Nisibis which, although it was besieged three times, valiantly withstood the Persian onslaught, no doubt with its inhabitants fully aware that, as Romans first, and Christians second, their chances of survival if they surrendered were zero.

To his credit, Constantius threw all his resources into this war, with no help from his brothers in the west, and prevented a Roman collapse in Mesopotamia. Eventually, it was Shapur who caved in first. In 350, news of steppe nomads invading the eastern Sasanian provinces – in this case a tribe called the Massagetae, who appear to have been close relations of the Huns – caused him to divert Persian troops to the east and call for a truce. So, Constantius was saved by the Persian challenge of having to fight on two fronts, itself so familiar a problem to the Romans.

No sooner could Constantius relax his efforts on the eastern front than developments took a turn for the worse in the west. For, in 350, as the truce with Shapur was agreed, news reached him that his brother Constans had been murdered and his position usurped by a general in the western army called Magnentius. He now had to contend with a major rebellion in the west.

6

Rebellion in the West

On a cold winter's night in central Gaul, the senior officers of the Rhine army were holding a dinner party. An officer stepped outside through an arch in the stone building that housed the officers' quarters. Waiting for him was his adjutant with a purple cloak. To wear purple was the exclusive right of the emperor and his family. For anyone else, it was an offence punishable by death.

He took the cloak and wrapped it round his shoulders. Then he re-entered the building. He was met with cries of *Augustus* by all the senior officers present. So goes the account of how Magnentius raised a rebellion on the night of 18 January 350, in the town of Augustulum (Autun) in Gaul. Urged on by his fellow officers, and in particular by another senior officer called Marcellinus, his revolt had the unequivocal backing of the Rhine army.

The background to this insurrection was, to begin with, the western emperor Constans' unpopularity with his army. It is difficult to ascertain the truth about his character since the Roman chroniclers could well have been biased, but apparently, he had become lazy and licentious. The spark that lit the fire seems to have been his preference for his own personal bodyguard of barbarian archers to the regular legionaries, causing resentment among the ordinary soldiers. Constans was apparently oblivious of this, and was happily engaged on a hunting expedition near the Pyrenees when Magnentius sent a small force to kill him. The hunter became the hunted, and Constans was seized and killed.

Magnentius, whose father was British and mother Frankish, had had a successful career in the Rhine army and was popular with his fellow officers and the rank and file. Given his partly barbarian ancestry, some historians have seen him as an example of the growing 'barbarisation' of the Roman army, meaning the growing presence of Germanic soldiers within its ranks, but he actually seems to have been thoroughly Romanised with a very successful army career, which began when he joined Constans' elite bodyguard, called the Herculians and Jovians, originally set up by Diocletian. As someone who had worked his way up by merit, he was probably not very different from the soldier-emperors, like Aurelian and Diocletian.

The armies in Britain and Spain quickly followed their Gallic comrades in declaring their support for Magnentius, who was keen to avoid war with Constantius. He tried to please him by issuing coins bearing his name and showing him as the senior Augustus. Hoping to establish some sort of legitimacy in Constantius' eyes, he married a great-granddaughter of Constantine I's, Justina. This worked for six months while Constantius was engaged fighting the Persians. But, when Shapur suddenly had to call a truce in the east because of an invasion of steppe nomads in the north-eastern rim of his empire, Constantius was free to focus fully on the west. Aware that if he acknowledged his brother's murderer, he might give up his own rights of legitimacy on the imperial throne, he decided on war.

By that time, Magnentius' power base had increased. He had usurped Constans' remaining territories, including North Africa and Italy. In Rome, there was a short-lived coup against him led by a man named Julius Nepotianus, a nephew of Constantine I, who unwisely bid for the purple, only to find that his supporters melted away when confronted by Magnentius' legionaries. He was arrested and executed.

Magnentius was now in a powerful position, with most of the western empire under his control. However, there was still one important territory which had remained neutral – Illyria (see Map 1) – and it was significant because it contained a powerful Roman army entrusted with the defence of the upper Danube. The Illyrian legions were the crucial remaining pawn in the power struggle between Magnentius and Constantius. If they had joined Magnentius, as he was urging them to do by sending envoys begging them to make terms with him, he would probably have been too strong for Constantius' eastern army.

However, the Illyrian legions went for a third option, and Constans' former *magister peditum* (commander of infantry), called Vetranio, was proclaimed emperor, forestalling Magnentius. Ultimately, this proved to be a stroke of good fortune for Constantius, since Vetranio was an old soldier and loyal follower of Constantine the Great. His fondness for the former emperor made him susceptible to the entreaties of Constantius' sister, called Constantina, who was Constantine the Great's eldest and most favoured daughter. She met him and persuaded him to stay loyal to her family. Accordingly, Vetranio agreed to meet Constantius at Serdica in late 350 and, before the assembled Illyrian legionaries, he abdicated and proclaimed Constantius the true emperor. The soldiers applauded and swore loyalty to Constantius. Some sources say the soldiers switching allegiance was spontaneous, in response to a rousing speech delivered by Constantius; more likely is that Constantius had been busy buying up the support of Vetranio's senior officers and promising him a comfortable retirement. Certainly, Constantius delivered on this last point and Vetranio was allowed to live in a luxurious villa in Bithynia until his death six years later.

It is worth mentioning that Constantina was one of a growing breed of imperial female power-brokers in the fourth and fifth centuries, which would ultimately culminate in the rule of the famous Galla Placidia in the fifth century. As Constantine the Great's favourite daughter, she still had considerable political influence over men like Vetranio. We will hear more about her shortly.

Vetranio's support for Constantius meant his army was now numerically larger than Magnentius'. He risked everything on a battle. After months of marches and counter-marches, on 28 September 351, the western and eastern Roman armies met at a town called Mursa, close to the Danube, which Magnentius was besieging. Various sources describe the battle, and all of them say that it was a bloody conflict. In the end, Constantius was victorious, helped by the defection of one of Magnentius' senior generals, called Silvanus, and, according to the account written by the future emperor, Julian the Apostate, by the success of the Roman heavy cavalry from the eastern army. But it was a pyrrhic victory. The chronicler Zonaras says that Magnentius lost two thirds of his army and that Constantius lost 40 per cent of his. Zosimus says that it critically weakened the Roman army's ability to counter its enemies. Constantius had won the battle. But the Roman Empire had lost the war.

Thereafter, Magnentius' support evaporated. Constantius briefly campaigned against the empire's enemies along the Danube, the Sarmatians, before invading Italy in 352, and then crossing the Alps. Magnentius sued for peace but Constantius knew he had the upper hand and wanted to finish the usurper off. Magnentius made a last stand in the Alpine foothills at a place called Mons Seleucus, where he was again defeated. Although we have virtually no details of the battle, it is safe to assume that it was a smaller and less bloody engagement than Mursa. Magnentius fled to Lugdunum in Gaul, where on 10 August 353, he committed suicide.

Constantius had achieved his aim of securing sole control of the empire. However, the military cost had been enormous, and with a resurgent Persia in the east, and growing pressures from the Germans along the Rhine and Danube, the Roman army was being stretched to breaking point.

Although Constantius was now sole master of the empire, he felt no more secure. Civil war was always just around the corner for the Romans, and Constantius' reign was no exception. Immediately after winning his first one, he helped to ignite another. The cause lay with his policy of installing relatives into positions of power, in the hope they would prove loyal to him.

For when he was fighting Magnentius, he had appointed his cousin, Constantius Gallus, as Caesar to administer the eastern provinces. Gallus was one of the few survivors of the 'massacre of the princes' in 337 when Constantius had murdered nine of his relatives, including the two co-emperors, Dalmatius and Hannibalianus. Now, in the strange politics of the late Roman Empire, Constantius seemed to have hoped that a blood link would be the foundation of loyalty.

This might sound surprising given that he had murdered most of his relatives, but Constantius placed a high value on legitimacy. It was much more important to him which family his appointees came from than if they were suitable for the job. Plenty of people, both in past and future history, would also try to keep power within the family, but it must be said that the best of the late Roman emperors tended to be those that could spot talent and promote it. Diocletian was a good example of this. But Constantius was no Diocletian, and his obsession with keeping senior positions within his family circle would ultimately prove to be his undoing.

In Gallus' case, he could not have chosen a less suitable governor for the eastern provinces. Ammianus Marcellinus is merciless about Gallus' complete lack of moral integrity. For example, once he took control of the eastern Roman administration, basing himself in Antioch, he accepted bribes in legal cases referred to him, even executing a nobleman in Alexandria apparently in exchange for a large bribe from the unfortunate man's mother-in-law.

This is where Constantius' sister, Constantina, reappears. For she had married Gallus when he was appointed Caesar in the east, and, according to Ammianus, she was even worse than him: 'She was a Fury in mortal form, incessantly adding fuel to her husband's rage, and as thirsty for human blood as he.'[11] The two of them conducted a reign of terror made even worse by the warring political factions in Antioch and Alexandria, who were more than happy to exploit Gallus and Constantina's corruption to have their own enemies exiled or killed. For example, again according to Ammianus, Constantina condemned an innocent nobleman to death simply in exchange for a valuable necklace she liked the look of.

It is worth digressing briefly to mention that Constantina's modern reputation is seriously at odds with her historical records. For, incredibly enough, in modern Rome she has her own church, Santa Costanza, where she is revered as a saint! You may well ask; how did that happen? The story is that she was buried in the church that her father, Constantine the Great, built for her, and which remarkably has survived to this day. In the Middle Ages, a legend developed about this church, which said that she was a wealthy woman, miraculously cured of leprosy, who devoted her life to supporting the poor of the city. Quite how that happened is, as they say, anyone's guess!

Meanwhile, back in the year 354, Constantius, who was in Milan at this time, was outraged at the news of what Gallus and Constantina were up to, and ordered the immediate recall of both. Constantina left first but, according to Ammianus, she died in Bithynia of a fever, although a more sinister cause of death is I think more likely. Gallus then reluctantly followed her, stopping to enjoy the chariot races at Constantinople, where he sat in the imperial box, much to Constantius' indignation. When he reached Pannonia, he was arrested and his interrogation began. He told them he was innocent and had been misled by Constantina. On hearing this, Constantius had him executed.

Having been so badly failed by Gallus, it is surprising Constantius still wanted blood relations to help govern the empire. But he did, and this time he chose his last remaining male relative, a young cousin, who in 355 was only 24 years old. He was about as different to Gallus as you could imagine. A young man who had spent most of his youth studying Greek philosophy and was troubled by the rise of Christianity. A man who would in due course become one of the most remarkable emperors in all of Roman history.

His name was Flavius Claudius Julianus. Posterity has called him Julian the Apostate.

PART II

The Empire of
Julian the Apostate

7

Julian in Gaul

The candle flickered. It cast long shadows on the coarse fabric of the army tent.

Silently, beside a small table, a bearded young man put down the papyrus scrolls he was reading. It was *The Gallic Wars* by Julius Caesar. He closed his eyes and imagined himself 400 years in the past at the battle of Alesia. It was Caesar's greatest victory over the Gauls. He thought how much Rome had changed in those 400 years. How much for the worse. Now, there were no longer sacrifices made to the gods. Instead, the Galileans had instituted their own stifling rules, enforcing the worship of their one god. He had no objections to much of their writings. Indeed, he sympathised with their vision of a heaven based on charity and forgiveness. But that was not what they practiced. They were intolerant. They claimed they alone had the one true god. That was not only patently untrue, but it was a mockery of Jupiter, Sol, Isis, Mithras and all of the gods they sought to crush. Socrates had said that he only knew one thing. That he knew nothing. The young man smiled to himself. *How much wiser*, he thought to himself, *than anything Jesus said.*

Then he laughed out loud. *Forget these thoughts*, he told himself. *For tomorrow you will die. Thirty thousand Germans, maybe more, are marching straight into Gaul and tomorrow we will face them in battle. At least*, he grimaced, *we will fight like Romans, and if we use Caesar's tactics, who knows what will be possible?* The young man was Flavius Claudius Julianus.

Let us begin Julian's story in 337, when he was only six years old. That was the year of Constantine the Great's death, and the year of the 'massacre of the princes' when Constantius executed most of his relatives. For the young Julian, it must have been traumatic, since among those executed was his own father, Julius Constantius, who was Constantine the Great's half-brother. Julian's mother had died in childbirth, leaving him parentless, and he was put in the hands of his maternal grandmother. Why did Julian and his half-brother Gallus survive the slaughter of most of his relatives? We shall never know, but perhaps it was a sense of remorse for these children that restrained Constantius, since Gallus was 11 years old and Julian six. Perhaps, against all expectations, even Constantius had a conscience.

Julian's childhood was secluded, living in Bithynia, where he spent most of his time reading, as he later described himself: 'Some men have a passion for horses, others for birds, others again for wild beasts; but I, from childhood have been infused with a passionate longing to acquire books.'[12]

And these books – or probably papyrus scrolls at this time – were to have a profound effect on him. In his early childhood, they were predominantly Christian texts, shown him by his personal tutor, Eusebius, the bishop of Nicomedia, but later he read many of the great ancient classical texts, including Homer, helped by another tutor called Mardonius. These were the works that meant the most to him, and he developed a fascination and love for ancient Greek and Roman civilisation. In contrast to this, he found the Christian teachings shallow.

One reason for his hostility to Christianity was that he felt oppressed by it. Not only was the new religion becoming ever more aggressive in its attacks on the ancient pagan gods, but it was also the religion of his uncle, Constantius II. And there was nothing very Christian in his uncle's murder of most of his relatives, which, later in his life, Julian denounced as a hideous crime.

But one thing is certain – anyone who saw him as a teenager could not have predicted his future. Julian himself, who has left us with copious writings, recorded that he was excessively bookish and introverted when he was growing up because he was forced to spend his teenage years in virtual solitary confinement. Constantius was so paranoid and suspicious of both Julian and his half-brother, Gallus, that he had them imprisoned on a royal estate in Cappadocia, called Macellum, simply meaning 'the enclosure'. In fact, this was probably better than it sounds, since the estate was a luxurious palace with extensive gardens. However, Julian later said that from the age of 12 to 18, he could not meet anyone his own age, or any of the friends he had met in Bithynia. He and Gallus were supervised by royal eunuchs, who gave the boys a Christian education, and otherwise they were left to being bored teenagers.

Except for Julian. Because the one activity not denied him was reading books. Indeed, he acquired a vast library, with the emphasis on Christian texts but also including all the major works of ancient Greek and Roman philosophy and literature. For him, this was a sort of paradise. It wasn't long before he taught the royal tutors themselves, who were astonished by his intellectual abilities. In 348, when he was 17, he was released from Macellum and allowed to study at Nicomedia. Meanwhile, Gallus was called to the imperial court at Constantinople. But this did not stop Julian continuing his studies at Pergamum and then at Athens, which was still the great centre of pagan philosophy and civilisation even though Christianity was increasingly intolerant of pagans. At Eleusis, just outside Athens, Julian was initiated into the Eleusinian Mysteries involving nine days of rituals, which remain a mystery to us today since the initiates took a vow of silence, and rather surprisingly, no-one ever publicly divulged what was involved. It was in these years that Julian himself later said he was fully converted to paganism.

In these years, Julian was the antithesis of a future emperor. At Athens, he was described by a church father who met him, called Gregory of Nazianzus, as an overly intellectual young man, withdrawn and totally unworldly. Some scholars have wondered whether he purposefully cultivated an eccentric personality in order to make himself less threatening. The emperor Claudius had famously done exactly this in the first century AD when, according to Suetonius, he appeared as a slobbering fool in his youth, making people believe he was a harmless imbecile. If this was Julian's intention, it certainly worked. For Constantius seems to have dismissed him as an idiot and allowed him to pursue his intellectual interests undisturbed.

Not so his half-brother, Gallus, who, as mentioned in the previous chapter, was given an important posting by Constantius in 351 to oversee the eastern provinces, only to be executed after succumbing to the temptations of corruption in 354. For Julian, things also looked ominous. When Gallus was summoned by Constantius to Milan to explain his misrule, he too was summoned from Athens. He was held a virtual prisoner for several days, fearing for his life, until he suddenly received very unexpected news. He was to be made Caesar and sent to Gaul to sort out the collapsing frontier with the German tribes.

What had happened?

Constantius' decision to entrust Julian with an important post has long surprised historians. However, there was one obvious reason. A second rebellion had broken out in Gaul. This time it was by a general called Silvanus, who had deserted Magnentius at the battle of Mursa Major to join Constantius, which may well have been decisive in his securing victory. However, Silvanus clearly felt inadequately rewarded, for he proclaimed himself emperor in August 355, in Cologne only to be killed by his own soldiers 28 days later, when they decided they had been backing the wrong horse. Constantius needed someone he could trust to serve as a figurehead in the west. In desperation, he turned to Julian, his last remaining relative, and in November 355, three months after Silvanus' rebellion, he promoted him to Caesar.

An important influence on his choice came from an unexpected quarter. This was the support given to Julian by Constantius' wife, Eusebia. This is an intriguing relationship, because, in his copious writings, Julian describes her in eulogistic terms. She had married Constantius after his first wife died in 350, and is said to have been exceptionally clever and beautiful. She exerted a powerful influence on Constantius, and met Julian a few years before 355. Our principal source on this relationship is Julian himself, and according to him, it was she who had persuaded Constantius to allow him time studying in Athens, and then again, according to Julian, it was Eusebia who persuaded Constantius to make him Caesar.

Historians have speculated whether Julian and Eusebia were having an affair, but there's no evidence of that, and she probably thought he was a capable young man who her husband could trust. As we will find out, she was correct on the first point, but less so on the second.

On 6 November 355, Julian stood on a rostrum, surrounded by soldiers and standards, as Constantius announced his elevation to Caesar and put a purple cloak around his shoulders. Observers have recorded that Julian looked downcast rather than elated. As part of the conversion to his new life, he was given a wife – Constantius' own unmarried sister, Helena. Unfortunately, Julian has left few kind words about her, suggesting the marriage was far from a love match. Helena was to die five years later in 360, although the cause has never been ascertained. However, Ammianus Marcellinus, our principal source, says that she had two miscarriages and even suggests that Constantius' wife, Eusebia, was instrumental in making these happen by sending her midwives who gave her poison. His allegation is that Eusebia was jealous of Helena, which provides further substance to the idea that Julian and Eusebia were in love with each other, although this is entirely conjectural.

However, what we know for certain is that Julian was despatched to Gaul in 355. And there, he found a truly desperate situation. The problem was that the Franks and Alemanni had taken advantage of Magnentius' rebellion, crossed the Rhine and occupied much of the west bank during the years between 351 and 355. Indeed, Constantius had even invited them to do this in order to divert Magnentius' troops. But once over the Rhine, the Germans would not go back, even when Constantius urged them to after he had defeated Magnentius. Indeed, the Franks were making good progress on the west side of the Rhine and had captured the important fortress city of Cologne in November 355.

So, what could Julian, the intellectual and introverted young man who looked completely the opposite of a soldier, do in this military crisis? To make matters worse, Julian himself and the historian Ammianus, who served in Julian's army and was a devotee of Julian's, say that Constantius denied him any proper authority and made him subordinate to the Roman generals who were already in Gaul. But history is full of surprises. Julian would now show everyone that he was not what he seemed.

8

The Battle of Strasbourg

Gaul was in a mess. The first thing Constantius wanted to do was to recover the west bank of the Rhine from the Germans. To do this, he planned a pincer movement against the German tribes, with the Roman army based in Milan advancing through Switzerland and into southern Germany, while the Roman army in Gaul – led not by Julian but by the main Roman general, Marcellus – advanced due east into Alsace. The two armies would then meet at Strasbourg, surrounding and capturing any Germans who did not retreat across the Rhine.

Unfortunately for Constantius, his plan did not work out. What actually happened was that both Constantius and Marcellus made slow progress, with the bulk of the Roman troops held up by the German defences. But to everyone's surprise, it was Julian who, leading a much smaller Roman force north of Marcellus' army, achieved some startling successes.

How did Julian turn himself into a successful soldier? Almost comically, to begin with at least, the answer lay with self-help books. On his way to Gaul, Julian says that he studied Julius Caesar's *The Gallic Wars*, in which the great general described his conquest of Gaul. Julian used this to make himself an expert in military strategy and tactics. Later, he even went on to write his own military treatises.

But just as importantly, he quickly showed he was no introvert. He rapidly won the respect of his men with his charisma, infectious enthusiasm, courage in battle (which was later to be his undoing), and his unusual insistence on sharing the hardships of army life with them. He always eschewed all luxury and was happy to eat the ordinary soldiers' porridge in his tent. Not just the rank and file came to love him, but experienced officers respected him; in particular, a senior officer, Salutius Secundus, became his trusted second in command and thereafter a lifelong friend.

Julian's first operations comprised hit-and-run guerrilla-type tactics that completely outwitted the Germans and sent them reeling back to the Rhine. He forced them back from besieging Autun, recovered Cologne, and then repelled a major German attack on Sens. And he did all of this with a relatively small number of men and no help from his senior general, Marcellus, who was so jealous of Julian's success that he actually refused to help him. In fact, Marcellus' jealousy did not matter, since Julian's tactics and the diehard loyalty he was earning from his troops were more than a match for the Germans.

Even Constantius was impressed. He sacked Marcellus for not supporting Julian, despite the latter's protests that Julian was plotting against him (which was untrue). For once, Constantius' paranoia gave way to genuine admiration for Julian. He promoted him to commander-in-chief in Gaul, and Julian in his turn appointed an exceptionally experienced and valued career soldier, Severus, as his senior general. It would be a superb choice.

But Julian could not prevent a much less capable commander, Barbatio, from taking command of the Roman troops in northern Italy. Like Marcellus, Barbatio was jealous of Julian's unexpected success. In 357, Julian began a second offensive to expel the Germans from the west bank of the Rhine in Alsace. But while he and Severus advanced into Alsace, Barbatio was halted by the Alemanni in northern Switzerland. They then attacked Lugdunum (modern Lyons) but failed to capture it, and it was Julian's troops who forced them to retreat. Indeed, Julian forced the Germans back along the entire Alsatian front. In contrast, Barbatio was making no progress and refused to help Julian, even burning his boats on the Rhine rather than sending them to help Julian cross the river. This did not matter, since Julian's soldiers, acting as lightly armed commandos, forded the Rhine, captured the islands in the river from the Germans and crossed over.

Meanwhile, Constantius was getting frustrated by Barbatio's lack of success. He ordered him to cross the Rhine. The result was a disaster. The pontoon bridge put across the river by Barbatio's men was smashed by trees the Germans floated downstream. Then they attacked the Romans and sent them reeling back towards Italy. Worse news was to follow. As Julian and Severus achieved their objectives, they heard that a massive German army, said to be 35,000 strong, with a host of tribes uniting against the Romans, was heading towards Strasbourg intending to conquer all of Gaul. Against them, Julian had about 15,000 soldiers.

He was about to face his greatest test so far.

We have exceptionally good records of the Battle of Strasbourg, or Argentoratum, as the Romans called it. Not only has Ammianus Marcellinus left us a detailed account, but we also have the account left by the fifth-century Roman writer, Zosimus, as well as Julian's own description.

The campaign began with the German army crossing the Rhine in late August 357, near to the Roman fortified town of Strasbourg, using a Roman bridge that had not been destroyed. What made it so large was that it was a united force of Alemanni who were still fragmented into tribal groupings. It was led by a fiery character called Chnodomar, nicknamed 'gigas', the giant, by the Romans because he was particularly tall and strong. With him were six other kings and ten princes, and a total army of 35,000, according to Ammianus.

Meanwhile, Julian's army had 13,000 men according to Ammianus, although some historians have suggested it might have been more like 15–20,000. Whatever the truth, the Romans were heavily outnumbered. There was a large Roman cavalry contingent, maybe up to 3,000 strong, comprising mailed horsemen and mounted archers, who were the battle-winning innovation of the Illyrian emperors in the third century. These were the tanks of the Roman army, and Julian hoped to use them to rout the Germans, who had only a few and relatively lightly armed cavalry. But the bulk of the army was infantry, although these included some of the best regiments. For example, the 5,000 or so legionaries (a late Roman legion had about 1,000 men, reduced from the 5,000-strong legions of the earlier empire) came from veteran units such as the Herculiani, the Ioviani and the Primani. These had been created by the Illyrian emperors as elite units in the third century. The rest of the infantry were equally highly regarded auxiliary units, mainly recruited from the German tribes themselves but trained after Roman methods. These included the celebrated Cornuti and Bracchiati vexillations (vexillations were smaller than legions) – the Cornuti are even displayed on the Arch of Constantine as elite soldiers in the battle of the Milvian Bridge.

Facing this Roman force, the German army was very different – mainly light infantry organised into tribal groupings with little discipline or coordination. Despite this, like the Franks and Burgundians, they were a highly militarised society with great emphasis placed on their warriors' individual bravery, strength and skill in battle. Tacitus recorded how, with the invasion of the Cimbri and Teutones back in the second century BC, the German women cheered their men on into battle, and would even kill those who dared to retreat! The Alemanni were of the same stock and not an enemy to mess with.

One important tactical difference compared with the Romans was the German use of cavalry. Being lightly armed, they could not match the mailed Romans in hand-to-hand combat, but they could still play a few tricks, as Ammianus described:

They [the Germans] realised that one of their warriors on horseback, no matter how skilful, in meeting one of our Clibanarii [armoured Roman cavalry] must hold bridle and shield on one hand and brandish his spear in the other, and could thus do no harm to a soldier protected by metal armour; whereas the infantry soldier in the hottest part of the fight, when nothing is apt to be guarded against except what is straight ahead of oneself, can move around low down and unseen, and by piercing a horse's side throw its unsuspecting rider headlong, whereupon he can be slain with little trouble.[13]

This tactic was to be used to devastating effect in the battle.

The first question for Julian was whether to retreat or give battle. He seems to have had little doubt that the latter course of action was the best, no doubt following Julius Caesar's advice that attack was often the best form of defence. His confidence was boosted by his excellent rapport with the officers and men in his army, and the knowledge that the troops he commanded were of an exceptionally high quality, probably just as good as those in Caesar's legions 400 years before.

So, in late August 357, Julian advanced to meet the Germans outside Strasbourg, where most of them had crossed the Rhine. The Romans sighted the Germans around midday. Julian deployed his army in a textbook fashion, with the infantry in the centre and the heavy cavalry on the right wing. He took personal command of the centre with his experienced general, Severus, commanding the left wing with a mix of infantry and cavalry.

Meanwhile, the Germans had prepared themselves well. Both sides used scouts and had gained a reasonable knowledge of each other's battle formations. Chnodomar positioned himself opposite the Roman heavy cavalry, expecting their attack to be the main Roman assault. He took what cavalry the Germans had. The great bulk of the German infantry faced the Roman legionaries in the centre. On the German right wing, a king called Serapion hid in a large wood with thousands of infantry and the few German cavalry, waiting to ambush Severus.

An incident just before the battle provides an interesting insight into the mentality of the German warriors. For they suddenly clamoured for their leaders to dismount from their horses and fight on foot. Their intention was to deny them an easy escape route in the event the Romans won. Chnodomar and the other kings obliged. This suggests Germanic society was surprisingly egalitarian. In contrast, it would have been unthinkable for the Romans to do the same. The Roman military structure was of course intensely hierarchical. The German behaviour suggests a lack of discipline. And this was to prove a decisive weakness in the forthcoming battle.

Shortly after the German leaders dismounted, the Roman trumpets heralded the attack. The Roman legionaries in the centre advanced in a tight formation while the Germans rushed to meet them, roaring their battle cry. Ammianus has described the terrifying spectacle of the German charge – 'they gnashed their teeth hideously and raged beyond their usual manner, their flowing hair made a terrible sight, and a kind of madness shone from their eyes.'[14]

There was an exchange of javelins, and then the Romans formed a tight shield wall in a testudo, or tortoise, formation, with the ranks behind the front line holding their shields high over their heads to protect them from the downpour of arrows and javelins. The tortoise formation was of course one of the most famous Roman tactics, especially in the early empire, and it is interesting to note that it was still widely used in the late empire.

While the Roman centre stood firm, the left wing led by Severus made some progress despite being ambushed by the Germans hiding in the wood. But it was on the right wing that the Romans fared badly. For the heavy cavalry which Julian had placed there, in the hope they would deliver the knockout blow against the Germans, found themselves embroiled in a desperate fight in which some of the German horsemen, as noted earlier, dismounted and infiltrated the horses, stabbing them from below and then butchering their unseated riders. In their heavy armour, the Romans found it difficult to fend off the German infantry, and when they saw a tribune wounded in this way and another armoured horseman, a clibanarius, thrown by his horse and badly injured, they decided their armour would not help them, so they turned and fled.

Julian, who was with the centre – and, as Ammianus described him, 'did not know the meaning of fear',[15] – spurred his horse towards them to restore order. Standing with his bodyguard and highly visible because of the purple dragon standard held aloft by a long spear (this type of standard had replaced the earlier Roman ones), he met the retreating horsemen and halted them. Or at least that is Ammianus' version, for Zosimus' account, although written many years later, says that Julian could not prevent the cavalry from retreating off the field. This is probably more likely. The Roman infantry in the centre were now exposed to the full fury of the German attack from both their left wing and the centre. It looked as if the Germans were going to win.

But then two things happened. First, Severus on the left wing held firm and pushed back the German right wing, so at least the legionaries in the centre did not need to worry about being outflanked on their left. Second, and this seems to have been the decisive factor, Julian called forward the elite infantry reserves which he had been holding back. These were the veteran Cornuti and Bracchiati auxiliary units who, as mentioned earlier, were exceptionally well-disciplined. They immediately proved their worth by stemming the German onslaught.

This was where Julian's careful reading of Julius Caesar's writing made the vital difference. Holding back a large reserve of high-quality troops was one of Caesar's most important tactics in his victories in Gaul. In the Battle of Strasbourg, it also worked. For despite the Roman cavalry being routed, the Roman wall of shields and testudo formations held firm. Only once did the Germans break through, whereupon they met the heavy legionaries of the Legio Primani – the *Praetorians* of the Roman army, as Ammianus described them – who Julian had held back in reserve. These soldiers 'stood as firm as towers and renewed the battle with increased spirit'.[16]

It was the injection of reserves that made the difference. The attacking Germans were pushed back, and with corpses piling up in front of the Roman shields, their morale broke. A lack of discipline among the Germans turned their attack into panic. Suddenly, groups of warriors turned back and fled. Then the entire German army broke up en masse and swarmed back towards the Rhine.

The Romans ran after them, killing them in their thousands. However, Julian, who as always was in the midst of the battle, showing no fear for his own safety, was apprehensive of a German counter-attack, again something Julius Caesar warned could follow a retreat by the enemy. So, he quickly ordered horns to call the Romans to a halt and pursue the Germans in a more orderly fashion to the bank of the Rhine, where the Roman archers could pick them off as they struggled to swim across, providing 'a stage show' as Ammianus described it, in which the Romans watched the barbarians drowning, swimming and being transfixed by Roman arrows and javelins.

It was a complete victory for the Romans. The German king Chnodomar was captured. Ammianus claims that 6,000 German corpses were counted on the battlefield, aside from the thousands that died in the rout and their desperate crossing of the Rhine. The number of Roman dead, according to Ammianus, was only 243 men and four officers, which seems unrealistically low.

Roman discipline had won the day. The battle showed that late Roman soldiers had retained many of the characteristics which enabled them to achieve success in the golden age of the Republic and early empire. This was despite a complete change in its ethnic composition, since Julian's army was predominantly Gallic and even had many Germans among the auxiliaries. However, the poor performance of the heavy cavalry, which had been the Romans' key to success in the third century, was an ominous sign for the future. After the battle, Julian made them put on women's clothing and perform a parade of shame while the infantry jeered them.

The battle was decisive in fourth-century Roman history in two important respects. First, it clearly saved Gaul from a serious Germanic invasion. But second, and more importantly, it would now set off a chain of events leading to Julian becoming the last pagan emperor of Rome.

9

Civil War

In the months after the Battle of Strasbourg, with his usual tireless energy, Julian exploited the opportunities afforded by the victory. He crossed the Rhine and ravaged Alemanni territory in punishment for their daring to invade Gaul. He also concentrated his now weary army on ridding northern Gaul of a Frankish presence which had developed during the years of neglect when Magnentius had revolted. Basing his forces in Cologne, he and Severus conducted several expeditions to recover territory from the Franks in what is now northern France, and then led a punitive campaign against another similar German tribe, called the Chamavi, who had occupied what is now the modern Netherlands, and used their command of the Rhine, Meuse and Scheldt waterways to cut off the grain supply from Britain. This supply had become important for the Roman army in Gaul really because of the Frankish devastation of the countryside in northern Gaul, which had also probably never fully recovered from the earlier destruction wrought in the crisis of the third century.

Meanwhile, all the time that Julian was building his reputation in Gaul, it is no surprise that Constantius was becoming more and more suspicious of his young cousin. This was despite Julian's diplomatic handling of the situation. Although he was actually applauded as Augustus (i.e., emperor) by his troops immediately after his victory at Strasbourg, he concealed this from Constantius and continued to send him lengthy panegyrics in which he praised the middle-aged emperor for his courage and sagacity.

But Constantius was not fooled. True to form, he began a cunning strategy to undermine his new Caesar. For example, he used the separation of the army and the administration of Gaul, implemented by Diocletian to prevent corruption, to his advantage by appointing his own administrative minister, Florentius, to hinder Julian in every way he could, even depriving his troops of pay because tax revenues had fallen sharply in Gaul. Constantius also recalled Julian's trusted second in command, Salutius Secundus, who was doubly important to him after the death of Severus, his able lieutenant who had helped him to victory at Strasbourg but died of natural causes soon afterwards.

Then, in January 360, Constantius went too far. He ordered Julian to send troops east to fight the Persians. And it was not just a small part of Julian's army he wanted. He ordered four of his best auxiliary regiments – the Aeruli, Batavi, Petulantes and Celtae – together with 300 men from every other legion and vexillation, to leave Gaul immediately to report to him in the east. This probably represented just under half of Julian's army, and would have left him with no real military strength. However, Constantius justified his order by saying that Shapur II had just launched another Persian offensive in which he had captured the major Syrian fortress of Amida, and was now threatening the whole of the east. This was true.

So, what could Julian do? Revolt against the emperor or go along with him? Historians are divided about what really happened. One version was written by Julian himself, who was a prolific writer during his lifetime, and thankfully many of his writings have survived. Of course, we also have the writings of the most reliable historian of this period, Ammianus Marcellinus. Both these accounts say that Julian was loyal to Constantius but what pushed him into revolt was the refusal of his troops to march east. They add that Constantius had misjudged the situation, especially the fact that the Gallic legions comprised Gauls who had no wish to depart for the east, leaving their families vulnerable to renewed Germanic attacks. So, according to these sources, the army of Gaul mutinied of its own accord, and in February 360, in Paris, they proclaimed Julian Augustus for a second time to prevent their having to march east.

But some historians think this version of events was propaganda invented by Julian and Ammianus after the event. They suggest that the soldiers' acclamation in Paris was engineered by Julian, who, working with his senior officers, decided this was the moment to make his bid for power. Whatever the truth, when Constantius heard this, he was at Caesarea in Cappadocia, and is said to have flown into a rage. However, neither he nor Julian wanted an open civil war at this stage. Constantius was actually more worried by the Persians than Julian. And Julian was mindful of his own precarious position. He knew he had little support outside Gaul and that Constantius was still seen by most Romans as the legitimate emperor. After all, he was Constantine the Great's son.

The result was a phoney war between them. Julian did not rush into any immediate confrontation with Constantius. It was business as usual in Gaul. He launched a campaign against the Franks in the summer of 360. We know from coins he issued in 360 and 361 that he used the title of Augustus, but some of his coins showed both him and Constantius as Augustus, suggesting he wanted joint rule. He also maintained a dialogue with Constantius, proposing that troops in Spain could reinforce the eastern front rather than his own Gallic soldiers.

But Constantius' paranoia was getting the better of him. He resorted to bribing the Germans to attack Julian, just as he had done with Magnentius, and Julian was compelled in 361 to campaign against the Alemannic king, Vadomarius, who had been paid by Constantius to attack Gaul.

This left Julian with little alternative but to go to war. Perhaps that is exactly what Constantius wanted, since he might have felt it was a war he could win, just as he had won against the rebel Magnentius. Certainly, he commanded most of the empire. Julian decided that attack was the best form of defence, and led a significant number of troops down the Danube on boats into the Balkans, occupying Illyria with little resistance, and then setting up camp at the town of Naissus on the border with Thrace and threatening Constantinople. Julian later claimed he had never wanted war and his advance was only meant to persuade Constantius that joint rule was in both of their best interests.

If this was true, it certainly did not look to be working.

For Constantius sent troops to seize Aquileia in northern Italy, to protect his control of Italy and the Adriatic. Constantius was still popular throughout most of the empire, especially in the city of Rome which he had visited in 357, and where he had put up a massive obelisk in the Circus Maximus in homage to the old capital of the empire. The moribund senate supported him, not Julian, despite Julian writing a letter to them, begging for their help.

Then, just as the empire looked on the edge of dissolving into a hugely damaging civil war, Julian's lucky streak continued. Constantius died. On his way back from the Persian front, returning to Constantinople, he contracted a fever and died in Cilicia (in modern Turkey) as he was about to travel through the Taurus Mountains. He was 44 years old and his death was totally unexpected. The empire was spared a civil war. What was even better for Julian was that, in his will, Constantius had previously nominated him as his successor, and he had not changed this despite the civil war between them. So Julian was now the sole and undisputed ruler of the empire. Catastrophe had been averted. On 11 December 361, Julian rode into the city of Constantinople, and the people turned out en masse to cheer him on.

A new chapter for the Roman Empire was about to begin.

10

The Philosopher Emperor

Julian's short reign, from 361 until his early death in battle in 363, was a pivotal moment in the history of the fall of the Roman Empire.

It was the last time that an emperor tried to recreate the golden age of Rome that had in reality been destroyed in the crisis of the third century. Julian is of course best remembered for his epithet 'the Apostate'. But it was not a term used in his lifetime. It was only used by Christians after his death, referring to his renunciation of Christianity. What this term fails to capture is Julian's positive energy and his yearning to revive the great civilisations of ancient Rome and Greece.

Julian is probably better described as the Philosopher Emperor rather than the Apostate, because he saw himself in the tradition of the philosopher kings that Plato envisaged in his great work the *Republic*. Julian was extremely well educated. His model as emperor was Marcus Aurelius, himself a philosopher and enlightened ruler, and Julian set himself on the path to becoming the same.

To begin with, Julian opposed Constantius' extravagant court. One story goes that, shortly after his arrival in

Constantinople, he sent for a barber. A richly dressed man appeared. When the barber revealed the huge salary Constantius paid him, Julian fired him on the spot, saying: 'I sent for a barber, not the head of the treasury.'[17]

Julian cut back the extravagant expenditure in Constantius' court, but this was a trifle compared with his attempt to make a wholesale restructuring of imperial administration. For Julian wanted to return to the empire of Augustus, and even wished to undo the centralisation of state that Diocletian had implemented to maintain power in the years of military anarchy in the third century.

Nothing Julian did was ever superficial. All of his actions were based on a deep understanding of ancient Rome. Now, he wanted to reduce the bloated imperial civil service and replace it with a strong civic authority, such as had existed in Augustus' reign and which had been the hallmark of the Pax Romana. At that time, the central bureaucracy running the empire was tiny, containing only a few hundred civil servants. Under Diocletian and Constantine, this had swollen to an estimated 35,000 civil servants. Julian slimmed this down by giving more power for tax collection and civil administration to the cities in the empire. He strengthened their resources by no longer requiring cities to present golden wreaths to the emperor. Cities had traditionally given the emperor a golden wreath every year as taxation. The wreaths could be huge and represented a considerable cost. Instead of sending these to him, Julian urged the city councils to spend their money on road maintenance and other amenities, which had been de-emphasised since the crisis of the third century.

A famous and very tangible example of his central cost reduction was his overhaul of the imperial courier system. The Romans had an extensive transport system for those travelling on government business, whether military or civil, throughout the empire. Thousands of staging posts and horses were maintained at enormous cost in all parts of the empire, and used by many officials. Julian restricted the perk of using them to essential business only and saved significant costs.

Besides this policy of decentralisation, Julian focused on bolstering the power of the senate in Constantinople. His aim was to make it equivalent to what the Roman senate had been in Augustus' era. He made a point of paying respect to the senate, just as Marcus Aurelius had done, by going on foot to the senate house instead of summoning the senators to his palace, as many of his predecessors had done. He took part in debates, giving his own speeches and accepting the votes of the senate, even if they went against his views, as binding in law. He passed legislation protecting the rights of senators and always described himself as a servant of the state, in a similar fashion to Augustus. This was a transformation compared with the autocratic rule of the emperors since Diocletian and Constantine. Julian was intent on restoring Rome to what it had once been – an essentially republican institution.

One area we have not touched on so far is Christianity and, of course, this is the area for which Julian is most famous. Reviled by Christian chroniclers in later centuries as the man who wanted to destroy Christianity, historians have long debated what his real objectives were. It seems to me that Julian was more enlightened and broad-minded than his critics say. At no point did he consider a persecution of the Christians. This simply did not appeal to his liberal mentality. He also knew that Diocletian's Great Persecution had been an abysmal failure which only served to strengthen the moral appeal of Christianity.[18]

Indeed, Julian always greatly enjoyed theological debates with Christians. One famous example was when he asked the blind bishop of Chalcedon, a man called Maris, why, if the Christian god was all powerful, he did not restore his eyesight, to which the bishop allegedly replied, 'So I might not set eyes on a tyrant like you.'[19] Julian was said to be delighted with his reply, describing it as clever and very witty. Other emperors would have had the man executed on the spot.

Julian's aim was to establish a level playing field between Christianity and the pagan religions. He was acutely aware that because Constantine had promoted the Christian Church, he had given it an advantage over paganism. For example, Constantine had exempted the clergy from taxation and spent state funds on church building. He and his son, Constantius, also persecuted those pagan religions which were out of favour, actually removing gold and precious metals from their temples. This resulted in quite a significant wealth transfer from pagans to Christians, which Julian wanted to stop. So, he banned all the tax advantages that the clergy and Christian Church enjoyed and which undoubtedly had helped Christianity to expand.

His next action was the edict of universal religious toleration – enacted on 4 February 362 – in which all religions were cited as equal before the law. There has been much debate about what his true intentions were, because religious toleration was in fact already enshrined in law, but this had become somewhat theoretical by the mid-fourth century. The truth was that Christianity was becoming more and more militant. The persecution of the Christians in the third century had been turned fully around and now it was the Christians who were ransacking temples and persecuting pagan cults. Many Christian bishops had a fanatical approach to conversion, and what Julian objected to was this loss of toleration in Roman society. With his edict, he emphasised that Christianity was not superior to other religions, going against both Constantine's and Constantius' attempts to make Christianity the official religion of the empire.

However, some historians see a more cunning agenda on Julian's part as they suggest he hoped to destroy Christianity by fomenting dissent between Christians themselves. The opportunity existed because the early Christian Church was deeply divided on many issues. As Ammianus Marcellinus noted wryly, 'No wild beasts are as dangerous to man as one Christian to another.' The Arian[20] division was a conspicuous one, not helped by the fact that the emperor Constantius was Arian, in opposition to many of the western clergy who were not. In the east, the bishop of Alexandria, Athanasius, was vehemently anti-Arian. Julian almost certainly hoped to strengthen these divisions and undermine the Church.

But his only direct attack on the Church was that banning Christians from being teachers and lawyers. This was damaging because it marginalised the Christian community. Julian's rationale was a clever one. He argued that since Christianity was monotheistic, it was not an enlightened religion and, as such, it was at odds with a liberal education and the rule of law. In concept, this was somewhat similar to the practice in modern French schools which have been secular since the French Revolution. However, Julian took it a step further by forbidding Christians to teach at all, whereas in modern France they can of course be teachers provided they do not teach religion.

To understand Julian's approach to Christianity, we must remember that, in his day, many Christians were militant, intent on promoting their faith as the only true religion and banning all others. None of his actions suggest he wanted to do more than limit Christian extremism, rather than ban the 'Galilean' faith, as he termed it.

Julian's aim was to restore Rome to its golden age and, just as he wished to revive the pagan gods, so he wanted to destroy its greatest rival – Persia. And in the last year of his life, he undertook what would be Rome's last great military expedition. The invasion of Persia.

11

War With Persia

In March 363, Julian departed from Antioch with a vast Roman army, maybe 90,000 strong. His aim was to destroy Persia, Rome's traditional rival.

This rivalry was central to how the ancient world worked. There had always been a sharp cultural divide between the civilisations of Rome and Greece, on the one hand, and Persia on the other. For Persia was not just Rome's lifelong enemy, it was also Greece's. The Achaemenid Persian Empire had tried to conquer ancient Greece only to be defeated at the famous battles of Marathon and Salamis, and this was followed by Alexander the Great's conquest of Persia, an event that changed world history.

Julian was profoundly aware of this historical relationship with Persia. Like most Romans, he regarded Alexander the Great as the military ideal to which he aspired. So, it is not surprising he regarded Persia's defeat as his greatest challenge. There were also some more pragmatic reasons why he wanted to defeat Persia. First, he wanted to secure the loyalty of the eastern army which had fought for Constantius, and which he had nearly come to blows with in the civil war that never happened. Second, he was a good general. His rise to power was entirely based on his capable leadership of the Gallic army and his string of victories in the west. He thought he could repeat these in the east.

And because he was the sole emperor, he also had the means to defeat the Persians. Constantius had never been able to unite the eastern and western parts of the Roman army against Shapur II, but Julian could do this in the way the great emperors of old had done. Incidentally, it is interesting to note that Julian's Gallic legions, who mutinied against Constantius' order to march east in 360, now changed their minds and were happy to fight in the east. This supports the view of some historians that the mutiny had been orchestrated by him as a pretext to seize power.

On 5 March 363, Julian left Antioch. But before we follow his campaign, it is important to mention that his stay in Antioch had been deeply unsettling for him personally. He had gone there in May 362 from Constantinople and had spent nine frustrating months arguing with both the Christians and pagans in the city. We have excellent records about this from both Julian himself and the historian Ammianus Marcellinus. So, what was the problem?

To start with, Julian was disappointed by how apathetic the pagans in Antioch were about his enthusiasm to revive the ancient gods. In particular, there was a grand temple to Apollo just outside Antioch, which he was particularly interested in reviving. But the inhabitants had largely forgotten about it and when he organised a ritual sacrifice, he was mortified to discover the priest had given up performing them and had to rush out to find a goose from a local farm to sacrifice.

Things got even worse when the temple burnt down shortly afterwards, probably because of the same negligent priest who Julian had flogged.

Julian was also shocked by how big the Christian community in Antioch had become. Antioch was probably split 50/50 between Christians and pagans at this time, but it had a rich Christian heritage, claiming to be the cradle of Christianity, where Paul the Apostle and Barnabas had established the first Christian community. Julian appears to have underestimated this, and he was annoyed by the ostentation and wealth of the Christians in Antioch. His indignation focused on the Golden Church, so-called because of its rich decorations, which had been built by Constantine and made even grander by Constantius. The burning of the temple of Apollo caused Julian to wonder if the Christians were responsible, and in retaliation, he closed the Golden Church.

In brief, Julian succeeded in alienating both Christians and pagans in this great city, and although he wrote one of his most famous pieces just before he left, called the 'Misopogon', or 'Beard Hater' – in which, with his characteristic humour and humility, he mocked himself as the eponymous bearded philosopher who everyone reviled, while also pointing out that the inhabitants of Antioch were superficial and hypocritical – he was clearly deeply disturbed by the whole experience and vowed never to return to the city.

While his troubles at Antioch were in themselves of little significance, they may have distracted Julian from the crucially important Persian campaign. This was to be his master plan. He had been working on it from the moment of

Constantius' death in 361, and over the previous 15 months he had not only built up an enormous army, but he had also devised a clever strategy. His aim was to capture the Persian capital, Ctesiphon – which had become symbolic in Roman minds with victory over Persia, having been captured three times by the Romans in the second century AD, when it was controlled by the relatively weaker Parthian dynasty, and then twice in the Roman recovery of the late third century.

Key to his plan was Shapur's brother, Hormizd, who had fled to Constantinople 40 years earlier as Constantine the Great's guest and rival to Shapur. Julian hoped to place him on the Persian throne as a vassal king. In retrospect, this seems more like a wild hope than an informed calculation but there may have been rebels in the Persian court who supported Hormizd that we do not know of.

His plan of campaign was well thought through, reflecting both his fascination with military tactics and his extensive reading of the past invasions of Persia, from the Athenian Xenophon to Alexander the Great and then to Trajan. He was well aware there were two ways of approaching Ctesiphon, either down the Euphrates or down the Tigris. Ctesiphon was actually located on the Tigris but this was a longer route than following the Euphrates (see Map 2). Trajan had attacked it by sailing down the Euphrates with a fleet and then digging a canal linking the Euphrates to the Tigris, so he could send his fleet from one river to the other to attack the city. This was the shortest route to Ctesiphon and Julian decided to copy Trajan, partly because he believed he had identified the same canal which Trajan had dug over 200 years before, although he knew the Persians had blocked it up.

Julian also wanted to trick Shapur into thinking he was taking the Tigris route, by advancing towards it and then splitting his army. He appointed Procopius as the commander of 30,000 men who would break away from his army and advance towards the upper Tigris as a diversionary attack, while he planned to head south along the Euphrates with the bulk of the army, probably around 60,000 men. Procopius was a maternal cousin of Julian's and someone he thought he could trust. Meanwhile, Shapur was indeed located with his main army in the north along the Armenian frontier, expecting Julian to launch his offensive there, which was the traditional battleground between Rome and Persia. Julian also made an agreement with the Armenian king, Arshak II, to join Procopius and form a formidable Roman and Armenian army which would keep Shapur engaged in the north while his army sailed down the Euphrates to Ctesiphon.

Julian's plan looked convincing, at least on paper. Buoyed up with his success in the west, Julian was keen to execute it. But historians have emphasised that this was not actually necessary. Shapur was not in fact a major threat to Rome at this time. His relations with Rome blew hot and cold, depending very much on what else was going on in his empire, in particular how dangerous the steppe nomads along his eastern frontier were. In 359, Shapur had inflicted a major defeat on Constantius by capturing the key Roman fortress city of Amida after a 73-day siege, but the Persians had suffered huge losses and made almost no other progress. Shapur was not intending to attack Rome. Indeed, it seems he was alarmed by the prospect of Julian's invasion and sent him envoys pleading for peace.

Despite this, Julian had set his heart on war and nothing would dissuade him from setting off from Antioch in March 363. His army is estimated to have been anything from 65,000 to 95,000 strong, and whatever the precise number, it was certainly one of the largest Roman armies ever mustered in Rome's entire history. Our main source, Ammianus Marcellinus, who was on the campaign with Julian, recounts omens of doom as the army set off, such as the collapse of masonry from an arch on the soldiers as they passed through the town of Hierapolis, killing 50 of them, and another incident when a huge haystack collapsed and crushed 50 grooms. But this sort of superstitious storytelling can be dismissed as being wise after the event.

Almost certainly, the army's morale was high as it set off in the knowledge that Julian, who was hugely popular with the western army, was leading it, and it was the largest army Rome had fielded since the days of Trajan. The prospect of booty and plunder would have been extremely enticing for the common soldiers.

After sending Procopius off on his decoy mission, Julian met up with a vast fleet that he had constructed, comprising maybe 1,250 ships and 50 pontoon vessels, to facilitate river crossings. These ships had been built further north near Samosata, and they joined Julian's army at the Roman town of Circesium. Together, the fleet and army set off down the Euphrates, with Julian travelling in a barge. The army was well supplied by the fleet. Everything seemed set for another of Julian's glorious victories.

On 6 April, just before they passed into Persian territory, Julian made a rousing speech to the army, which Ammianus

Marcellinus recorded. In it, Julian called the expedition a historic event, and claimed the defeat of Persia would be like Rome's triumph over Carthage:

> *...the emperors Trajan, Verus and Septimius Severus returned victorious from Persia. Angered by the fate of our captured cities and defeated armies, I am resolved to make our territory safe and strong. Should I be killed in battle, it will be as a willing sacrifice for my country. We must destroy Persia as our ancestors destroyed Carthage. What I ask from you is steadfast discipline in achieving this aim.*[21]

With these words, Rome's last great army marched into the shimmering sunlight of Persia.

12

The Spear of Destiny

Julian liked taking risks.

His Persian expedition was the biggest risk he had undertaken since his revolt against Constantius. With that, he had been fortunate in that Constantius had unexpectedly died of natural causes. Much of Julian's success so far had been because of a large dose of luck. And, as everyone knows, luck is fickle.

As he marched into Persia in early April 363, his army was so large that it spread for ten miles alongside the Euphrates. After it left the last outpost on the river, the frontier city of Circesium, its initial advance into Persia was reasonably successful. The first Persian city they encountered, called Anatha, surrendered without a fight, and the garrison commander even joined the Roman army. They also liberated a prisoner of war who was nearly a hundred years old and had been captured when he had fought for Diocletian's co-emperor, Maximian, back in the third century. The old soldier was overjoyed and told Julian that he had always known he would eventually be freed.

Although Shapur II himself was not in the area, the Persians were by now aware of Julian's offensive along the

Euphrates, and Shapur sent the Surena, his deputy and the head of the Sasanian army, to command the forces opposing Julian. Growing numbers of Persian troops harried the Romans as they marched down the Euphrates. At one point, Hormizd, Shapur's brother and Julian's would-be pretender for the Sasanian throne, was nearly captured while out on reconnaissance.

Finally, in late April, the Romans reached Porisabora, the first well-defended Persian city. This was Julian's first test, since it had a strong garrison of regular Persian troops, maybe some 2,500 strong. Using their powerful reflex bows, the defenders took a heavy toll on the attacking legionaries, even when they used their famous tortoise formations. Ammianus Marcellinus recounts Julian joined one such formation in an attack on a gate, risking his life. When the bombardment of arrows and stones from the Persians was too much, Julian and his legionaries retreated. Ammianus says Julian later told him he was copying what he read Scipio did when attacking Carthage. Although Julian's bravery was beyond reproach, there was a recklessness in risking his own life that set an ominous precedent for the future.

The siege was helped by Julian's fascination with siege warfare – he had even written a book on the different siege engines. He ordered the construction of a gigantic siege tower armed with catapults and battering rams, which Ammianus called a 'helepolis' or city-taker. When the city's outer walls had finally been breached, this monster was dragged through the streets to the citadel, where the Persian garrison was making a last stand. Confronted with such a machine, which was actually taller than the citadel walls, and knowing that they were incapable of resisting it, the defenders lined the walls, lifting their arms in the air in surrender. Their commander was lowered on a rope to negotiate with Hormizd and Julian, who spared their lives.

It was a victory but fiercely fought for, and suggested this would not be an easy campaign. This impression was reinforced the next day when a Persian cavalry unit, led by the Surena himself, attacked three Roman cavalry squadrons. A Roman standard was captured and Julian personally led a relief force to chase the Persians off. Julian was so discouraged by the poor Roman performance that he punished the cavalry squadrons by putting to death ten of their company. This was unusually severe. Perhaps to compensate for this, the same day he called the army together and promised to pay each man a hundred pieces of silver in additional pay – the type of donative that had become customary to offer the army. This was actually less than what he gave the Gallic army when they proclaimed him Augustus in Paris in 360. The soldiers voiced their disappointment, upon which Julian made a speech saying that if they defeated the Persians, the plunder would be spectacular, and he would be better placed to reward them than if he paid Rome's enemies for peace, as had become normal under his predecessors.

This seems to have motivated the soldiers sufficiently for the army to continue its march down the Euphrates to the next Persian city, Maiozamalcha, on about 8 May. Again, this was a powerful stronghold, sited on a rocky outcrop, with tall walls and well garrisoned. Displaying both his bravery and recklessness in equal measure, Julian took a small reconnaissance force to scout out the city's defences. He was nearly killed when ten Persians leapt out from behind a concealed postern gate. Ammianus says that the emperor actually killed one of them with his sword and the rest were driven off.

Although the soldiers were pleased to hear of Julian's bravery, it did not help them take the city. The heavily armed Persian defenders poured arrows and stones down on the attacking legionaries. Midday temperatures reached 40 degrees centigrade. Things were becoming desperate. Julian was also worried about the proximity of Shapur with the main Persian army. He had received no news from Procopius, either. So, using his extensive knowledge of siege operations, he put together a group of sappers to mine under the walls. To hide the noise they made, he organised a series of attacks on the walls to distract the defenders' attention. This strategy paid off and the Roman sappers, led by a capable tribune called Dagalaifus, opened the mine at night just behind the walls and burst through, slaughtering the Persian guards who were singing songs to keep themselves awake.

Within minutes, the Romans opened the gates and legionaries streamed in, killing the townspeople and soldiers alike. What followed was carnage. Ammianus says that many of the defenders threw themselves to their deaths from the walls. There was a wholesale slaughter of the inhabitants, although Ammianus says many of the women were spared since 'Persian women are renowned for their beauty'. There was also plenty of booty to delight the soldiers' greed. Julian made a point of telling the troops that the plunder was all theirs, and he would keep for himself only three gold coins and spare the life of a dumb boy whose skill in sign language impressed him.

The campaign was now reaching a critical point. Ctesiphon was only a few days' march away. Julian wanted to get there before Shapur. It was then that he implemented a potential masterstroke. He identified the canal that the emperor Trajan had dug 250 years before to link the Euphrates and Tigris. The Persians had filled it in, and instead used a canal below Ctesiphon to link the two rivers, where it would be difficult for an enemy fleet to sail upstream to attack the city. Trajan's old canal was cleared and the dams restraining the water were broken. Ammianus described a great head of water pouring through the canal, after which came the Roman fleet. In horror, the inhabitants of Ctesiphon looked out from their city walls to see the Tigris filled with Roman ships.

Meanwhile, the army marched beside the canal towards the city. The soldiers found themselves in the green and well-watered hinterland to Ctesiphon. They reached the Persian king's zoological garden, replete with lions, boars and exotic animals, which unfortunately they butchered with bloodthirsty delight. But Persian resistance was stiffening as they approached Ctesiphon. A fort in front of the city put up a daunting resistance, first nearly killing Julian himself when he, yet again recklessly, reconnoitred it. His armour bearer was wounded by a hail of arrows sent in their direction, and Julian was only just able to scramble away unscathed. Then a night attack on the fort was unexpectedly met by the defenders opening the gates and sallying out. In the ensuing fight, a tribune was killed, and in the night-time confusion, the Romans were pushed back. Julian was furious and subjected the fort to a ferocious attack on all sides, killing its defenders to the last man and leaving it a burning wreck.

The Romans were now in full sight of the Persian capital. But while the fleet encircled it, the army was on the wrong side of the river, since Ctesiphon was on the left bank of the Tigris with the army on the right. A substantial Persian force, led by the Surena, was also ready to meet the Romans. Ammianus describes the gleaming plate-mail of the Persian cavalry, together with the terrifying elephants that the Sasanians regularly used in their larger army groupings, 'like walking hills'.[22] And this was not even the main Persian army, which was still marching south with Shapur.

Julian knew he had to move quickly if he was to capture Ctesiphon before Shapur reached it. So, he devised one of the daring commando-type raids he had used so successfully against the Germans. At nightfall, he sent Count Victor, who Ammianus describes as a daring commander, across the Tigris with five boats full of soldiers: 'Under fierce attack from fire bombs and every sort of combustible.'[23] Count Victor secured a bridgehead on the opposite bank of the Tigris. This was followed by an amphibious assault, and hundreds of Roman ships and soldiers rowed across the river and took up position in front of Ctesiphon and the Persian army.

Julian's dream of capturing Ctesiphon now looked possible. On 29 May, the Romans attacked. The Roman infantry formed a solid mass and advanced 'in their gleaming crested helmets, slowly swinging their shields...'[24] There was a fierce melee, in which the emperor galloped from side to side encouraging his officers, before the Persian ranks broke and fled. The Persians were still cautious about fighting the Roman legionaries. And so it proved on this occasion. Ammianus says 2,500 Persian dead were left on the battlefield compared with only 70 Romans. This seems hard to believe, but the Romans had certainly won a victory and there were celebrations in the camp that night.

It proved to be a hollow victory. Ammianus says that when the Persians retreated, the Romans were in a suitable position to storm Ctesiphon. However, it was the daring commander, Count Victor, who called the Romans back. He himself was wounded, hit in the shoulder by an arrow, and he feared that an assault on the city would end in disaster. He may have been right.

This proved to be a turning point not just for this campaign, and not just for Julian, but for the entire history of the Roman Empire. For the Romans' failure to capture Ctesiphon marked a decisive turning point. Never again would a united Roman Empire be in a position to achieve such a triumph.

So, what went wrong?

Ammianus is our most reliable source since he was actually there. He says that at a council of war held the day after the battle, most of the Roman generals told Julian that a siege of Ctesiphon would fail for two reasons: first, the city was impregnable, and second, Shapur was about to arrive and the Roman army could be caught between the Surena in Ctesiphon and Shapur's army.

He goes on to say that while Julian accepted this argument, he refused to agree to a retreat. Instead, he wanted to advance east into Persia, apparently to continue the invasion and subjugation of the Sasanians. Ammianus says that he was misled by Persian deserters, who told him they could lead him to victory.

Julian then made a critical strategic error. He burned the massive fleet that had transported the army down the Euphrates and across to the Tigris. He was afraid it would otherwise fall into the hands of the Persians and burning it freed up 20,000 soldiers who had been manning the ships.

Then the errors started multiplying. It was discovered that the Persian deserters had tricked Julian into thinking there was a straightforward path into the Persian interior. Orders were given to stop the burning of the fleet. But to no avail. The fleet disappeared in a fiery tumult, much to the army's disappointment, with only 12 ships left out of 1,250.

Continuing with Ammianus' account, he says that Julian continued with his plan to advance east into Persia. Initially, this met with success. The Romans found themselves 'in a rich region which provided food in abundance'.[25] Perhaps Julian had been right after all? This proved not to be the case. The Persians quickly implemented a scorched earth policy that denied Julian's troops forage and water. His offensive ground to a halt.

Julian resorted to asking the gods what to do by taking omens, in other words inspecting the entrails of slaughtered animals. Ammianus almost mocked him for this despite the fact he too was a pagan. It was the first time he showed a lack of confidence in Julian's judgement. The omens failed. They provided no clear guidance about what to do. The troops wanted to return home and were frustrated that the ships had been burned, although Julian pointed out that it would have been impossible to sail them upstream against the current anyway. He decided to march north along the Tigris to meet up with Procopius and Arshak, whose whereabouts were still a mystery. It was about all the Romans could do.

But no sooner did they set off, than a great cloud of dust was spotted in the distance. Some optimistically thought it was Procopius' army, but it turned out to be Shapur's. Perhaps surprisingly, the Romans were not discouraged. Just the opposite. Ammianus describes how the troops relished the prospect of fighting the Persians. The first skirmishes between the two armies went in favour of the Romans and Ammianus says 'the enemy squadrons scattered after suffering a serious reverse'.[26] The Persians continued to harry the Romans with mixed results. A Persian satrap, a senior general, was killed and Julian rewarded the soldier who had killed him lavishly. But a Roman cavalry unit, the Tertiaci, was accused of cowardice by the legionaries and punished by Julian.

Finally, a few miles further up the Tigris, the full Persian army gave battle to the Romans. Ammianus describes the endless ranks of heavily armoured Persian horsemen, the ferocity of the Persian archers and the terrifying elephants. But when battle was joined, the legionaries again proved their worth, and the Persians were the first to leave the field – after suffering much heavier casualties than the Romans, according to Ammianus.

It was a Roman victory but far from decisive. The next day, Julian's army continued its march north to meet up with Procopius. The Persians were now afraid to give battle but constantly harried the retreating Romans. At one point, Persian cavalry attacked the rearguard, and Julian, who always wanted to be in the midst of battle, rushed to organise the Roman resistance. However, in his eagerness, he forgot to put on a breastplate. The Persians then switched their attack to the advance guard. Julian galloped there. But another Persian cavalry unit attacked the Roman centre with elephants. Julian rushed to deal with that and led a Roman counter-attack which put the Persians, including the elephants, to flight. But then disaster struck. He got caught up with a mass of fleeing Persians, and, just as his bodyguard were trying to catch up with him, a cavalryman threw a spear which caught him in the side and lodged in the lower part of his liver. When he pulled it out, he cut his fingers on the blade. Then he fell from his horse and was carried back to camp.

While a battle raged outside, which the Romans won, Julian lay in his tent being tended to by his doctors. At first, he and they thought his wound was not fatal, and he issued instructions to tell his officers he would soon be well. But it quickly became clear this was not the case. As he lost more blood, he became weaker until, realising that he was at death's door, Ammianus says he discussed philosophy just as Socrates had done before his death. He then died at the age of 32, having been emperor for just under two years.

That at least is the record which Ammianus has left us, and it deserves serious attention because of course he was the only person to leave an account who was actually there. But his account raises more questions than answers, such as why did Julian give up his idea of capturing Ctesiphon so quickly? Historians have suggested possible reasons. One is that the land around Ctesiphon was apparently waterlogged (Ammianus mentions this) because the Persians had purposefully opened all the floodgates from both the Euphrates and Tigris in order to make it more difficult for the Romans to advance. This meant an increased risk of malaria. Ammianus says that storms of insects were plaguing the Roman army outside Ctesiphon and perhaps Julian felt a prolonged siege would cause a malarial outbreak that could devastate the Roman army? If so, his decision to abandon the siege was far from foolish.

Another possible reason is that Julian was relying on the pretender, Hormizd, having spies in Ctesiphon who would open the city gates. If these had been discovered and eliminated, it makes sense that the Romans would have had to change their plans. Ammianus says Julian was tricked by Persian deserters into thinking it would be better to abandon the siege and invade Persia instead, suggesting there was some level of subterfuge going on.

The non-appearance of Procopius' army also remains a mystery. No record of a defeat exists to explain it. We can only assume that either the Persians slowed down his advance south, or that Procopius was incompetent or downright treacherous. Incompetence seems the most likely reason.

Another controversy exists over the identity of Julian's killer. This is because a tradition developed among later Christian chroniclers to credit Julian's death to a Christian Roman soldier. However, there is absolutely no evidence of this. Its origin lies with the Christians' argument that no Persian ever claimed responsibility for Julian's death. Yet whoever did it could easily have been killed themselves shortly afterwards. Or perhaps they did not realise they had mortally wounded the emperor.

Another problem created by Julian's death was that he did not nominate a successor. Interestingly, one historian has suggested this could have been because he actually took longer to die than just the single day recorded by Ammianus. His theory is that a wound to the liver would have caused an infection that probably killed him in three days, during which he may have believed he would live, not needing to nominate a successor.

In conclusion, Julian's death and the failure of his Persian expedition were transformational. What would have happened had he lived is one of the biggest 'what ifs' in Roman history. Would paganism have been restored? Would Christianity have been crushed? Would the fall of the Roman Empire have been postponed or put off altogether? Many historians, writers and thinkers, from Voltaire and Gibbon to Gore Vidal, have offered their thoughts about this. But there will never be an answer.

The reality was that Julian had failed. And only 47 years after his death, in 410, the city of Rome itself would be sacked by the Goths. Yet the rapidity of this collapse cannot be ascribed solely to Julian's failure. His defeat was a blow to Rome but it was not fatal. Something worse was about to happen.

The Huns were coming.

PART III

The Road to Disaster

13

The Huns

The heat shimmers across the parched earth of the steppe-land. Once, this land was green with vegetation. Now, the wind blows over dry streambeds and sand dunes. Against a vast panorama of cruel mountain peaks in the east, thousands of steppe nomads ride tough small ponies, their belongings in carts dragged by skeletal cattle, and behind them thousands of starving sheep and goats are driven forward by herders.

The men have long black hair and small, brightly coloured shields strapped to their backs. Quivers of arrows are at their sides. In the carts are women and children. This is an entire people on the march. A people fleeing not a human enemy but a natural one. Drought has brought them here, in search of pasture for their flocks. They are the Huns.

Suddenly, a shout goes up from Hunnic horsemen at the front of the column of travellers. Ahead of them is a band of warriors with metal breastplates and iron helmets. The Alans. An Indo-European people. Behind them lies their land of green valleys and well-watered springs. They are here to protect it. Lines of horsemen, several deep, assemble ready to charge the oncoming refugees. The glaring sun shines off their armour. The mass of Alans trot forward, then break into a canter. They hold long spears. The earth pounds with the beat of hooves. Dust swirls all around them. They gather pace as they move towards the long caravan of travellers.

But they never get there. As fast as a lightning bolt, the Huns have massed together. Dry dust billows from their horses' hooves into the air so that you can scarcely see what is happening. The air is filled with arrows. Thousands of razor-sharp, flint-headed arrows pour out of the sky into the oncoming Alans. They tear through their shields. They pierce heads, arms and shoulders in a deadly storm. The Huns encircle them in a crescent formation, taunting them and drawing them forward. They loose arrow after arrow, restringing their bows as effortlessly as if they were nimbly threading a wicker basket. The Alans drown in a storm of arrows. Their own horse archers shoot their arrows but they fall short, without the power or the range of the Huns.

Soon, the Huns close in on their kill. Drawing sabres and maces, they butcher those that have survived the dreadful aerial onslaught. The ground is covered with bodies. The screams of the wounded fill the air as they are tortured to death, and then the Huns cut the heads off their leaders and fix them to spears in triumph.

As Julian lay dying in Persia, a new enemy was approaching the Roman Empire that would transform the ancient world. They were the Huns.

The Huns had already overrun China but it was not until the fourth century AD that they came anywhere close to Europe. In the 360s, they first appeared on the eastern edge of what is now modern Ukraine. Thereafter, the history of the

Roman Empire would become inextricably linked with that of this new and violent race.

The Huns are one of the most under-researched peoples in global history. Yet their impact on the ancient world was nothing short of phenomenal. At one time or another, they conquered and dominated all the major civilisations in Eurasia from China to India, Persia and the Roman Empire. Their story began in Mongolia with a tribe called the Xiongnu (see Maps 3 and 4). They first came into conflict with the powerful Han Chinese Empire in the third century BC. Indeed, the Great Wall of China was originally built to keep them out. But under the rule of a remarkable leader called Modu, they broke through the wall, slaughtered the Chinese armies and then subjected Han China to a form of vassalage. Modu turned the skulls of his enemies into drinking cups and took the Chinese emperor's daughter as one of his many concubines. He created an empire that stretched from Manchuria to Kazakhstan and was larger even than that of Alexander the Great. On his death in 174 BC, the Xiongnu Empire was probably the most powerful state in the whole of Eurasia.

After that, the balance of power see-sawed between the Xiongnu and China for the next five centuries. While Han China momentarily rid itself of the Xiongnu in the first century AD, they returned with a vengeance in the fourth, actually conquering Jin China (the Jin dynasty replaced the Han), and burning its capital Luoyang to the ground. Thereafter, the Xiongnu and Chinese continued to fight while also becoming increasingly integrated. One historian[27] has argued that China's whole military, political and administrative development was effectively taken over by the Xiongnu. He sees what the Chinese called a 'barbarian' military aristocracy (i.e., the Xiongnu) ruling over the Chinese people with the help of native bureaucrats. Interestingly, this has parallels with the Germanic kingdoms that developed in the western Roman Empire in the fifth century.

So, the Huns played a major role in ancient Chinese history, but how did they affect Rome? The Romans themselves were clear on this point. Our most reliable historical companion of the fourth century, Ammianus Marcellinus, summed it up succinctly when he wrote: 'The seed-bed and origin of all this destruction and of the various calamities inflicted by the wrath of Mars, which raged everywhere with extraordinary fury, I find to be this: the people of the Huns.'[28]

The immediate threat the Huns presented in the fourth century was not a Hunnic invasion of Europe (this would come later in the mid-fifth century, led by Attila) but, like a ripple spreading across a lake, the domino effect they created by pushing the Germanic tribes west into the Roman Empire. Bishop Ambrose of Milan summed this up with impressive clarity: 'The Huns fell upon the Alans, the Alans upon the Goths, the Goths upon the Romans, and this is not yet the end.'[29]

This view is now widely accepted by historians as the primary reason for the fall of the western empire. However, two questions stand out: first, why were the Huns able to push the German west relatively easily, and why did they migrate to Europe in the first place? Europe is, after all, a long way from Mongolia.

Let us start with a Roman description of the Huns. Ammianus provides us with a vivid description of them, the best outside Chinese sources: 'The people of the Huns, who are mentioned only cursorily by ancient writers, and who dwell beyond the Sea of Azov [Palus Maeotis] near the frozen ocean, are quite abnormally savage.'[30]

The frozen ocean appears to refer to the Arctic Circle, which is a bit too far north, but ancient geography was not perfect. He describes them as barely human:

> *They have squat bodies, strong limbs, and thick necks, and are so prodigiously ugly and bent that they might be two-legged animals, or the figures crudely carved from stumps which are seen on the parapets of bridges. Still, their shape, however disagreeable, is human; but their way of life is so rough that they have no use for fire or seasoned food, but live on the roots of wild plants and the half-raw flesh of any sort of animal.[31]*

You may be forgiven for thinking that Ammianus is describing Orcs out of J.R.R. Tolkien's *The Lord of the Rings*. Indeed, it would not surprise me if Tolkien's inscription was derived from Ammianus. But, aside from the ferocity of their alleged physical appearance, why were they so terrifying?

The answer is they were good at fighting. And this was because they fought in a different fashion from both the Germans and the Romans. As usual, Ammianus gives us an insightful description:

> *The Huns enter battle drawn up in wedge-shaped masses...And as they are lightly equipped for swift motion, and unexpected in action, they purposefully*

divide suddenly into scattered bands and attack, rushing about in disorder here and there, dealing terrific slaughter... They fight from a distance with missiles having sharp bone, instead of their usual points, joined to the shafts with wonderful skill; then they gallop over the intervening spaces and fight hand to hand with swords.[32]

Another key writer for this period, Zosimus, said that, 'The Huns were totally incapable and ignorant of conducting a battle on foot, but by wheeling, charging, retreating in good time and shooting from their horses, they wrought immense slaughter.'[33]

So, the Huns were typical steppe nomads, deadly with their bows, after which they would gallop in and finish their enemies in close combat. But there seems to have been something unusually frightening about the Huns, and one historian[34] has ventured an explanation. This is based on the few remains we have of Hunnic bows, which suggest they were particularly large and powerful.

A feature of all the steppe nomads was that they had more powerful bows than those in Europe because they did not use a single stave of wood to make a bow, which was the norm in Europe for thousands of years, including the famous longbows of the Middle Ages. These involved shooting an arrow by pulling a string, which forces the wood into a concave shape. But the steppe nomads used what are called composite recurve bows, more complicated to make than their European counterparts, and comprising separate sections of wood and bone, glued together to create strength, making the shape of the bow look a little like a 'W'.

The Huns then did something on top of that. Whereas most nomad bows were about 30 inches long, the Huns' bows were much longer, between 50 and 60 inches. So, how did they fire a bow that was so long from the saddle? It is clearly easy for an infantryman to have a long bow since he can stand up to shoot it. But shooting from the saddle normally requires a shorter bow. The Huns' answer was to make the bow asymmetric, with the upper half of the bow longer. Why did their opponents not do this? The reason was skill and comfort. There was considerably more skill required to shoot an asymmetric bow. It was also larger and less easy to carry. But the Huns considered the power and distance of the shot outweighed those disadvantages. For example, the Huns' asymmetric bows gave them the ability to shoot arrows through the armour of the Alans, the Indo-European people who they first encountered in the west. Then when they came up against the Goths, who rarely wore metal armour unless they had taken it from the Romans, the ferocity of their archery was overwhelming.

It is worth clarifying that the Huns were not helped by stirrups at this time. They used heavy wooden saddles which allowed them to grip the horse with their legs and create a firm firing platform. Stirrups were unknown in Europe until the Dark Ages, although historians think they were being used in the fourth century in some parts of India and China.

This brings us to the second question: why did the Huns go west?

The Chinese sources[35] provide us with a clue. They suggest that Han China's resurgence in the first century AD forced a group of breakaway Xiongnu to move to the west of China to the Altai Mountain region (where modern Kazakhstan, China, Russia and Mongolia converge). Historians are now broadly agreed that these 'western' Xiongnu were the same Huns who invaded both Europe and Persia/India in the fourth and fifth centuries. However, the Huns did not appear on the edge of Europe (in modern Ukraine) until the AD 360s, meaning there is a gap of over 200 years between their move to the west of China and their subsequent migration over a thousand miles to Europe. This has become known as the 'missing 200-year interlude' and historians have struggled to explain why the Huns should have migrated so far west during this time. However, recent research has come up with an explanation that is truly groundbreaking.

It was climate change.

14

Climate Change and Rome

It is normal to measure human history in terms of technological change. The Stone Age gave way to the Bronze Age, followed by the Iron Age and now the Nuclear Age. But there is another force that has shaped human history over a much longer period, which is still surprisingly ignored by many people: the climate.

While today we may think of planet Earth's climate as being stable, historically it has been extremely volatile. Over the last 2–3 million years, the planet has shifted between glacial and interglacial periods. These shifts seem to have taken place every 40,000 to 100,000 years. The last glacial phase, or ice age, when most of Northern Europe and America were covered with sheets of ice, ended about 10,000 years ago, and was followed by our current interglacial period, called the Holocene.

We still do not fully understand what caused the extreme volatility of the climate in the past. A famous Serbian scientist, Milankovitch, developed the theory a hundred years ago that it was small changes in Earth's rotation and orbit around the sun that caused a cycle of alternating ice ages and interglacials. Since then, scientists have added a host of other possible causes, including volcanic activity, sunspots, tectonic plate motion, and most recently the addition of greenhouse gases into the atmosphere by human beings.

But one thing we know for certain is that the Holocene climate has favoured humanity. During its brief time, humans have evolved from hunter-gatherers to the creators of a terrifying nuclear age. The human population has skyrocketed, particularly in the last 50 years, rising from only 1 million 10,000 years ago to its current 8 billion.[36] While most humans regard this planetary conquest with either satisfaction or horror, the question of why the Holocene has been so kind to humanity is often overlooked.

The answer is that, after the melting of ice sheets, the climate became warmer and wetter. A period called the Middle Holocene (c. 6250–2250 BC) distinctly favoured human activity. Modern humans had spread from Africa a long time before this, but now they could travel more easily into the northern hemisphere. The Sahara was green, and the Mediterranean was more fertile than it is today. Human expansion across it accelerated.

However, even within the Holocene period, there has been variability in climatic conditions. Indeed, starting from around 2250 BC, the Late Holocene period became less favourable for humanity. There was a southward drift of the Intertropical Convergence Zone, where the easterly trade winds converge around the equator. The Sahara became a desert. Rainfall diminished. Summers in the northern hemisphere became cooler. In the Mediterranean, summers became hotter and drier. The climate became gradually more challenging for humans. Some climatologists believe we are due another ice age in about 50,000 years. However, almost all regard human-made global warming as likely to postpone this for hundreds of thousands of years. While that might sound positive, rest assured it is not. The advent today of the so-called 'anthropogenic' climate, meaning one that is dominated by human activity, may postpone another ice age, but climate scientists also believe it will bring a Pandora's Box of misfortunes on humanity as droughts, climatic volatility and environmental disasters escalate in a way that we are still struggling to comprehend.

And that is where the history of Rome might help us to understand the potential impact of the climate on human history. Because, it is now increasingly clear that even minor changes in climate during Rome's long history (long in human terms but short in climate terms) had a material, and even life-threatening, effect on it.

First, let us look at the early and middle Roman period. What is immediately striking is the abundance of archaeological and literary evidence pointing to the fact that the climate was more favourable in the Mediterranean basin than it is today. Most striking was the exceptional fertility of North Africa in the Roman period. It is well known that Egypt and modern Tunisia (where Carthage was situated) were called 'the granary of Rome' by the Romans. Today, both countries are grain importers. Yet during the Roman period, from Morocco to Egypt, a line of coastal cities produced vast quantities of corn, wine and fruit, as well as breeding horses. Wild animals also lived much closer to the Mediterranean than today, providing an abundant source of exotic creatures to be massacred in the Roman amphitheatres. For example, Pliny the Elder said that elephants roamed the Atlas Mountains. Today, they are long gone.

Aside from the agricultural fecundity of North Africa, the Romans have left copious records of Tiber floods. Roman Italy seems to have had far more rainfall than today. Pliny the Younger and Ovid recorded frequent Tiber floods during the summers. Pliny even described Roman furniture floating down the streets in floods during Trajan's reign. By contrast, in the Middle Ages, the Tiber never seems to have flooded. Another example is agricultural production. Pliny the Elder said that not only was Italian wheat excellent but that it was grown in the mountains, suggesting warmer but also wetter conditions than today. In Greece, ancient heavy olive-crushing installations have been discovered high above the modern levels of olive cultivation, again suggesting that Greece was wetter and more fertile.

So, there is plenty of literary and archaeological evidence to suggest that the Mediterranean enjoyed a more favourable climate for agriculture in the Roman period than it does today. Climatologists are now in broad agreement that there was a period of warm, wet and stable climatic conditions that lasted from around 200 BC to AD 530, and have called it the 'Roman Warm Period'.

This was replaced by the 'Late Antique Little Ice Age', which is a widely recognised period of cooling that lasted from 536 to about 660, and which climatologists believe was almost certainly caused by a series of major volcanic eruptions around the world, starting in 536. Volcanic eruptions tend to cause cooling because the ash, dust and gases they release into the atmosphere normally reflect the sun's rays. This proved catastrophic for the eastern Roman Empire since it caused harvest failures, famine and may have contributed to the great plague in Justinian's reign, which devastated not just eastern Rome but the whole ancient world. In a subsequent book in this series, I will discuss this in more detail as a key contributor to the breakdown of the eastern Roman Empire in the sixth and seventh centuries.

It is also worth noting that even before the volcanic eruptions of the sixth century, one historian[37] has recently argued that the Roman Warm Period was replaced by a less favourable climate from as early as 150. The primary evidence for this lies with increased drought and crop failures, especially in Egypt in the 240s. For example, in 244, for the first time in centuries, the Nile failed to flood. In 245 or 246, it is uncertain which, the flood was yet again weak. This was a challenge for the Romans since Egypt, like Carthage, was a principal supplier of grain to the city of Rome. To add to the problem of drought in Egypt, evidence suggests that the whole of North Africa was increasingly vulnerable to drought in the mid-third century. Cyprian, the bishop of Carthage, best known for his records of the plague that carry his name, recorded drought in Carthage in the 230s–240s. Jewish records tell of drought in Galilee and Judea at around the same time.

But the biggest revelation of all lies in the fourth century, and although it did not concern climate change in the Roman Empire itself, its effect would prove even more deadly. For, recent developments in paleoclimatology have revealed groundbreaking new insights into the history of the Huns.

In particular, studies analysing millennia-long juniper tree-ring records[38] – and yes, it might sound surprising that there are still trees dating back thousands of years, but they do exist – show that in the fourth-century Asian steppe-lands, there was a prolonged period of drought, indeed what climatologists call a megadrought. The evidence suggests the drought was most intense between around AD 310 to 360. This type of prolonged drought would have caused any nomadic people to look for more fertile ground to graze their flocks of goats and sheep. The timing fits well with the Hunnic migration since it occurred just before the Huns appeared on the edge of eastern Europe. In conclusion, the evidence is strong that the Huns were refugees from climate change.

Why was there a period of prolonged drought in the fourth century AD? Again, paleoclimatology has made some interesting progress in answering this question as well. The latest climate evidence suggests the central Asian steppe suffered from prolonged La Niña-like conditions in the fourth century AD. El Niño and La Niña refer to the cycle of warming and cooling of water in the eastern tropical Pacific Ocean cycle. El Niño is warm and La Niña is cold. The effect of this cycle on the Pacific has quite a profound and variable effect on the climates of other places on Earth. And for the Asian steppe, El Niño produces rain while La Niña produces drought. Climatologists are now fairly sure that in the fourth century AD there was a prolonged La Niña in the Pacific, which would therefore have contributed to the aridity of the Asian steppe, supporting the juniper tree-ring evidence for a megadrought.

Another relevant point supporting the view that the Huns were climate change refugees is that, although it may sound counter-intuitive, nomads do not actually like to travel too far. They need a good reason to migrate hundreds or thousands of miles. The celebrated Roman historian, J.B. Bury, speculated over a hundred years ago that the Huns' appearance in Europe could be explained simply because they were nomads. This view is now rejected by most historians. The reason lies in the word itself. For 'nomad' comes from the Greek *'nomas'*, meaning someone roaming in search of pasture. Most anthropologists now believe that nomads prefer *not* to travel too far. Being nomadic refers to the alternation of grazing land between summer and winter. In the Asian steppe-land, this is required because it comprises two types of pasture. Upland summer pasture which provides abundant grass in summer but is too cold for grass to grow in winter, and lowland winter pasture where there is a lack of rain in summer, while in winter there is plenty of rain. Asian steppe nomads alternated between upland and lowland pasture, typically within a 100-mile radius. The Huns' priority was grazing their flocks which were their most precious asset, meeting all their needs in terms of milk, meat and providing leather for clothing.

This means that for the Huns to have migrated all the way from Mongolia to the edge of ancient Germania required something very unusual indeed. Historians used to think it was defeat by the Chinese Han dynasty in the first century AD that propelled the Huns (or a segment of them) west. There would have been other political conflicts as well about which we know nothing. But, even if these did influence the Huns' westward migration, climate change is looking increasingly likely as the main reason for it.

This analysis fits with a growing awareness of how the impact of climatic change has been underestimated in other periods of history. For example, one historian[39] has focused on the Medieval Warm Period, between AD 800 to 1300, when there was a noticeable rise in surface temperatures that changed climate worldwide. While this benefited Europe, with longer summers and more bountiful harvests producing population growth and cultural flowering, in other parts of the world it did the opposite, bringing prolonged drought and famine. In particular, it led to droughts which are now widely considered to be the main killers of two great medieval civilisations – the Mayan civilisation in Central America, and the Khmer Empire in Cambodia.

As part of the same Medieval Warm Period phenomenon, and in a close parallel to the Roman experience with Hunnic expansion, paleoclimatology increasingly points to the creation of the great Mongol Empire by Genghis Khan in the thirteenth century as a response to droughts in central Asia similar to those that may have caused the Huns to migrate west in the fourth century.

Historians are increasingly focused on the climate as a major causal factor in history. It should help us to understand the past better. It should also help us to understand the potential effects of climate change today.

Figure 1: Augustus was the first Roman Emperor and established the Pax Romana (Author's Collection).

Figure 2: Statue of the four Tetrarchs or co-emperors established by Diocletian. Note how the artistic style changed in the late Roman Empire (Author's Collection).

Figure 3: This head of the emperor Constantine was originally part of a colossal statue in the Roman Forum (Author's Collection).

Figure 4: Gold solidus depicting the emperor Julian the Apostate. He tried but failed to restore the empire to its former military glory and pagan ethos (Classical Numismatic Group, Wikimedia Commons).

Figure 5: The Arch of Constantine next to the Colosseum built by the Roman Senate to commemorate Constantine's victory over Maxentius at the Battle of the Milvian Bridge in AD 312. Christian chroniclers claimed he was converted to Christianity shortly before the battle (Author's Collection).

Figure 6: The Arch of Constantine has no Christian symbols. Instead, it has depictions of the pagan Roman god Sol Invictus, as shown here riding his chariot. This suggests Constantine was converted to Christianity at a later date (Author's Collection).

Figure 7: This ivory diptych is thought to represent Stilicho, his wife Serena, and son Eucherius. Stilicho is wearing clothes typical of a late Roman soldier with a long sword, spear and oval shield (Monza Cathedral, Wikimedia Commons).

Figure 8: The Colosseum in Rome was completed in AD 80 and could hold up to 80,000 spectators. Construction began under the emperor Vespasian, who used plunder from the sack of Jerusalem to fund it. The last gladiatorial fight was held around 435. In the Middle Ages it became a castle (Author's Collection).

Figure 9: The Pantheon is the best preserved of all ancient Roman buildings. Originally commissioned by Marcus Agrippa during the reign of Augustus, it was rebuilt by Hadrian. It became a church in the seventh century (Author's Collection).

Figure 10: The interior of the Pantheon contains a perfectly preserved Roman concrete dome, nearly 2,000 years old. An oculus at the top allows some rain and sunlight into the building (Author's Collection).

Figure 11: The Roman Forum was the heart of Ancient Rome. This view is from the Tabularium looking east to the Temple of Antoninus and Faustina (six pillars shown in photo). Beyond that is the Basilica of Maxentius and the Colosseum (Author's Collection).

Figure 12: The emperor Aurelian built walls surrounding Ancient Rome which bear his name to protect the city from barbarian attack during the 'crisis of the third century'. Running for 12 miles, they are well preserved today (Author's Collection).

Figure 13: The Goths breached Rome's walls in AD 410 through the Salarian Gate, which no longer stands since it was demolished in 1921 to open the area to road traffic. It looked reasonably similar to the Porta Latina Gate shown here (Author's Collection).

Figure 14: Milan (called Mediolanum by the Romans) replaced
Rome as the capital of the western empire during much of
the fourth century. It had sturdy walls which resisted various
barbarian sieges, although it finally fell to Attila the Hun in 452.
This tower is all that remains of its walls (Author's Collection).

*Figure 15: The Columns of San Lorenzo in Milan
survived Attila's sack of the city in AD 452
(Author's Collection).*

*Figure 16: This mosaic is one of the earliest depictions of Christ
and shows him wearing a Roman toga. It is in the Basilica of San
Lorenzo (Chapel of Saint Aquilino) in Milan.
(Author's Collection)*

15

Bursting a Blood Vessel

As the Huns were first appearing on the edge of Europe, the emperor Julian lay dying in Persia. On 26 June 363, he had been mortally wounded. His precise date of death is not known, but it was almost certainly one to three days afterwards. The Roman army was left stranded beside the Tigris in Persian territory. Julian's great Persian expedition had failed, but worse was to follow. He left no successor and it was up to the army to proclaim a new emperor. There were two factions in the army, Constantius' former officials and Julian's Gallic officers. Since Constantius and Julian had been enemies, these two factions were fairly hostile to each other. But there was one person they all admired and this was Salutius, Julian's trusted second in command. So, they agreed to offer the throne to him. Unfortunately for them, Salutius was a wise old man and turned the offer down, presumably guessing that it would only bring him trouble. Next, they offered it to another compromise candidate, Jovian, the commander of Julian's guard, who accepted.

Thus began the brief reign of Jovian, widely regarded as one of the most damaging in late Roman history. And the reason for this was that he negotiated a humiliating peace with Shapur, which put the Romans on the back foot with the Persians for the next 100 years.

Ammianus, who was there, says that this treaty was unnecessary. The Roman army had inflicted heavy losses on the Persians, and the army was also so incensed by Julian's death that it was 'set upon avenging its illustrious chief rather than upon self-preservation, and intended to extricate itself from its pressing difficulties by either complete victory or a glorious death'.[40] Shapur was aware of just how dangerous the Romans still were and did not want to engage them in battle. Ammianus believed Jovian could have led the army to safety, since a fertile region called Corduene was only a hundred miles away, where the Romans could have recuperated.

But Jovian did not care about the army's honour and even less did he care about Julian's reputation. Instead, he seems to have been motivated purely by a wish for his own self-preservation. This meant that when Shapur sent envoys to negotiate a treaty, he caved in far too easily. The deal that was hammered out was a virtual Roman capitulation. In exchange for the army being allowed to cross the Tigris and limp back to Antioch, Shapur demanded the cities of Nisibis and Singara, as well as the five satrapies, as the Persian provinces were called, that Diocletian had taken from Persia 60 years before in the Peace of Nisibis in 299. Peace for 30 years was also agreed. Hostages were exchanged to ensure the terms of the treaty were kept.

Ammianus highlighted that the peace did not gain anything for the Romans. Even after the treaty was signed, the Roman retreat was still very costly, resulting 'in loss of life on a large scale'.[41] This was because the Persians were not required to supply the Romans with food, the shortage of which was their major problem. In addition, they picked off stragglers and any Romans who unwisely wandered too far in search of provisions. Finally, Roman morale seems to have broken down, resulting in a chaotic crossing of the Tigris in which many soldiers drowned.

The Romans also promised not to intervene in Armenia, which meant it quickly fell under Persian sway. In fact, Shapur invaded the kingdom shortly afterwards and the Armenian king Arshak II was imprisoned, never to leave the so-called 'Castle of Oblivion' to which he was confined.

Jovian's embarrassing climb-down in 363, known as the Second Peace of Nisibis, was not well received by the Romans. When safely back in Roman territory, he had the audacity to say that the peace represented a Roman victory. This was going too far. The citizens of Nisibis, who were forced to evacuate the city before handing it over empty to the Persians, were so outraged that they stoned to death one of Jovian's senior officers. When the army limped back to Antioch, its citizens did not conceal their anger and rioted against him. Only too late did they realise they should have backed Julian.

It is intriguing to speculate what might have happened had Jovian chosen to fight his way out of Persia. If Ammianus was right, and there is every reason to believe he was since he was actually there, then the Romans might well have fended the Persians off, perhaps even defeating them, and the status quo before Julian set out might have been preserved. But the reality was that Rome had now lost its dominant position in the east. This, together with Julian's death, were the first steps on the path towards the fall of the Roman Empire.

As for Jovian, he never got very far. Just as he had caved into Shapur, so he tried to appease too many of the factions in the empire. He was a Christian, which made it easy for him to secure the support of the powerful Christian communities by repudiating Julian's pagan sympathies. But he also courted favour with the pagans, for example, by sacrificing and consulting the omens in Persia before offering his peace terms to Shapur. Therefore, even the Christians turned against him.

Despite growing resentment, Jovian was keen to take control of the empire. But the storm clouds were gathering. Not only were there riots denouncing him in Nisibis and Antioch, but in Gaul, his father-in-law Lucillianus, who he had sent to take over from Julian's commander, was murdered by the troops furious that their hero Julian was dead.

Leaving Antioch for Constantinople to stamp his authority on what was effectively the capital of the empire, Jovian never made it. He died in February 364 in Ancyra, apparently asphyxiated in a fire in the house he was staying in. Ammianus says there was a cover-up about the true cause of death, and it is very likely he was murdered by his own soldiers, who had by now realised their mistake in making him emperor. It was in no-one's interests to disclose this and so it never was.

There was no obvious successor to Jovian. The senior army officers who had accompanied him on his last journey to Constantinople, turned again to Julian's favourite, Salutius, as they had done immediately after Julian's death. But again, Salutius turned them down, presumably because, like the last time, he felt the job was more trouble than it was worth. Instead, the throne was offered to a senior army officer called Valentinian, who was the tribune of an elite infantry regiment called the *Scutarii*. Valentinian had little to commend him apart from the lack of other more suitable candidates. However, he jumped at the opportunity, and quickly appointed his brother, Valens, as his co-emperor in a junior role to him.

For the next ten years, Valentinian and Valens tried to keep the empire going. But their attempt bore little comparison with the efforts of their predecessors like Julian or Constantine. Lacking inspiration and imagination, it was very much a case of keeping their heads above water rather than trying to find a true solution to the empire's woes, as Julian had tried to do. In the end, Valens would go down in history as the man who sent the empire into a death spiral at the Battle of Adrianople in 378.

Their first action was to divide the empire between them, with Valentinian taking the west and Valens the east. However, almost immediately, there was a challenge to their authority. This was probably because they were a little too heavy-handed in removing some of Julian's supporters, and when they tried to arrest his cousin, Procopius, the one who had mysteriously failed to come to Julian's aid in the ill-fated Persian campaign, he escaped to the Crimea. There, he plotted against them. He arrived in Constantinople in September 365, and set up a rival government, claiming legitimacy due to his Constantinian ancestry.

He seems to have enjoyed reasonable support among both the people of Constantinople and the army, which included two Thracian legions stationed in the city, suggesting that Valens was not popular. Meanwhile, Valentinian in the west decided not to go to his brother's aid, preferring to keep his troops guarding the western frontiers, and, according to Ammianus, saying quite sensibly: 'Procopius was merely his own and his brother's enemy, whereas the Alemanni were the enemies of the whole Roman world.'[42]

For a while, it looked as if Procopius' bid for power might succeed, especially when he occupied Bithynia and appealed to the Goths to send him troops. But Valens was also busy on his side, persuading the eastern army to back him. Given that Julian had never fully won over the eastern army's loyalty, since most of its senior officers were men appointed by his rival Constantius, and given that Procopius was of course Julian's cousin, the bulk of the eastern army opted to support Valens. This enabled him to muster sufficient forces to advance on Constantinople and defeat and execute Procopius.

Procopius was the last male relative of Constantine the Great, and after his death, Valentinian and Valens faced no further dynastic challenges. However, there were still external threats. And plenty of them. Valentinian fought an almost continual war with the Alemanni along the Rhine, together with a growing Saxon menace in the English Channel, and soon he was also confronted with a full-blown collapse of Roman rule in Britain and North Africa.

Starting with the Alemanni, as mentioned, Valentinian did not help Valens fight Procopius because he was too concerned with their recovery after Julian's devastating victory over them at the Battle of Strasbourg. In 365, they crossed the Rhine en masse and invaded Gaul. Valentinian preferred to send his generals to fight them rather than risk the disgrace of defeat himself. Two generals, Charietto and Severianus, were defeated and killed. It was only when another general called Jovinus took command that the Alemanni were finally fought to a standstill.

Compounding Valentinian's problems, in 367, there was a full-scale collapse of Roman rule in Britain called the 'Great Conspiracy', since it involved a three-way invasion by the Picts from Scotland, Irish tribes sailing across from Ireland, or Hibernia, as the Romans called it, together with Saxons sailing from Germany. In addition, some of the Roman army in Britain actually joined the revolt, probably because it had not been paid for some time. Apparently, the few legionaries still left on Hadrian's Wall conspired with the Picts to invite them in and share their plunder.

When this invasion happened, Valentinian was fighting the Alemanni, and could do little other than send Jovinus to reconnoitre the situation. But in 368, the Romans finally broke the Alemanni offensive at the battle of Solicinium. This meant that in that year, Valentinian could divert troops to recover Britain, led by Count Flavius Theodosius, the father of the future emperor Theodosius the Great. This included elite legionary and auxiliary units who succeeded in retaking Londinium and going on to clear Britain of the Picts, Irish and Saxons. The ease with which this was achieved suggests that the invaders had never intended to stay, and once they had obtained the plunder they wanted, they were quite happy to go back home. A wise move of Theodosius' was to grant an amnesty to Roman army deserters, who were allowed back to their posts to bolster the depleted British legions.

The success of the British campaign prompted Valentinian to make Theodosius his senior general, the *magister equitum*. In this position, Valentinian sent Theodosius on further military expeditions, first against the Alemanni in 370 and then against the Sarmatians in Illyria in 371. Theodosius rapidly became the western empire's most successful and celebrated general.

His skills were needed across a wide range of fronts. In North Africa, there was a complete breakdown of Roman rule. This happened because a corrupt Roman governor called Romanus was forcing African towns to pay him protection money to stop attacks by Berber tribesmen with whom he was in league. He would give some of the protection money to the Berbers and pocket the rest himself. This outrageous abuse of power prompted a rebellion of the Roman inhabitants against him, led, rather surprisingly, by a Berber prince called Firmus who seems to have been as outraged as the local Romans. With Firmus claiming to be the champion of the Romans against their corrupt governor, a bit like an African Robin Hood, Valentinian had no choice but to send Theodosius to restore order. Taking legions from Pannonia and Moesia, Theodosius landed in Mauretania (modern-day Tunisia and Algeria), arrested Romanus and then fought a difficult guerrilla war with Firmus, who retreated into the African interior. Finally, he tracked Firmus down and captured him in 374.

The African revolt was another source of irritation for Valentinian, who was still hard-pressed on the Rhine and Danube frontiers. In 373, the German tribe called the Quadi, living on the upper Danube south of the Alemanni, protested against Valentinian's policy of building forts on the east side of the Rhine and Danube rivers. They regarded the east bank as theirs. This ignited a series of events that ultimately led to Valentinian's death.

This strange tale began with the Quadi sending deputations to the Roman governor in Pannonia protesting about Valentinian's programme of fort building. In response, the Roman governor, Marcellianus, invited them to a grand banquet to settle their differences, only to trick them and murder the Quadi king, Gabinius. This was broadly in keeping with official Roman policy to deceive and, where possible, murder barbarians who had accepted their hospitality. But this time it backfired badly. Several of the legions defending this part of the frontier had been sent to Africa to deal with the rebellion there, and legionaries were thin on the ground. Therefore, it was relatively easy for the Quadi to join with the Sarmatians, cross the Danube, try to hunt down the double-dealing Marcellianus and pillage Roman territory south of the Danube for good measure.

Not surprisingly, Valentinian was none too happy with this turn of events, especially since he was forced to gather legions from the Rhine and march to the Danube to restore order. The Quadi and Sarmatians retreated over the Danube and requested a peace treaty with Valentinian. They insisted on an audience with Valentinian himself, to which he reluctantly agreed. At this meeting, the Quadi, quite reasonably, argued that the war had been started by Marcellianus' treachery in killing their king. They also repeated their opposition to Valentinian's policy of building forts on what they considered to be their land.

Valentinian was not the sort of emperor who you would have wanted to get into an argument with. According to Ammianus, he was famous for losing his temper, as well as being capable of extreme cruelty. For example, he kept two bears in an iron cage which he took with him on his journeys. Servants who displeased him were put in it to be ripped apart by the bears. Ammianus adds that on the morning he went to see the Quadi delegation, he was in a particularly bad mood, and when he had difficulty mounting his horse, which reared repeatedly, he ordered that the groom holding the horse should have his right hand cut off.

Fortunately for the young groom, the tribune of the stables deferred the sentence. Valentinian went to meet the Quadi, where their insistence that they had been wronged by the Romans made his temper rise. This brought on such a paroxysm of anger that, 'boiling with fury', he collapsed on the floor and within a few hours was proclaimed dead. Valentinian had burst a blood vessel. This made him the only Roman emperor to die literally from losing his temper. He was 54 years old and had reigned for just under 12 years.

Aside from the comedy or tragedy of Valentinian's death, his reign in the west had been reasonably successful. Faced with incessant warfare along the Rhine and Danube, together with a collapse of Roman government in Britain and North Africa, he had at least kept the empire together. But he was certainly no visionary. His skills were not remotely comparable with those of Rome's great emperors like Aurelian, Diocletian or Julian. At its moment of greatest peril, Rome was not favoured with gifted emperors. Valentinian's brother, Valens, his co-emperor in the east, would prove far worse than him.

As the barbarians were gathering at the gates of the empire, there were only fools to meet them.

16

War With the Goths

The Huns arrived beside the mighty rivers Don and Volga sometime around AD 360–70. There they met and subjugated the Alans, a steppe people with strong links to the Germanic world, and, according to Ammianus, skilled metal workers capable of fielding armoured cavalry. But the Huns' deadly arrows made short work of them, and the Alans were forced to join the Hunnic armies. Then the Huns advanced south over the Dnieper River and into the Gothic lands in modern-day Romania. The Goths tried to stop them and, although the details are limited, Ammianus says there were many battles but the Goths were always defeated. He says one Gothic leader, Ermanaric, even offered himself to be sacrificed to appease the gods whose displeasure was seen as the cause of the Gothic defeats.

By the 370s, the Goths were in full retreat. In desperation, they even used old Roman defensive systems to fend the Huns off, in particular a long Roman wall on the Olt River, in the former Roman province of Dacia, which Aurelian had evacuated 100 years before in the crisis of the third century. But all to no avail. The Huns were triumphant and, by the summer of 376, hundreds of thousands of Goths arrived on the Danube to ask the Romans for asylum from this terrifying enemy. Ammianus Marcellinus wrote:

> ...*outside our frontier, terrifying rumours got about of a new and unusually violent commotion among the people of the North. Men heard that over the whole area extending from the Marcomanni and Quadi to the Black Sea, a savage horde of remote tribes, driven from their homes by unexpected pressure, were roaming with their families in the Danube region. Our people paid little attention to this at first, because news of wars in those parts generally reached distant hearers only when they were already over or at least quiescent. Gradually, however, the story gained credence, and it was confirmed by the arrival of the foreign agents begging and praying that the host of refugees might be allowed to cross to our side of the river.*[43]

Ammianus says that the number of these barbarians was so vast that, 'To try to find their number is as vain as numbering the wind-swept Libyan sands.'[44] Another source says that there were over 200,000 of them.

What was happening was a huge migration of Goths. And the word here is migration. This was not the usual raid, designed to get rich quick. Two entire Gothic tribes, the Greuthungi and Thervingi, had fled to the Danube, including men, women and children. They wanted asylum. They were refugees from the Huns.

The man caught in the eye of this Gothic storm was Valentinian's brother, Valens. Until 376, Valens had enjoyed an easier time than his brother. As described earlier, his first challenge had been to put down a rebellion by Julian's cousin, Procopius, in 364. Next, he had to face a Gothic invasion because Procopius had called on the Goths to support him. But the invasion was not very serious. The Goths protested to Valens that they had been invited to invade by Procopius, so they were only doing what the Romans wanted. Valens easily persuaded them to return over the Danube. In 369, he made peace with them and rather generously awarded himself the title 'Gothicus Maximus'.

The next challenge was Persia. Just as with the Goths, to begin with, this seemed to go alright. The bone of contention was, as ever, Armenia, the traditional buffer state between Rome and Persia, and an interminable source of conflict. Thanks to Jovian's humiliating treaty in 363 with Shapur, Rome had passed control of Armenia to Persia. Taking advantage of this, the Persians had imprisoned the pro-Roman Armenian king Arshak II, but his son, Papas, or Pap as he was known, escaped and, in 369, Valens supported his attempt to recover the throne. Shapur was not too pleased about this and, seeing it as a breach of the treaty, which it was, responded by invading Armenia and overrunning most of the country. Pap narrowly escaped with his life and appealed to Valens, who, with the Goths now under control, was able to send 12 legions to Armenia, where they scored a victory over the Persians at the battle of Bagavan in 370. Shapur was distracted by attacks on his eastern frontier by the Kushans, and so let Rome get its way in Armenia. Valens had won his first round with the Persians.

However, Pap overstepped his authority, and demanded control of Roman towns like Caesarea and Edessa. Advised by his generals that Pap could be a traitor, Valens had his general, Traianus, invite him to dinner and murder him, a tactic the Romans were fond of. Valens replaced him with a more loyal Roman stooge called Arazdat.

This infuriated Shapur, who could not respond because he was distracted by a war in the east against the Kushans. By 375, the situation with the Kushans had stabilised, and Shapur was ready for a fight in Armenia. But Valens was not. And the reason was the Goths, who appeared on the Danube in 376.

With preparations for war in the east ongoing, the Danube frontier was short of Roman troops, and because of this, Valens initially adopted a conciliatory stance towards the Goths. Requests for asylum were not unheard of. Even the emperor Tiberius in the first century AD had allowed 40,000 Germans to settle in Gaul, according to the Roman historian Eutropius.[45] This practice had continued during the Pax Romana, albeit with fairly small numbers involved.

However, as Rome's decline began, the numbers grew. Marcus Aurelius allowed several barbarian groups to settle in the empire in response to the major Germanic invasions during his reign. But the Romans followed strict rules, only allowing barbarians to settle on Roman territory once they had been defeated, disarmed and integrated politically into the empire as farmers. Valens broke this rule by allowing some of the Goths to cross the Danube still fully armed and remaining an independent political unit. It would prove a costly mistake.

Why did he do it? There were several reasons. One is that he knew the Gothic leader of the Thervingi tribe personally and trusted him. He was called Fritigern, and he had helped Valens in the First Gothic War in 367–9, when Valens successfully beat off the Goths who had come to support the Roman rebel Procopius. These Goths were led by a Thervingi chief called Athanaric. Fritigern was a rival of Athanaric's and more than willing to help Valens fight him. Fritigern also converted to Christianity. So, when seven years later, Fritigern appeared on the Danube asking for asylum, he was someone who Valens thought he could do business with.

The second reason is that he did not give the Goths carte blanche to cross en masse. He only allowed Fritigern's Thervingi to cross. He forbade the other Gothic tribe with them, the Greuthungi, from crossing. These were at least half of the 200,000 Goths in total. He also insisted that Fritigern's senior followers convert to Christianity as Fritigern had done.

Hostages from the Thervingi were taken to guarantee honourable conduct, and the Goths agreed to supply soldiers for the Roman army. This latter point was important to Valens because he was building his army to fight Shapur, and he did not mind having a few additional regiments of Gothic auxiliaries. Fritigern's men had been helpful fighting against Athanaric, so why not against Shapur?

All of these reasons influenced Valens' decision to allow the Thervingi to cross the Danube. He clearly thought he had the situation under control. But one thing he underestimated was the sheer number of Goths. The Thervingi were around 100,000 people – men, women and children – and suddenly having an additional 100,000 mouths to feed in the Thracian countryside inevitably put pressure on food supplies. Suspecting that there might be trouble, the Romans wisely moved the harvest of 376 to fortified strongpoints which could resist the Goths. This seemed a good idea, but it also made some unscrupulous Romans think they could exploit the situation.

According to Ammianus, it was Roman greed that lit the Gothic bonfire. For the Roman governor of Thrace, Lupicinus, and a general called Maximus, decided that the hungry Goths were an opportunity to get rich quick by selling them overpriced food. Allegedly, they even gathered up stray dogs for the Goths to eat, offering one dog for a child to be sold into slavery. Whether or not that was true, it was no surprise that tensions between the Romans and Goths started to rise.

Exasperated with Roman corruption, the Goths protested outside the legionary fortress at Marcianople, in eastern Thrace, close to the Black Sea. Lupicinus, who should go down in history as one of the most incompetent governors of all time, responded by gathering his troops stationed along the Danube to intimidate them. This only meant that the other main Gothic tribe, the Greuthungi, who had been barred from crossing the Danube, took advantage of the absence of Roman river sentries and crossed over to join their cousins the Thervingi. So, double trouble.

Faced with an ever-increasing number of Goths, and sensing that things were about to get out of hand, Lupicinus resorted to an old Roman tactic. He invited the Gothic leaders to a grand banquet intending to kidnap or kill them. As mentioned before, this was a favourite Roman fourth-century trick. But it was also one that seldom succeeded.

Lupicinus spectacularly mismanaged the kidnapping and/or assassination attempt. Ammianus suggests that this was because he was enjoying the banquet too much himself: '[Lupicinus] who, after a long sitting at an extravagantly luxurious meal followed by a noisy floor-show, was muzzy and dropping with sleep.'[46] What followed is not entirely clear from the Roman sources, but it seems Lupicinus failed to spring his trap on Fritigern immediately. Perhaps the two of them were actually becoming friends as they enjoyed the floor-show. But what spoilt the party, literally, was that, during this banquet, fighting broke out between the Goths and Roman soldiers outside the town, as the Goths demanded food and the Romans refused them. When Lupicinus heard this, he panicked and seized Fritigern, killing his bodyguard. Fritigern cleverly saved his own life by persuading Lupicinus that if he killed him, the Goths would storm the town. Instead, he persuaded the incompetent Roman that if he released him, he would pacify his followers and everything would be fine.

Why Lupicinus fell for this is anyone's guess. Perhaps he had drunk too much, as Ammianus says. But whatever the reason, he released Fritigern, who rejoined his Goths outside the town, to their rejoicing, and immediately went back on his promise to Lupicinus by telling his men the Romans had betrayed him and it was now war.

Lupicinus had done the exact opposite of what Valens told him to do. He had started a war. The very next day, he asked his soldiers to sort out the mess he had caused. Gathering his men, he marched to meet Fritigern. But his performance on the battlefield was no better than at the banquet. We do not have any details about the battle other than the knowledge that the Goths trounced the Romans, who, according to Ammianus, suffered considerable casualties, losing their standards with several tribunes killed. Lupicinus managed to escape; as Ammianus says, 'While others were fighting, his one aim was to get away.'[47]

Part of the explanation for the miserable performance of the Roman troops was probably that they were second-rate garrison troops, the *limitanei*, as the Romans called them, and not the field army, or *comitatenses*, which would have had better soldiers. This, together with Lupicinus' incompetence, now ignited a Roman Gothic war that would last from late 376 until 382, and which would prove to be a turning point in Rome's history.

By eliminating Lupicinus' regiments, the Goths had gained control of the countryside of Thrace, since the only other substantial Roman forces were those in Illyria under the western emperor's command, and Valens' eastern units which were massing in faraway Syria to fight the Sasanians. The western emperor by this time was Gratian, Valentinian's son, who succeeded him after his father died from losing his temper with the Quadi.

The problem for the Goths was that they had control of the countryside but not of the towns. This was because all the major towns were heavily fortified, and the Goths had no expertise in siege warfare. The credit for these strong defences must go to Diocletian, whose idea it had been in the third century to construct extensive fortifications in all the frontier provinces, especially the major towns and cities. What archaeological evidence we have suggests these walled towns were extremely well fortified, with tall walls and often huge U-shaped bastions designed to carry the brutally effective Roman wall artillery. Against this, the Goths stood little chance.

So, what they did was to pillage the Roman villas that dotted the countryside. Archaeological evidence shows substantial numbers of these in the regions around Marcianople and Adrianople. The area had enjoyed great prosperity during the fourth century, benefiting from the hitherto relatively safe frontier along the lower Danube. These affluent centres were now put to the torch, and their inhabitants, if they had not already fled, were killed, raped and enslaved. In addition, considerable numbers of slaves and poorer peasants chose this moment to rise against their masters and take revenge for their mistreatment.

In another example of Roman misfortune, the Gothic ranks were also swelled by a regiment of Gothic auxiliaries stationed in Adrianople. Still led by their two chieftains, Sueridas and Colias, these auxiliaries were otherwise loyal to the empire. Or at least they were until they received orders to march immediately east to get them out of the way of the oncoming Thervingi. When they hesitated to leave, the town governor and the citizens turned on them and tried to force them out of Adrianople, perhaps understandably worried that there might be a Gothic coup in the city. However, according to Ammianus, the citizens were as incompetent at dealing with the Goths as Lupicinus had been. The Gothic auxiliaries did not like being viewed as potential traitors and came to blows with the citizens. There was some fighting, in which Ammianus says many citizens were killed, and the Goths left Adrianople, but only to join Fritigern.

While all of this was going on, Valens was still in Antioch. It is not difficult to imagine his reaction to the news of this Gothic invasion when he was putting the finishing touches to his projected offensive in Armenia against the Sasanians. The last word he had received about the Goths was they were seeking asylum in the empire and could provide a valuable source of auxiliary troops. Now, there was a full-scale war in Thrace in which the Roman army had been trounced and tremendous damage done to a hitherto prosperous and peaceful province close to the empire's new capital. Although Valens did not burst a blood vessel as his brother Valentinian had done, he might understandably have come close to it.

Nevertheless, once he had absorbed the bad news, his response was measured and sensible. He had already asked his nephew, the new western emperor Gratian, for help to fight the Persians, and now he sent messengers urgently asking for help to fight the Goths. Second, and probably with great reluctance, he cancelled his whole Persian expedition. He sent his general, Count Victor, who had been a hero in Julian's ill-fated Persian campaign, to sue for peace with Persia. Shapur demanded that the Romans gave up their attempts to control Armenia, and recognised his own king in the kingdom of Georgia in the Caucasus, known as Iberia, which was Christian and pro-Roman. These demands were reluctantly accepted and the Persians yet again strengthened their position in the east.

With the Persian frontier secure, Valens began the difficult process of moving the eastern army hundreds of miles west to Thrace. By the summer of 377, two generals from the eastern front, Traianus and Profuturus, arrived with the first batch of troops from the east. Gratian sent a small force under his general, Richomer, through the Succi pass, in what is now western Bulgaria, to join them. The Goths retreated north towards the Danube. The two Roman forces joined up and offered battle to the Goths. At a place called Ad Salices, in the narrow piece of land between the Danube and the Black Sea, the two armies met. There are no detailed accounts of what happened, but it seems to have been a bloody slogging match that resulted in a draw. Ammianus describes the battlefield littered with corpses. The Goths withdrew into the safety of their wagon circle for a week, suggesting they had sustained heavy casualties, and the Romans withdrew to Marcianople.

It was now a stalemate until the Goths were reinforced by a large number of Huns and Alans, who, having heard of the enormous booty to be stolen from the Romans, were eager to take part in the raiding and plunder. This encouraged them to venture towards Constantinople once again, but they were put off, according to Ammianus, when some Goths near the city were attacked by a group of Arab auxiliaries working for the Romans, who took them prisoner, slit their throats and drank their blood. The Goths were appalled by this behaviour and never ventured near the city again.

Meanwhile, the Romans were also getting stronger. By early 378, the bulk of Valens' eastern army arrived near Constantinople. However, Valens did not want to commit to a fight unless he had Gratian's support from the west. This meant that the Goths, with their Hun and Alan allies, were able to devastate Thrace yet again. 'The barbarians poured over the wide extent of Thrace like wild animals escaping from their cage,'[48] as Ammianus put it. This time it was even more brutal than the last time, if that was possible. 'Everything was involved in a foul orgy of rape and slaughter, bloodshed and fire and frightful atrocities.'[49]

However, the major cities and Constantinople itself were safe. The Goths were in awe of Constantinople's powerful walls, even though these were not yet the famous Theodosian walls which can still be seen in modern Istanbul.

Meanwhile, the ever-growing Roman army in Constantinople merely looked on at the horrific devastation of Thrace and did nothing. The reason was that Valens was waiting for Gratian. But the western army had been delayed. In early 378, just as he was setting out to join Valens, Gratian had been diverted by a major assault on the Rhine frontier by a tribe of Alemanni called the Lentienses. This happened in February 378 and the ensuing conflict was not resolved until May, when Gratian won a resounding victory. Ironically, this Roman victory in the west only made matters worse in the east, for it put pressure on Valens. His army had been sitting in Constantinople doing nothing for months when the news of Gratian's victory arrived. Although Constantinople itself was safe, its citizens, with whom Valens had never been popular, ridiculed him for his cowardice in not attacking the Goths, even calling for him to be replaced by Gratian.

By August 378, Gratian was on his way but still only in Illyria. Other news reached Valens. One of his generals, Sebastian, had won a resounding victory over a minor Gothic war-band near Adrianople. Fritigern was sufficiently alarmed to withdraw to the north of the city. Valens was encouraged by this and wondered whether he could defeat the rest of the Goths by himself and boost his image.

Tempted by this, he advanced the eastern army towards Adrianople. Scouts informed him that only the Thervingi were in the area, led by Fritigern. The Greuthungi and their

Hunnic and Alan allies were widely dispersed, foraging around Thrace. The Thervingi warriors were reported to number about 10,000. Against this, Valens had around 30,000 troops, including the elite regiments of the eastern army. Valens was tempted to attack on his own. The taunting of the Constantinopolitan mob, the months spent waiting, and, according to Ammianus, his growing jealousy of Gratian, meant that Valens was a man with a lot to prove. As Ammianus said: 'He was eager to put himself on a level with his nephew, whose exploits irked him, by some glorious deed of his own.'[50]

Just at that moment, Gratian's general, Richomer, arrived in person, to say that the western army was only a few days' march away. Valens called a council of war and asked his generals for their opinion. Although some seasoned veterans, like Count Victor, advised him to wait, Count Sebastian boasted of his recent victory over the Goths and said that they could easily win without Gratian. Ammianus says the flattery of others decided Valens in favour of battle: 'They urged immediate action to prevent Gratian sharing in a victory which in their opinion was already as good as won.'[51]

Meanwhile, when Fritigern heard Valens was considering marching straight for his camp, he played for time. Knowing he was heavily outnumbered, he wanted to delay battle to give time for the other main Gothic tribe, the Greuthungi, as well as the Alans, to join him. On the same night that Valens held his council of war, Fritigern sent a Christian priest to him as a peace envoy. But Valens would have none of it. He had decided on war and the priest was sent packing. The next day, Valens rode north with his army from the city of

Adrianople to meet the Goths who were encamped only a few miles away.

He rode to meet his destiny, but it was not to be the destiny he hoped for.

17

The Battle of Adrianople

The day of 9 August 378 would prove to be a fateful one. As the sun rose that morning, the roads and fields north of Adrianople would have been packed with Roman legionaries and cavalry. At the top of a steep slope, a huge circle of barbarian wagons, a couple of miles long, came into sight. Still trying to buy time, Fritigern sent a last-minute deputation to discuss peace. The emperor Valens accepted and discussions began.

Meanwhile, the Roman army deployed into its battle formation. A mixture of cavalry and infantry mustered on each wing, with the bulk of the heavy infantry in the centre. The August sun was burning. The Roman legionaries felt they were being cooked in their heavy armour. They were already tired and sweating from the eight-mile march to reach the Goths. Then the Goths set fire to the dry grass in front of them and the air became even hotter and more oppressive for the Romans.

Both sides waited while Fritigern played for time by making offers of peace. His deputies even promised that he would come to meet Valens himself if high-ranking hostages were exchanged. The western general, Richomer, courageously offered himself as a hostage, and was actually on his way towards the Gothic lines when something completely unexpected happened.

On the Roman right wing, a couple of regiments began an unauthorised attack on the wagon circle. But no sooner did they advance than they retreated back. Richomer wisely decided not to offer himself as a hostage. Negotiations ended, and the battle began. Ammianus' account is the best we have but even it is a little disjointed, and unlike the emperor Julian's Persian campaign, where Ammianus was present, we know that he was not at Adrianople and relied on second-hand information.

What seems to have happened was that, although the first fighting was on the Roman right wing, Ammianus says that it was the Roman left wing which made the most progress, advancing right up to the Gothic wagon circle. But then disaster struck for the Romans. The Gothic cavalry arrived. These were the Greuthungi and Alans who Fritigern had been waiting for. They transformed the battle. Ammianus says, 'They shot forward like a thunderbolt and routed with great slaughter all they could come to grips with…'[52] Their onslaught seems to have destroyed the Roman left wing, and because of this the Roman legionaries in the centre found themselves outflanked by the Gothic cavalry, while also facing a horde of Gothic infantry in front of them.

Although these soldiers were the elite regiments of the eastern army, and probably as good as Julian's Gallic legions, whose steadfastness defeated the Alemanni at the Battle of Strasbourg in 357, this time they were too penned in on all sides to use their weapons effectively. Ammianus says they were:

> *...so closely huddled together that a man could hardly wield his sword or draw back his arm once he had stretched it out. Dust rose in such clouds as to hide the sky...In consequence, it was impossible to see the enemy's missiles in flight and dodge them; all found their mark and dealt death on every side.*[53]

They were using the densely packed testudo formations, normally what gave the Romans a competitive advantage, but this time they did not work against the Goths. 'The barbarians poured on in huge columns, trampling down horse and man, and crushing our ranks so as to make orderly retreat impossible.'[54] Despite this, for quite a while the legionaries held their ground. Ammianus describes a bloody battle with both sides taking heavy casualties: '...you might see the barbarian towering in his fierceness, hissing or shouting, fall with his legs pierced through, or his right hand cut off...'[55]

Finally, Valens' legionaries '...weak from hunger, parched with thirst, and weighed down by their armour...'[56] broke under the pressure of the Gothic attack. Only the most elite Roman regiments, like the Lancearii and Mattiarii, kept fighting while the others fled. The result was slaughter. 'The barbarians spared neither those who yielded nor those who resisted.'[57]

It was one of Rome's most disastrous defeats. Contemporaries were unanimous in acknowledging its significance. Ammianus said it was the worst defeat since the disastrous battle of Cannae in 216 BC, when Hannibal had destroyed most of the Roman army in Italy and left the Republic on the brink of collapse. Two thirds of the eastern Roman army were killed by the Goths, maybe 20,000 legionaries and cavalry. What was particularly damaging was that most of the eastern army's elite regiments were destroyed. These soldiers were extremely difficult to replace, and their loss was so damaging that it would not be until the sixth century, over a hundred years later, that the emperor Justinian and his general, Belisarius, could create an army as professional and experienced as that destroyed at Adrianople. And of course, by that time, the western empire had long fallen. So, Adrianople was more than just a battle lost, it was a mortal blow to the Roman army.

The roll call of Roman dead was truly astonishing. It included the eastern emperor Valens himself, and almost all his senior military officers – 35 tribunes (commanders of legions and so equivalent to generals), as well as the magister peditum and magister equitum (Traianus and Valerianus respectively, the two most senior commanders in the eastern army and equivalent to field marshals). No-one knows exactly what happened to Valens. He was either killed randomly on the battlefield, or one story recounts he fled to a farmhouse which was burned down and he died in the flames.

Even had he survived the battle, it is doubtful Valens would have lasted long. His contemporaries were absolutely certain that the disaster at Adrianople was his fault. To begin with, had he waited for Gratian's army, a Roman victory probably would have been achieved. Even excusing his jealousy of Gratian, his management of the army on the day of the battle was appalling. First, he relied too heavily on the faulty intelligence of his scouts, who suggested the Greuthungi were not in the area, and which prompted him to think he had a numerical advantage. Second, he made a decisive tactical error in marching his soldiers for eight miles to the battlefield, so that they were already tired even before the battle began. Experienced and skilful generals, like Julius Caesar and Julian the Apostate, would never have made these sorts of basic mistakes. Third, he was deceived by Fritigern's delaying tactics, and wasted time negotiating with the Goths even after he had committed to battle. On every measure that mattered, Valens failed miserably. The only consolation for the Romans was that he paid the ultimate price for his failure. He died at the age of almost 50 after a reign of little less than 14 years.

The day after their victory, the idea seized the Goths that Adrianople contained a vast treasure belonging to Valens. According to Ammianus, they poured towards the city, determined to take it at any cost: '…like wild beasts maddened by the taste of blood…'[58] But the city's tall walls, equipped with the brutally effective Roman artillery, and manned by soldiers and every able-bodied citizen, were waiting for them. Like waves crashing against rocks, they threw themselves against the Roman defences, only to suffer horrendous losses as missiles and artillery poured down on them. Eventually, terrified in particular by the enormous stones thrown at them by the Roman artillery, they retreated, cursing that they had ever entertained the idea of taking the city.

What the Goths encountered at Adrianople set a standard for the rest of the Gothic war. They simply did not have sufficient knowledge about siege warfare to take any walled city. After Adrianople, they marched to Constantinople. But one look at its walls, even though these were not yet the mighty Theodosian walls, which would be built over 30 years later, convinced them it would be impossible to take the city.

The result was a stalemate. The Goths could not take any of the Roman cities but the Romans did not have an army left to face them in the field. Or at least not in the east. In the west, of course, there was still a formidable Roman army, and this prevented the Goths from advancing west to the Adriatic. To the east, they were also confined by the Bosphorus, which prevented their crossing into Anatolia. This meant the Goths stayed in Thrace, plundering whatever it was they had missed in the previous two years.

Meanwhile, the Romans prepared to take their revenge. The western emperor, Gratian, appointed Theodosius in January 379 to replace Valens. Theodosius was a soldier without any dynastic claim to the purple, but he was the son of Valentinian's famous general, also called Theodosius (we shall call him Theodosius senior to avoid confusion), and he was appointed to shake up the eastern army and secure a victory over the Goths.

To help him, Gratian gave him control of Illyria, which formally belonged to the western empire, so that Theodosius had direct control of all the Roman forces in the Balkans. However, that was the limit of Gratian's help. He did not send the western army to fight the Goths, as had been the original idea before the Battle of Adrianople. The reason was probably Gratian's fear of a collapse in the west should the western army also be defeated by the Goths. This was understandable but perhaps a missed opportunity.

As for Theodosius, we know very little about him before the Battle of Adrianople. It seems he was stationed in the Balkans close to Thrace, where the trouble with the Goths began in 376, but luckily for him, he somehow did not take part in the Battle of Adrianople.

His background had been troubled since his father, Theodosius senior, fell victim to a court intrigue after Valentinian's death and a jealous minister, Maximinus, executed him for reasons that have never become apparent. Theodosius junior was exiled to Spain. However, the Theodosian family's fall from grace was short-lived. By 376, Gratian had Maximinus executed, and effectively took over full control of the western empire, side-lining his younger half-brother, Valentinian II. He restored Theodosius to an army command in Moesia along the upper Danube.

Gratian seems to have respected and trusted Theodosius, and he gave him the task of rebuilding the eastern army and leading it to victory over the Goths. The problem was that the defeat at Adrianople had eliminated nearly all the elite regiments of the eastern Roman army. Rebuilding an army to anything like the same level of experience and ability would take years, if not decades. And Theodosius had just over a year to do it. He recruited from three sources – veterans were recalled to the ranks, new troops were called up and trained, and he also gathered barbarian mercenaries. But clearly this new army would not be anything like as good as the one that had been destroyed at Adrianople.

Strangely, Theodosius did not realise this and, in the summer of 380, only 18 months after he became emperor, he tested out this rooky army by offering the Goths battle. It was a poor decision. He should have waited longer to train it. There are no detailed records of the battle but it was a clear Roman defeat. Theodosius had failed.

Nevertheless, while he had clearly misjudged the military situation, he was a shrewd and cunning politician. For not only did he survive the court intrigues that developed in Constantinople against him after his defeat, but he also found a diplomatic solution to the problem of the Goths. This became a possibility because, after six years of war, the Goths were exhausted and just as keen to make peace as the Romans. Although they had now defeated two Roman armies – one at Adrianople in 378, and Theodosius' new model army in 380 – they were incapable of taking any of the Roman towns and cities. The western army was successfully pinning them into the Balkans and preventing their migration westward towards Italy. Running out of food, they were ready to negotiate.

In October 382, Theodosius agreed a landmark settlement with the Goths. Hailed by his courtiers as a Roman victory, the treaty of 382 was, in fact, the opposite. It was the first agreement the empire had made in its history to hand over a portion of territory for occupation by a foreign invader. Theodosius agreed the Goths could settle in an area south of the Danube, and although we do not know precisely where it was, it seems to have been mainly in Moesia and Macedonia. This meant that the Goths evacuated Thrace, and the devastated region returned to Roman rule. Indeed, archaeological evidence suggests that the wealthy Roman villas that the Goths had destroyed were rebuilt within the safety of the towns and cities which had never fallen to the Goths.

Our knowledge of the details of the peace treaty are virtually non-existent. We only know three things for certain. First, the Goths were still fully armed and autonomous, and they were not Roman citizens. This was a Roman admission of defeat, for never before had a group of barbarians succeeded in settling in Roman territory while fully armed. Second, there was a regime change demanded by the Romans. Fritigern disappears from the history books, presumably on Theodosius' insistence. This makes sense since he had become the symbol of Gothic defiance. It may also suggest that his own political standing had fallen. The Goths wanted peace and they were willing to oust Fritigern.

Third, the Goths promised to supply troops, albeit under their own commanders and not Roman ones, should they be called on. This would be important in future years, and the Goths would take this commitment seriously, suggesting they saw themselves now as Roman allies. And of course, Rome had a long history of forming alliances with barbarian tribes, but hitherto they had always been with tribes outside Rome's borders, not within them.

There was an interesting spin put on the peace treaty by a Roman senator called Themistius, many of whose writings have survived to this day. He was a consummate politician and lived through the reigns of most of the emperors of the fourth century. His skill was to flatter his lords and masters, and he did his best to present the treaty of 382 as a Roman victory. To do this, he argued that although the Goths were an independent nation being admitted into the empire, there was a clear precedent from history showing that they would be absorbed and incorporated into the Roman world.

The example he chose was a major Gallic invasion of Greece back in the third century BC, so over 600 years before the Battle of Adrianople. What had happened then was that an enormous group of Gauls had migrated, rather similarly to the Goths, south of the Danube, into the territories of the Greek successor states to Alexander the Great's empire. The Macedonians had only just beaten them and diverted them across the Bosphorus into Anatolia, where they set up a Gallic state that survived for a couple of hundred years before fading away and being incorporated into the Roman Empire. Indeed, the Greeks called a large part of Anatolia Galatia in reference to the Gallic presence.

Themistius claimed the Goths would eventually be just like the Gauls. They would be absorbed into the Roman Empire. But he conveniently forgot to mention that, in fact, a century after the Greeks had failed to defeat the Galatians, the Roman army had managed to defeat them and only then were they incorporated as a subject race into the empire.

But this time there was no Roman victory. The truth was that the Goths had won. Their crushing victory at Adrianople, and the Roman army's subsequent inability to defeat them, set a new and perilous precedent. For the first time in Rome's history, it had had to acknowledge defeat at the hands of a foreign power and the cessation of territory to that invader, albeit at this point only a small part of the empire.

If the Gothic settlement had been a one-off, then it would not have mattered to Rome. No doubt that is what Theodosius hoped. But it was not to be. Roman capitulation to the Goths marked the beginning of what has become known as the *Völkerwanderung*, or 'wandering of the peoples', a time during which the whole of the western empire would ultimately be swallowed up by the barbarians.

18

Making Matters Even Worse

The last thing the Romans needed in the 380s was civil war. Yet that is exactly what happened.

This occurred during the reign of Theodosius the Great – and we will return in the next chapter to the question of whether his reign was actually so great – when there were two major civil wars, both of which are often underestimated as important causes of Rome's decline and fall. In addition, there was a significant conflict both within the Church and between the Church and the emperors, essentially about the doctrine of Arianism. This was led by a man who would become a central figure in the development of the Catholic Church, Ambrose, the bishop of Milan. Again, this served as an unhelpful distraction for the imperial government during a period of intense external crisis.

Let us start with the civil wars. The first began soon after Theodosius had secured his peace treaty with the Goths in 382. The direct cause was dissatisfaction with the western emperor, Gratian. This has never been satisfactorily explained by the Roman sources which, it is worth mentioning, suffer from a marked deterioration in quality after 378, when our most reliable chronicler on fourth-century Roman history, Ammianus Marcellinus, finished writing. Although he is thought to have lived until the 390s, he decided not to record Theodosius' reign, leaving us to rely on other sources, most of which are incomplete. The best record we have for the period from 378 until the fall of Rome in 410 was written by a Greek historian, Zosimus, who lived in Constantinople a hundred years later, around AD 500, and was a pagan. Unlike Ammianus, he did not live through the times he recorded, and he seems to have put together his history from the works of other more contemporary writers, most of which have been lost.

This can sometimes create a bewildering picture of these vital years in Rome's history. A good example is the unsatisfactory explanation of Gratian's demise. Zosimus rather mysteriously says it was because he favoured his bodyguard of Alan tribesmen over the regular Roman soldiers. The Alans were excellent horsemen and Gratian's close friendship with them stemmed from his passion for hunting. Apparently, Gratian liked to give them generous presents, and even enjoyed dressing up in their clothes, to the annoyance of the regular Roman troops and the Germanic auxiliaries.

Zosimus' portrayal of Gratian presents us with a puzzling contrast to his earlier career, when he was highly regarded as a soldier, even being lauded as a suitable replacement for Valens back in 378. Edward Gibbon suggests one interpretation is that Gratian was always incompetent, but he covered it up well through the good advice of his counsellors and generals, who deserted him later in life. This sounds as plausible a reason as any to explain why he lost the confidence of his troops. The first to rebel were the British legions, often a discontented section of the army because of their marginal position in the Roman world, who declared a popular general called Magnus Maximus emperor in early 383.

Based in Britain, Maximus had enjoyed an impeccable military career. He had served under the emperor Theodosius' father, who had helped Valentinian I to subjugate revolts in Britain and North Africa. Once he was declared emperor, Maximus crossed over to Gaul, where Gratian gathered what troops he could, and advanced to meet him in battle near to Paris. But Gratian's troops went over to Maximus, and Gratian fled to Lugdunum, where he was caught and killed.

Maximus was following in the footsteps of the rebel Magnentius, whose rebellion also began in Britain, and ended up being put down by Constantius in 353. But with Maximus, it took a while for a proper civil war to develop since, in Constantinople, Theodosius initially adopted a conciliatory stance towards him, although Zosimus says that he was '…at the same time privately preparing for war, and endeavouring to deceive Maximus by every type of flattery… '[59] Theodosius' problem in 383 was that he was busy with yet another Persian war on his eastern front, this time with Shapur II's successor Shapur III, and there was little he could do to oppose Maximus.

We have to wonder whether Theodosius might have been better off accepting Maximus and trying to work with him? Indeed, it is surprising he was not more favourably impressed by Maximus' loyalty to his father, and the fact he was a capable general, which was exactly what the empire needed at this point. But Theodosius was firmly set against him. The real sticking point seems to have been dynastic, in the sense that Maximus was a usurper and had murdered Gratian, who was the legitimate emperor. It was also Gratian who had elevated Theodosius to the rank of eastern emperor in the first place, so Theodosius may have felt a sense of loyalty to him.

However, the person most directly in Maximus' line of fire was not Theodosius but Valentinian II, the third reigning emperor, in control of Italy. Until this moment, no-one had paid much attention to him because he was still only a child. In 383, when Maximus killed Gratian, Valentinian was only 12 years old. And before his death, Gratian had in fact ignored his younger half-brother and ruled the western empire alone. Now things changed, although not so much because of Valentinian but because of his mother, Justina. She had been Valentinian I's second wife, and was a force to be reckoned with. Apparently devastatingly good-looking, and distantly related to Constantine the Great, she was the sort of woman who was not going to be bossed about by an upstart general like Maximus.

On hearing that Maximus had murdered Gratian, she immediately sent the Italian legions to block the Alpine passes and made sure that he could not advance into Italy. Justina, Maximus and Theodosius then agreed the empire should be ruled jointly. Valentinian II and Justina remained in control of Italy, based in Milan. Maximus ruled the rest of the western empire, including North Africa, from Trier on the German frontier, and Theodosius ruled the east from Constantinople. For four years, this regime worked well and there was peace between the three emperors.

But Justina and Valentinian had another problem aside from Maximus, which was that they were Arians. The fourth-century Christian Church had long been divided by a bitter theological dispute between the Arians and the non-Arians which went back to the council of Nicaea in 325, when the emperor Constantine convened the first great council of the Christian Church to agree a single version of Christian belief and ritual.[60] Constantine and the bishops did a pretty good job. They agreed on things like one statement of faith, a date for the celebration of the main Christian festival, which was Easter and not Christmas (which is a more modern invention), and also the basics of how the Church was to be organised and run.

But there was one point of doctrine that defied agreement, which was whether Christ and God were the same, or whether Christ was the son of God and therefore subordinate to him. This may seem obscure to us today, but in the fourth century it exerted an almost obsessive fascination for most clerics. A bishop called Arius said that since Christ was the son of God, he could not have existed for eternity, and must be subordinate. Although some bishops agreed with this, especially those in the east, the majority did not. Constantine had little interest in Christian doctrine, and it is almost certain that he had no interest at all in the Arian debate. At Nicaea, he decided in favour of the non-Arians simply because this was the majority view. It became known as the Nicene Creed, and is still the foundation of the modern Catholic Church.

Without probably realising it, Constantine made this dispute worse because, just before his own death, he was baptised by his favourite bishop, Eusebius of Nicomedia, who happened to be an Arian, as were many of the bishops in the eastern Roman Empire. This meant that in the east, Arianism survived and prospered, especially within the imperial family. Constantine's son, Constantius II, and the ill-fated Valens were both Arians.

In line with imperial family practice, Valentinian II and his mother, Justina, were also Arians. But the problem for them was that they were in a minority in Italy. In the west, most Christians were not Arian. And to make matters worse, the non-Arians in Italy were championed by a charismatic new bishop called Ambrose, the bishop of Milan.

Matters came to a head between Ambrose and Justina when he refused to allow Arians to worship in the churches in Milan. This was supported by most Christians in the city, but it was a direct attack on Justina and her son Valentinian. Justina demanded that two churches in the Milan diocese should allow Arian worship – one inside the city and one just outside. Ambrose not only refused, but he went to the church in the city, the Basilica of the Apostles, and barricaded himself in. Justina sent troops to evict him, but they backed off without a fight, and Ambrose won the day.

It was the first time in history that a Christian bishop had stood up to a member of the imperial family and won. The incident set an ominous precedent for the future relations between Church and state. It also gave Maximus, who was not an Arian, a pretext to invade Italy. In 387, he crossed the Alps with his army and entered the Po Valley. Justina and Valentinian fled to Thessalonica. There, Justina appealed to Theodosius for help against Maximus. According to Zosimus, she cleverly arranged for Theodosius to meet her sister, Galla, who, like Justina herself, was exceptionally beautiful. Again, according to Zosimus, Theodosius fell in love with her and promised to fight Maximus. A more likely explanation is that Theodosius was already planning an offensive against Maximus, and the reason he was now free to do this was because he had secured peace on his eastern front by making a humbling treaty with Shapur III, giving control of most of Armenia to the Sasanians. A marriage with Galla was convenient because it enabled him to cement his alliance with Valentinian and Justina.

Theodosius was quick to strike at Maximus, who had advanced from northern Italy into Illyria. In the summer of 388, two battles were fought, one at Siscia and the other at Poetovio. In both of them, pitted against each other, were the main regular Roman regiments from east and west, together with Maximus' Germanic mercenaries and Theodosius' Gothic *foederati*. Unfortunately, we have almost no details about either battle although Theodosius secured a victory in both. What we can say is that the western army must have sustained casualties it could ill afford. Maximus fled to the legionary fortress at Aquileia, where he was betrayed by his men, surrendered to Theodosius and was executed.

Thus ended the first civil war. Theodosius would have to face another and even more dangerous civil war in 392, but for the moment, he had triumphed, and he moved to Milan. There, he encountered the fiercely independent bishop Ambrose. Although Theodosius was committed to the Nicene Creed, and had actually issued an edict condemning the Arians in 380, he and Ambrose fell out over a peculiar incident in the Greek city of Thessalonica in April 390.

This concerned the Gothic commander and governor of the city, Butheric, who arrested a popular charioteer for the alleged rape of a cup bearer. This act of homosexuality was apparently particularly repugnant to the Goths, but not to the Greek population of the city, who were indignant that their favourite had been punished in this way. They rioted, demanding the charioteer's release. When Butheric refused, the mob lynched him. Theodosius reacted angrily to the news of this disturbance and allowed the garrison, which may have been mainly Gothic, to enter the hippodrome and restore order. Things got out of hand and the angry Gothic soldiers were said to have killed 7,000 of the spectators. To add insult to injury, the Goths were almost certainly Arians.

When Ambrose heard of the incident, he condemned Theodosius for ordering the garrison to restore order in such a brutal manner, and refused to grant him communion for eight months as a penance. During this time, he had to attend church without his imperial robes. It was unprecedented for a bishop to impose his will on the emperor. Edward Gibbon saw it as an example of how the early Christian Church triumphed over the Roman state, and suggested this as one of the reasons for the fall of the Roman Empire.

It was so extraordinary that historians now wonder whether it even happened or if it was in fact made up by an overzealous bishop called Theodoret of Cyrus, whose account of it is the only source for the story. If Theodoret did invent it, then the Christian Church was extremely clever in using it as a precedent to justify the Church's authority over the state, something that was to become a source of perennial conflict not just during the last days of the western empire but for centuries afterwards in the Middle Ages.

Whatever we make of the truth about Ambrose's

humiliation of Theodosius, there is no doubt imperial authority was being challenged by the Church. Constantine's conversion to Christianity was not serving his successors as well as he would have expected. Nor was the threat of civil war reducing in the late Roman Empire. Externally, there was the new power of the Goths, the threat of Persia, and the endless conflict with the German tribes along the Rhine frontier.

The storm clouds were gathering over the Roman Empire.

19

Theodosius the Not So Great

By the year 391, Theodosius had spent three years in Milan since his victory over Maximus in 388. During this time, the western empire had been his focus. In that year, he returned to Constantinople to rule the entire empire from what was now its real capital. And in the west, he thought he could rely on two loyal supporters. One was the young Valentinian II, now 20 years old, and the other was the man who he had entrusted with the military command of the west, a general of Frankish origin, Flavius Arbogastes, better known as Arbogast.

Arbogast's titular position was *Magister Militum in Praesenti*, which literally meant 'commander of the armies attending the emperor', but, unlike in the east where there were several generals at the magister level, he had absolute command over all the western armies except for those in Africa. So, he was the de facto ruler in the west. His loyalty to Theodosius was thought to be beyond reproach. He had fought for Theodosius in his Gothic campaigns and against Maximus, and had even undertaken a mission to kill Maximus' son, Victor.

So, you would think that everything was set for excellent cooperation between him and Theodosius, similar to the way Diocletian had relied on his trusted general, Maximian, to rule the west? Unfortunately for Theodosius, this proved not to be the case, and the situation developed into one of the worst civil wars ever to hit the Roman Empire. The direct cause was the unsatisfactory position of the young Valentinian II. For Valentinian was now 20 years old and no longer a child emperor, although the problem was that everyone still treated him as just that. His forceful mother, Justina, had died in 388, leaving him without any prop on which to lean.

Compared with him, Arbogast could not have been more different. He was a tough, experienced soldier. It is, frankly, difficult to see how a rupture between the two of them could have been avoided. For Valentinian understandably wanted to wield power and Arbogast stood in his way. Tension between the two of them was bound to rise and, ultimately, Theodosius must be blamed for the falling out, since he had created a situation that was unmanageable. In 391, Valentinian tried to remove Arbogast by summoning him to his residence in Vienne in Gaul. From his throne, he handed Arbogast a letter dismissing him. Arbogast read it and laughed, saying that he took orders from Theodosius, not Valentinian.

What happened next has always puzzled historians. Shortly after his bust-up with Arbogast, Valentinian was found dead, hanged in his own quarters on 15 May 392. Arbogast protested he had no hand in it, although Zosimus says he organised his death, and may even have carried it out himself. The official verdict was suicide, but, whatever the truth, the finger of suspicion pointed at Arbogast.

This put Theodosius in a difficult position. On one hand, Arbogast had no pretensions for the purple himself, since he accepted that his Frankish blood ruled this out, and he was a competent general who respected Theodosius. If Theodosius had been a wiser and better emperor, he might have judged that coming to terms with Arbogast was in his best interests. But Theodosius was not far-sighted. He was also married to Galla, Valentinian's sister, who was outraged by her brother's death and blamed Arbogast.

Theodosius was typically indecisive. He prevaricated for months, neither accepting Arbogast nor condemning him. By ignoring him, Theodosius put him in an impossible position. For, since Arbogast did not have the presumption to take the purple himself, he found it difficult to govern the western empire from a practical standpoint. For example, legally, he could not issue instructions and edicts without being an emperor. So, Theodosius' silence forced Arbogast to find his own emperor. And this turned out to be Eugenius, who had been Valentinian's chief secretary. According to Zosimus, he was not power hungry and only reluctantly accepted the position. He was also a Christian, which softened the fact that Arbogast was a pagan. Eugenius immediately sent two embassies to Theodosius seeking friendship. He minted coins with himself and Theodosius as the two consuls in the west to show that he was not a threat. The tradition of having two consuls, one or both of whom were emperors, was meaningless but still symbolic, and still survived from Augustus' time as a nod to the Republic. Even Ambrose, who was still in Milan, supported a compromise with Eugenius.

But Theodosius was having none of it. In January, he raised his young son, Honorius, to the full rank of Augustus, implying that he was the emperor of the west, not Eugenius. War was now inevitable. In April 393, Arbogast's troops moved into Italy unopposed and occupied Milan, which Ambrose left to go to Bologna. This move is widely seen as the last reassertion of paganism. Arbogast was a pagan and most of the senate in Rome were still pagans. They asked for the restoration of their cherished Altar of Victory. This was one of the mains symbols of the classical pagan Roman Empire. A gold statue of the goddess Nike, or Victory, it was originally captured over 600 years previously in the war against the Greek king Pyrrhus when the Roman Republic was quite young. Octavian gave it special significance by placing it in the senate house to commemorate the battle of Actium, which marked the effective birth of the Roman Empire. Ever since then, it had been central to Roman tradition, with senators burning incense and offering prayers for the empire's welfare daily. Constantius II had removed it in 357, only for it to be reinstated by Julian, and then removed again by Gratian in 382.

Eugenius' restoration of the Altar of Victory sparked a pagan revival in Italy. Eugenius appointed a pagan Praetorian Prefect of Italy, Flavianus, who encouraged temples to be restored and pagan festivals and sacrifices to be celebrated. Ambrose wrote to Eugenius in protest: 'Even if imperial power is great, consider how great is God...was it not your duty, Augustus, to refuse what was so injurious to Holy Law?'[61]

In early 394, both sides prepared for war. Arbogast

controlled the west – including Italy – but not North Africa, where Gildo, Theodosius' loyal appointee, could have stopped the grain shipment to Rome. Theodosius decided against this, perhaps hoping to persuade the Roman populace to come over to his side.

The two sides mustered their forces. What was striking about Theodosius' army was the very high proportion of barbarian mercenaries, especially Goths who had agreed to supply troops to the Romans in the peace treaty of 382. He also hired Alans and Huns. Many of his main generals were also of barbarian descent, including Stilicho, the future commander of the western army, who first appears in our historical records at this time.

Against him, Arbogast gathered what was probably a more Roman army with a higher proportion of legionaries, including the Gallic legions, arguably still the best units in the Roman army just as they had been in Constantine's and Julian's armies. He also recruited a fair number of barbarian mercenaries, including Franks and Alemanni. Barbarian mercenaries were now becoming as important in the Roman army as the legionaries. This is an important subject to which we will return in later chapters.

Another striking feature of this conflict was its religious significance. Christian chroniclers have gone to great lengths to emphasise that it was Christianity's greatest test yet, and that Arbogast and Eugenius' army was a pagan one while Theodosius' was Christian. While they have probably exaggerated this, it was certainly true the Roman senate, championed by the Praetorian Prefect of Italy, Flavianus, saw this as an opportunity to reassert paganism if not to actually destroy Christianity. Flavianus boasted that when Arbogast defeated Theodosius, he would force Italian monks to join the army and turn the holy churches into stables.

The two armies met in Illyria, in the area that is now modern Slovenia, in a strategically important pass that linked northern Italy with the Balkans beside the Frigidus River. Arbogast's army blocked the pass, and on 5 September 394, Theodosius launched an attack led by his Visigothic mercenaries. There was a bitter fight with heavy casualties on both sides, but the western legionaries, with their Germanic mercenaries, repelled Theodosius' Goths who retreated, leaving as many as 10,000 dead.

In the western army's camp, there was jubilation. Eugenius thought that victory was his. Arbogast then made a fatal mistake. He sent a significant number of troops in an outflanking manoeuvre to occupy the passes behind Theodosius, intending to encircle the eastern army and destroy it. It was a superb tactical move and should have brought him complete victory. But history moves in unpredictable ways, and the commander of these troops turned out to be a traitor, who joined Theodosius in exchange for an enormous sum of money. We know nothing about the individual concerned, but his actions literally changed the course of history, for the next day, Theodosius felt strong enough to launch another assault.

However, this second attack also began to falter when another unexpected event happened. This was a natural phenomenon – a cyclonic wind known locally as the 'Bora'. The cold air in this region coming from the mountains can produce an unusual atmospheric pressure effect which creates a temporary cyclonic wind of over 60mph. This was exactly what happened during the second day of the battle. Arbogast's army was desperately unlucky because the full force of this wind blew against them. It pressed against their shields, blinded them with dust, deflected their missiles backwards, and gave their opponents an irresistible tailwind to hurl themselves forward. Not surprisingly, the Christian chroniclers saw this as an example of divine intervention.

The result was that Arbogast's army eventually broke and scattered. Theodosius' soldiers stormed his camp and captured Eugenius alive. He pleaded for mercy but Theodosius had him beheaded, and his head impaled on a spear and paraded before the prisoners of the western army. As for Arbogast, he escaped to the mountains but after a few days he decided his position was hopeless and committed suicide.

Theodosius was now the sole emperor of the entire Roman Empire. He was the last man to hold that position. But not for long. For less than five months later, he was dead. He died on 17 January 395, aged 48, and had ruled for 16 years. He probably died from heart failure due to a weak heart or caused by overindulgence in eating and drinking. Although his health had always been poor, his death was unexpected and he left the empire in the hands of his two young sons, Arcadius in the east, and Honorius in the west. But they were both too young to rule. Arcadius was 17 and Honorius was only 11. On his deathbed, Theodosius appointed regents to govern for his sons, including Stilicho in the west and the Praetorian Prefect, Rufinus, in the east.

What was Theodosius' legacy? His epithet of 'The Great' suggests he had achieved something spectacular for the

Roman Empire. However, with two costly civil wars and the 'barbarisation' of the Roman army, the evidence suggests otherwise. History, as they say, is written by the victors, and our sources for Theodosius are a good example of this. The only victor from Theodosius' reign was the Catholic Church, and it is no surprise that it was the Catholic bishops who called him 'The Great'.

Their veneration of him is understandable. His piety was beyond reproach. He was a committed Christian and a believer in the Nicene Creed, and vehemently opposed to the Arians. He enacted pro-Catholic legislation early in his reign, in 380, with the 'Edict of Thessalonika', which stopped Arians from attending churches in Constantinople, although not in fact elsewhere in the empire. He was passionately anti-pagan. An edict issued in 392 clearly stated that Christianity was the empire's favoured religion and that paganism was all but banned. Theodosius' religious zeal may have stemmed from his recovery after a severe illness in the year 380, which prompted him to be baptised in gratitude for what he thought was divine deliverance.

But while the Catholic Church had good reason to celebrate his reign, the Roman Empire had none. His rule was a disaster for the Roman army. Unlike Aurelian and Diocletian, who rebuilt the Roman army during the crisis of the third century, Theodosius completely failed to rebuild it after the catastrophe at Adrianople. His inability to defeat Fritigern's Thervingi and avenge Adrianople clearly showed this. There was nothing like the reinvention of the cavalry arm which saved Rome in the third century. Instead, virtually all the elite regiments of the eastern army that had been destroyed at Adrianople were not rebuilt, meaning that the eastern army became second-rate.

He compensated for the downgrading of the eastern legions by using the Goths as mercenary troops. This worked well in the short term, but in the longer term for the Roman Empire it proved disastrous, since the Goths and other barbarians effectively replaced Roman soldiers as the elite regiments in the Roman army. Then, just as Theodosius failed to revive the eastern Roman army, so he nearly destroyed the western army. At the beginning of his reign, it was still a premier fighting force, just as it had been under Julian when it won the Battle of Strasbourg in 357. But Theodosius' two civil wars undermined it. In particular, at the battle of the Frigidus River, it suffered huge casualties which left it as a shell of its former self.

In summary, there was nothing great about Theodosius' reign. Only 15 years after his death, the city of Rome itself was sacked by the Goths. More than any other emperor in Rome's history, he sowed the seeds for its downfall.

PART IV

The Fall of the West

20

The Roman Empire Divided

A summer breeze blew gently, making the long grass outside the city walls ripple like waves in the sea.

It was a hot night on 24 August 410. The ghostly moonlight illuminated the walls of Rome, built by Aurelian over a hundred years before. The sentries were at their posts. There was a stillness in the air. The tents of the Gothic camp were visible in the distance. But the sentries rested on their spears. This was the third time the Goths had come to the city. Each time, they had waited and not tried to attack. Now, in the stillness of the night, there was a sense of peace, almost as if they were old friends returning from their travels.

The centurion in charge of the Salarian Gate did not notice the slaves as they moved in the shadows of the city. They passed along the street, stooping low, hiding themselves against the sides of the buildings. They were armed with daggers and a butcher's knife. A legionary standing at the bottom of the gate saw them. But it was too late. Two of them grabbed him from both sides and held him down as a third slit his throat. He tried to scream, but all he could do was utter a stifled sigh. The centurion thought he heard something. He looked down from the wall, first beyond the city walls, towards the Goths. But he saw nothing. No sign of movement. Then, he turned round and looked down towards the road in the city that led to the Salarian Gate.

'Decius!' he called out. That was the dead sentry's name.

But there was no answer. Puzzled, he walked down the steps to the bottom of the gate. Then, coming out of the shadows, he saw three men. The butcher's knife caught the side of his head while a dagger was planted in his back. He was knocked to the ground. His helmet rolled off, making a clinking sound the slaves knew would be heard by the other sentries. They left the centurion rolling in a pool of blood and ran to the gate, where they heaved off the heavy wooden bars that held it firm. Then they dragged the great doors open. They could hear the sentries rushing down the steps, shouting out to their comrades. At the same time, the Goths, who had been waiting concealed in the long grass beyond the city walls, stood up and rushed towards the gate. Within minutes, all three of the slaves were dead, killed by the sentries. But they, in their turn, were butchered by the hordes of Goths that were now pouring through the gates. There were too many Goths and too few sentries.

The sack of Rome had begun.

Fifteen years before, on 17 January 395, Theodosius I had died, leaving his two sons, Arcadius and Honorius, his successors in the east and west. Although it had always been his carefully nurtured plan to leave the empire to his two sons, his death had occurred much earlier than anyone had expected, and this meant there were two major problems.

First, both his sons were too young to rule. Arcadius was 17 and Honorius was only 11. If Arcadius had been an exceptionally gifted young man, then he might have risen to the challenge. But unfortunately for the Romans, neither Honorius nor Arcadius were exceptionally gifted. Indeed, they were the opposite. And although Theodosius had hoped to train them for the demanding roles they were to inherit, his premature death prevented this. The result was a critical failure of leadership just when the Roman Empire needed it most.

Second, because of these two exceptionally weak emperors, the empire became increasingly divided between east and west. Indeed, historians normally mark the division of the Roman Empire from Theodosius' death in 395 even though there was no formal division at this time. Indeed, contemporaries still regarded the empire as united. Yet a real division was created when the imperial courts at Milan and Constantinople vied with each other as enemies.

Of course, the tendency for the empire to fragment was an old problem. Ever since the crisis of the third century, it had proved increasingly difficult for one emperor to rule the entire empire in the way the emperors from Augustus to Septimius Severus had done. And the real reason for this was that the empire had too many enemies. One emperor could not fight on the Rhine, Danube and the Tigris at the same time. To solve the problem, Diocletian had instituted the tetrarchy – the division of the empire into four separate zones each with its own emperor or junior emperor – and although this worked well during his lifetime, it depended on his charismatic personality to succeed. Without a truly authoritative emperor like him, the system was not sustainable.

After Diocletian's death, Constantine spent most of his life fighting one civil war after another until he had secured full control of the empire for himself. Thereafter, he divided it between his three sons. This tripartite division of the empire differed from Diocletian's because it was dynastic – i.e., sharing the empire between members of the same family. And this was how the empire operated henceforward for most of the fourth century and into the fifth. Indeed, in the fourth century there were only 15 years when the empire was ruled by just one man.[62]

From 395 onwards, the emperors were simply too young – and when they became older, too untalented – to rule effectively by themselves. In the west, the man who would dominate Roman history from Theodosius' death in 395 until his own in 408 was Stilicho. Stilicho was a rising star in Theodosius' army, although we have very few details about the roles he had until 395. Stilicho's parents were a Vandal father, serving in the Roman army, and a Roman mother. All we know about his early life is that he joined Theodosius' imperial guard and his main career breakthrough came when he married Theodosius' niece, Serena.

How did an ordinary guardsman end up marrying Theodosius' niece? It was probably a genuine love match. Serena may have noticed Stilicho, who was no doubt a handsome soldier, when he was on his duties around the palace. She fell in love with him, and he with her; all the evidence suggests they were a genuinely devoted couple throughout their lives, with her supporting his career in every way she could.

Serena was the key to Stilicho's early rise to prominence. She introduced him to Theodosius and asked if she could marry him. She was Theodosius' niece but he was apparently very fond of her, so much so that he made her his adopted daughter, and although Stilicho's social rank was far below hers, he allowed them to marry in either 383 or 384.

It was almost unheard of for an ordinary guardsman to marry an imperial princess, so Theodosius must have been impressed with Stilicho as a capable young soldier who could be useful to him. When he allowed them to marry, he promoted Stilicho to head of the Imperial Guard and then made him a general. Stilicho's meteoric rise continued as he remained one of Theodosius' favourites. We know little about his appointments in the ten years between 384 and 394, but Theodosius increasingly used him as one of his inner circle of trusted favourites. For example, he sent him as an envoy on the peace mission to Persia, which ended in 387 with a truce that enabled Theodosius to divert troops from the eastern front to fight Maximus in the west. Then, in 394, after the battle of the Frigidus River, Theodosius made him the commander-in-chief of the western army. This was a massive promotion, making him one of the most important people in the empire.

Things continued to work in his favour. A couple of months later, Theodosius' health deteriorated and he started planning for his succession. In late 394, he made Stilicho *parens principum*, or principal guardian, of the 11-year-old Honorius, the emperor designate in the west. And finally, Stilicho claimed that, just before he died, Theodosius made him guardian of Arcadius in the east as well, giving him authority over both the boy emperors. However, this claim remained controversial because there were no witnesses to it, and Arcadius and his court in Constantinople immediately rejected it.

Indeed, Stilicho's ambition for power in both the east and west fractured relations between the two halves of the empire. Arcadius' Praetorian Prefect of the east, Rufinus, saw him as a direct threat to his own authority. Rufinus was, according to all the surviving sources, a nasty piece of work who had eliminated his rivals except for one – a eunuch called Eutropius who was Theodosius' imperial chamberlain. Eutropius proved to be no pushover and won an important victory over Rufinus by getting Arcadius to marry a young woman, Eudocia, who was a protégé of his.

The story was that Rufinus was planning to get Arcadius to marry his own daughter when Eutropius found and befriended an exceptionally beautiful young woman called Eudocia. He showed a portrait of her to Arcadius, who was immediately captivated, and, according to the chronicler Zosimus, Eutropius deceived Rufinus into thinking that Arcadius was about to marry his own daughter when he had already persuaded him to marry Eudocia. Eudocia was herself a tough operator and would henceforth hold considerable power over her weak-willed husband, and became yet another important political player.

Another character who would play a crucial role in Roman politics was the famous Galla Placidia. She was Theodosius' daughter by his marriage to his second wife. We should remember that Honorius and Arcadius were born to Theodosius' first wife. This caused tension between them, which would become another destabilising force in the imperial family. She would play a key role in the early fifth-century Roman Empire, but in 395, she was at most seven years old, and lived with Stilicho and Serena because she had fallen out with her stepbrother Arcadius in Constantinople.

Perhaps the most important figure of all in Roman politics from 395 to 410 was Alaric, king of the Goths, the man who would sack Rome in 410. But, in 395, such an idea would have seemed ridiculous. Theodosius had made peace with the Visigoths in 382. They had fought loyally for him at the battle of the Frigidus River in 394. Yet they were not Roman citizens, they were armed, and in 395 they surprised the Romans by revolting.

The reason was that they felt betrayed by Theodosius. They had honoured their agreement, made in the treaty of 382, to fight as mercenaries for the Romans if requested, but Theodosius had abused this trust by using them as his first line of attack against Arbogast's western army in the battle of the Frigidus River in 394. They had borne the brunt of the fighting and been effectively defeated by the legionaries of the western army. According to one source, they had suffered 10,000 casualties.

This became a source of resentment against the Romans, especially as Theodosius failed to reward their loyalty with a donative or special concessions. Instead, after the battle of the Frigidus River, he told them to make their way, in winter, back to their homes in lower Moesia along the middle Danube. Although he rewarded their king, Alaric, with a Roman military title – *comes rei militaris* (count of the military), this was not enough to pacify either him or his followers.

Alaric put pressure on the Romans to make more

concessions by raising a rebellion in the Balkans. Some historians think that part of his motivation was to bring all the disparate Gothic tribes under his control since, although he was referred to as king of the Goths by chroniclers, he was probably actually only king of the Thervingi. To make his point, Alaric led his Gothic army to threaten Constantinople itself.

The result was panic in the city. No eastern army existed to meet the Goths since it was either in the west with Stilicho, having just fought the Frigidus battle, or had been sent east to Armenia to confront a Hunnic invasion through the Caucasus. Although the Goths were still no better at siege craft than they had been when they failed to capture any significant Roman cities after the Battle of Adrianople, and it is extremely unlikely that they could have taken Constantinople, Rufinus was sufficiently scared, according to Zosimus, that he agreed to meet Alaric and promised that he could ravage Greece unopposed if he left Constantinople. He almost certainly also bought him off with a payment of gold.

Meanwhile, in the west, Stilicho was in command of the remains of both the western and eastern Roman armies that had fought at Frigidus. When he heard of Alaric's rebellion, he was both incensed that this former Roman ally had betrayed his oath to Rome, and alert to the opportunity to claim power in the east by defeating Alaric and saving Constantinople.

Stilicho marched through Illyria and confronted Alaric in Thessaly. But it was at that very moment, just when he seemed to have Alaric within his grasp, that the Romans scored a massive own goal. This happened because the treacherous Rufinus, afraid that if Stilicho defeated Alaric, he would next get rid of him, persuaded the young emperor Arcadius to order a halt to Stilicho's advance.

The result of this Roman rivalry was that Alaric escaped. The eastern army simply marched back to Constantinople rather than working with Stilicho to defeat the Goths. An unexpected twist followed. When it reached Constantinople, the emperor Arcadius and the Praetorian Prefect Rufinus came out of the city to greet it. Rufinus was normally protected by his Hunnic bodyguard, but not on this occasion due to the emperor's presence. As speeches were being delivered, a group of soldiers surrounded Rufinus and hacked him to death.

Why did this happen? Historians have come up with a host of possible explanations. The most likely is that Stilicho had to obey Rufinus and let Alaric escape because his wife, Serena, and his children were resident in Constantinople, making them potential hostages. In revenge, he arranged for eastern soldiers, sympathetic to his cause, to kill Rufinus.

Whatever the truth about Rufinus' bizarre assassination, it transformed the political situation in the east. His rival, Eutropius, quickly stepped into his shoes and assumed power under the auspices of Arcadius' wife, Eudocia, who supported her benefactor. Eutropius and Stilicho now cemented an understanding that healed some of the division between east and west. Eutropius was an astute politician, utterly different from the small-minded Rufinus, who only cared about his own political survival. Eutropius' genuine worry was the Huns, who were at that moment in Armenia and Mesopotamia, pillaging both Roman and Persian cities. But before striking at them, he wanted to get control of the army, and he spent 396 securing the replacement of the two major generals in the eastern army – Timasius and Abundantius – with men of his own choosing. This took some time, since he had to organise false allegations of treason against them. But such was the brutal nature of Roman politics.

As a gesture of cooperation with Stilicho, he let him take control of the half of Illyria that had originally been part of the western empire before it was ceded to the eastern empire by Gratian. Its return to the west was a welcome sign of greater unity between the two halves of the empire. Meanwhile, Stilicho marched his army back to the west to deal with the Rhine frontier, where he led successful attacks against the Franks, securing Roman defences and also raising recruits from the German tribes to augment his Gallic legions.

By winning some small-scale victories over the Germans in the west, Stilicho was also hoping to boost the western army's morale, as it was still demoralised from its defeats at the Frigidus battle and the earlier conflict between Theodosius and Maximus. In addition, Stilicho secured the support of the Roman senate by giving it more legislative power and in return he was supported by a prominent senator called Symmachus.

This renewed détente between the east and west was all well and good but it did not solve the main problem facing the empire, and one that was about to detonate in everyone's faces. That problem was Alaric. While Stilicho and Eutropius were securing their own power bases, Alaric was running amok in Greece. After his escape from Stilicho's clutches, he invaded Greece and besieged one city after another, although the larger cities like Thebes and Athens were beyond his grasp.

Alaric's survival depended on keeping the western and

eastern empires apart. If they fielded a joint imperial army against him, he knew he was finished. So, he curried favour with Eutropius by limiting the destruction wrought by his Gothic horde in Greece. The Goths extorted protection money from the Greek population rather than destroying property. Eutropius began to regard Alaric as someone he could do business with.

Meanwhile, Stilicho was intent on destroying Alaric and solving the Gothic problem once and for all. Alaric's defeat would give him the prestige to leverage his claim to Constantinople, as Eutropius was only too aware. So, he got ready to strike again at the king of the Goths. In early 397, he crossed the Adriatic with an army of legionaries and German mercenaries, landing at Corinth in Greece, which was part of the eastern empire. He did not ask permission from Eutropius, who interpreted his actions as, in effect, an invasion.

Stilicho's campaign started well. He defeated the Goths in several small skirmishes. Eutropius began to panic at the prospect of Stilicho arriving in triumph at Constantinople. Just as the Goths were retreating, and a Roman victory was finally within sight, Eutropius did his best to thwart this by persuading the emperor Arcadius to declare Stilicho a *hostis publicus* (public enemy) of the state. In this way, any pretence of cooperation between east and west was fully shattered, enabling Alaric to take full advantage of the divided Roman Empire. The eastern army allowed the Goths to retreat east unopposed and out of the grasp of Stilicho's legionaries. Pursuit was hindered by the Greek cities closing their gates to his men and depriving them of food. After a campaign of only some ten weeks, Stilicho gave up and returned to Italy.

Eutropius had ensured Alaric's survival. Now, he wanted him to act as a buffer against Stilicho. He made an alliance with the Gothic king and even gave him an official position within the Roman army as magister militum of Illyria. He instructed the Goths to occupy some of Illyria, right on the border with the western empire. Alaric and his followers settled down to enjoy the benefits of Roman pay as frontier guards.

The tragedy for the Romans was that if the western and eastern halves of the empire had cooperated against Alaric they probably could have eliminated him. But the debilitating division between east and west enabled Alaric, the chief architect of Rome's demise, not only to survive but to prosper.

21

Drifting to Disaster

In 395, the Huns invaded the eastern Roman Empire.

It was an event so poorly recorded that most historians pay little attention to it. Yet it was potentially more significant than the petty squabbles which dominated the fractured relations between the western and eastern empires at this time.

Never before had the Huns directly attacked the Roman Empire. Previously, they had only indirectly influenced the Roman world by pushing the Goths west into the Roman Empire. But in 395, a large force of Huns crossed over the Caucasus Mountains, between the Black Sea and the Caspian Sea, and invaded Roman and Persian Armenia before advancing west into Roman Syria and south towards the Persian capital Ctesiphon.

Unfortunately, we have almost no source material on this invasion. All we know is that the Romans said the Huns reached Antioch, the great Roman metropolis of Syria, and the Persian capital Ctesiphon. However, they did not sack either city. In 398, the eastern Praetorian Prefect Eutropius led the eastern army against the Huns, who retreated back into the Caucasus. The Persian army was also engaged trying to stem their onslaught around Ctesiphon. That is pretty much all we know about this Hunnic invasion, apart from the fact that Eutropius claimed a glorious victory.

However, no source actually mentions a battle, which is very strange. So, what really happened? We will probably never know the full story, but one contemporary source, the Roman writer Priscus, writing decades after the event, said that the Huns' aim was only a short-term raid to relieve the pressures of a famine on the steppe-lands. This could well have been related to the mega drought that brought the Huns into contact with Europe in the first place. It seems plausible that drought north of the Caucasus (which is where the Huns were located at this point) caused a famine on the western edge of Europe which compelled them into making a raid into the Roman and Persian empires to replenish their supplies. The invaders appear to have been a collection of disparate Hunnic tribes, without a dominant political leader such as Attila would become in the fifth century. Our limited sources say the Huns were keen to capture and transport livestock, which makes sense if their own herds of cattle had been depleted.

This could also explain why Eutropius claimed a victory over the Huns, despite there being no mention of a battle. The truth was probably that there was no battle and no Roman victory. After the Huns had got what they wanted, they simply went back home. But of course, Eutropius did not need to present the story in that way. Instead, it was easy for him to claim that he sent them packing. And that is exactly what he did. However, it is highly unlikely that the eastern Roman army, still suffering from the loss of its professional core at the Battle of Adrianople, was capable of defeating the Huns.

After 398, the European Huns switched their focus from east to west, and that was the main reason behind the deluge of Germanic invasions that broke across the western empire in the years 406–10, as we will discuss in the next chapter. Meanwhile, as the Hunnic threat in the east receded, the Roman Empire could get back to doing what it did best – squabbling between east and west.

In 397, the east/west dispute took a new and unexpected turn. The Roman governor of North Africa, Gildo, switched his allegiance from west to east. The reason for this lay with a bitter family dispute. Gildo had fallen out with his brother, Mascezel, who had fled to Rome after Gildo had murdered his wife and two sons. Mascezel petitioned Stilicho for justice, and Gildo sought help from the eastern empire, where his daughter, Salvina, had married a relative of the emperor Theodosius, and was resident in Constantinople.

Eutropius welcomed Gildo's defection as an opportunity to undermine Stilicho. When Gildo announced his switch, he also reduced the grain supply from North Africa to Italy. He did not cut it completely; he just reduced it a bit to intimidate Stilicho. But Gildo's strategy badly backfired. There was considerable alarm in Rome about Gildo's revolt, especially the cut in the grain supply. Stilicho was popular in the senate and had a powerful ally in a prominent senator called Symmachus, which he used to his advantage. He gave the senate increased powers, and they used these to declare Gildo a hostis publicus – enemy of the state – just as the senate in Constantinople had done with him. He also arranged for supplies of grain from Gaul to be rushed into Italy to prevent a famine. With the senate and the people of Italy backing him, he proposed an attack on Gildo. He showed good judgement in not choosing to lead the expedition himself, which would have taken him away from the court politics in Milan and Rome, but chose instead Gildo's brother, Mascezel.

What better choice than the wronged brother who was itching to avenge the murder of his wife and sons? Stilicho gave him 5,000 legionaries and, in November 397, he set sail for Africa from Pisa. The sources are brief on what happened next, but Mascezel defeated his brother fairly easily and Gildo fled and committed suicide. Victory had been achieved more quickly and completely than anyone had expected. Not only was the grain supply to Italy restored, but Gildo's lands were confiscated for the state, providing Stilicho with some much-needed revenue to pay his army.

Mascezel returned triumphantly to Milan. But his own glory was short-lived. Stilicho was alert to his growing popularity as the man who had restored the grain supply. When he was crossing a bridge with Stilicho, he apparently slipped and fell into the river, where he drowned. Although Stilicho protested his innocence, the accusing finger was pointed at him by the historian Zosimus. This was almost certainly accurate. Stilicho had neatly eliminated a potential rival, and the Roman senate and people were more than happy to believe his version of events.

Things were going well for Stilicho. The senate and the 14-year-old Honorius regarded him more favourably than ever before. Things got even better when his main rival,

Eutropius, was toppled from power as quickly as he had risen. This happened because he made several major political blunders. First, to celebrate his so-called victory over the Huns, he secured his own nomination for consul in 399. While the appointment of consuls was more symbolic than anything else, for Eutropius there was one problem – he was a eunuch. Never in Rome's entire 1,000-year history had there ever been a consul who was a eunuch. Eunuchs were accepted in many jobs, and there had been government ministers who were eunuchs, but a eunuch being a consul was something altogether different. Eutropius had not realised how shocked Roman society was. The western senate in Rome rejected him outright. The weak-willed Arcadius accepted him, but not for long, since Eutropius' blunders continued to multiply.

His next error came with the army. After his victory over the Huns, he tried to run the army down to prevent any of its generals from becoming too powerful. But he still promoted Alaric to a rank equal to them. Promoting a rebellious Gothic leader over the heads of loyal generals was simply too much. A Roman Gothic commander called Tribigild rebelled in Anatolia. Eutropius sent the only general he trusted against him, a Roman named Leo, but he was defeated and killed. Eutropius turned to another Gothic general, Gainas, to put the rebellion down. Gainas had fought with Stilicho against Alaric, and also felt slighted by Alaric's promotion. So, he refused to fight Tribigild and petitioned the emperor Arcadius to get rid of Eutropius, in return for which both he and Tribigild would swear their loyalty to the emperor.

Eutropius' third blunder sealed his fate. This was to offend Arcadius' wife, Eudocia. It was, of course, Eutropius himself who had found and introduced Eudocia to Arcadius as a way of increasing his own influence over the emperor. But that was now some time ago, and she had become more influential with Arcadius than Eutropius now was. Not only did she completely dominate the emperor, but she was also irritated by Eutropius, who resented her growing independence.

One story is that she finally decided to get rid of him when Eutropius was so afraid of losing his own control over the emperor that he insisted he had to approve all meetings booked in the emperor's diary, even those with his own wife. She demanded that Arcadius dismiss Eutropius, which he did reluctantly, since he was apparently very fond of him. Eutropius was exiled to Cyprus in 399, and at an unknown later date was executed for treason.

So much then for Eutropius. The consequences of his fall from power were not exactly what you might expect. First, he was replaced by a minister called Aurelian, previously the Prefect of Constantinople. He was anti-German and hostile to the Gothic general, Gainas. Sensing trouble, Gainas struck first, exiled Aurelian and made himself commander-in-chief of the eastern army, similar to Stilicho's position in the west. However, a German grabbing power in this way did not go down well with the Roman population of Constantinople. When Gainas entered the city, he was given a hostile reception. In addition, the emperor's wife, Eudocia, whose political power was strengthened when she was crowned empress on 9 January 400, also had little sympathy for the Germans.

When she fell out openly with Gainas, he decided it was in his best interests to leave the city, feigning illness. He was followed by 7,000 of his Gothic troops. But the Roman population rose against the Goths as they marched through the streets, and slaughtered them to a man. Gainas took his remaining Gothic soldiers into Thrace, which he pillaged until he was defeated by the new Roman commander-in-chief, Fravitta. Fravitta was another Goth but a highly Romanised one, with a Roman wife, and had always been a loyal soldier in the regular Roman army. Gainas fled across the Danube, where he sought refuge with a group of western Huns led by Uldin. He made the wrong choice. Uldin regarded the Roman Empire as an ally against the Germans, who were their prime focus for subjugation. Uldin promptly beheaded him and sent his head to Arcadius in Constantinople. In recognition, Arcadius rewarded Uldin with the Roman title of *comes* (count or senior general).

With Gainas' removal, the anti-German minister Aurelian was recalled from exile and the eastern empire embarked on a more anti-German course than the west. In time, this would become a crucially important differentiator between the two halves of the empire, and one which would enable the east to resist the growing germanisation, or 'barbarisation' as historians call it, of the Roman army.

Second, there was a rapprochement between the two halves of the empire. After Eutropius' dismissal, the condemnation of Stilicho as hostis publicus ceased. The news that Eudocia had given birth to a son in 401, called Theodosius, having already had three daughters, also caused Stilicho to give up any claim to being parens principum over Arcadius in the east, which had been the main cause of Rufinus' and Eutropius' hostility towards him. He recognised that the

Theodosian dynasty in the east was now secure, although, of course, it was the empress Eudocia who was running the show rather than the still-clueless Arcadius. In 402, the two halves of the empire expressed their newfound friendship in a joint declaration that their respective emperors, Arcadius and Honorius, were joint consuls.

However, while the Roman world was celebrating a return to something approaching normality, there was someone who was nervous about both the improving relations between east and west, as well as the growing anti-German sentiment. And that was Alaric.

Eutropius had been Alaric's chief supporter, and his demise meant Alaric was cast into the wilderness. Indeed, after 400, it is likely that Aurelian, Eutropius' replacement, stopped paying him as magister militum for Illyria. In addition, although both of the main generals in the eastern army, Fravitta and Sarus, were Goths, they were of a more highly Romanised variety than Alaric, and both of them detested him. Alaric was well aware that it would probably not be long before the eastern Roman army was despatched to destroy him.

Always resourceful, Alaric tried a new strategy. He offered his services to Stilicho, his arch enemy. But this did not work, since both Stilicho and the Roman senate saw through his game. It is perhaps surprising that Stilicho did not move against Alaric at this point but he was probably mindful that it might damage the fragile peace with the eastern empire.

Rebuffed by Stilicho, Alaric turned upside down the adage of 'if you can't beat them, join them' by declaring war on Stilicho. External factors also played a part here. In the autumn of 401, a group of Vandals and Alans invaded Roman Raetia and Noricum in modern-day Austria, causing Stilicho to rush the bulk of the Italian legions to confront them. Alaric saw an opportunity. With Stilicho's legionaries engaged in Raetia, he invaded Italy. A new and shocking war had begun.

22

Alaric's First Invasion of Italy

Alaric's march towards Italy began in western Illyria, which belonged to the western empire. There, he met little resistance since most of the Roman troops were with Stilicho in Raetia. He advanced past Sirmium and crossed the Julian Alps – so-called to this day in honour of the road that Julius Caesar built through them – into Italy, in November 401, just before they became blocked by winter snow. His destination was Aquileia, a vast Roman legionary fortress and town, at the top of the Adriatic. But unlike the Alpine passes, this was well defended, and since the Goths were still relatively unskilled at siege craft, he could not take it. In early 402, he abandoned the siege and advanced into the Plain of Venetia, with Milan, the Roman capital of the western empire, now his destination.

Meanwhile, Stilicho was trapped by the winter in Raetia to the north of the Alps. He could not do anything to stop Alaric other than to issue a flurry of commands, ordering the legions in Britain and along the Rhine to head south to save Italy, as well as recruiting mercenary troops from the Germanic tribes along the Rhine, and even issuing an edict inviting slaves in Italy to volunteer for military service.

In Italy, there was panic. The emperor Honorius tried to flee from Milan to Arles in Gaul, but Gothic cavalry intercepted him and forced him to take refuge in the fortified town of Hasta (modern Asti), which boasted impressive defensive walls. Meanwhile, in Rome, the concern was such that work to strengthen the Aurelian walls began in earnest. The walls of Milan, like those of Hasta, proved substantial enough to hold the Gothic army at bay. Yet again, the Goths' inabilities at siege craft saved the Romans.

Milan's defences held out for two months until, in February 402, Stilicho finally led the Italian army back over the Alpine passes, where the snow had thawed sufficiently to allow a crossing, and by early March, he reached the city. In a night attack, he broke through the Gothic lines and entered the city, to scenes of wild rejoicing. Alaric was dismayed and withdrew west.

After Stilicho raised the siege of Milan, he rescued the emperor Honorius from Hasta. Then he took a very significant decision for the future of the western Roman Empire. He moved the capital from Milan to Ravenna. The rationale was that Ravenna was easier to defend. Surrounded by marshes, and with a port providing good access to the sea, there was only one land route to it and it could be defended better than landlocked Milan.

Some historians have seen the move as a reflection of the new politics of the fifth century, when men like Stilicho dominated weak emperors like Honorius, who needed to be kept safe in secure locations, a bit like a trophy stored in a display cabinet. It is true Stilicho needed the emperor's support, and any removal of Honorius would have threatened his own grip on power.

But there was also something else going on. The move to Ravenna signalled that the military effectiveness of the western empire was starting to fail. It would have been unimaginable, even relatively recently, under emperors like Theodosius and Valentinian, to move the western capital to what was effectively a hiding place. Under emperors like Julian and Constantine, it would have been unthinkable. And it does not bear thinking what Augustus or Hadrian would have made of it.

The move to Ravenna throws into stark relief the different situations in the two halves of the empire. In the east, Constantinople was secure. The city was becoming bigger and stronger by the day. The eastern empire did not need to cower like its western cousin even if the Huns were threatening on the Danube. In contrast, the western empire was starting to fade. Its army was looking increasingly vulnerable to the hordes of barbarians along its frontiers. The move to Ravenna was an admission that the days of the western empire were looking numbered.

But it was not dead yet. For, despite the move to Ravenna, Stilicho was doing well to keep Roman hopes alive. He had forced Alaric to retreat from Milan, and as he retreated west towards Gaul, he was in hot pursuit and caught up with him near the city of Pollentia. Although the sources for the battle are limited, we know for certain that Stilicho attacked Alaric's forces on Sunday, 6 April 402. We know this because it was Easter Sunday, the most important religious festival in the Christian calendar. Although the Goths were Arians and the Roman army was orthodox, both sides would have normally avoided fighting on such a day. Perhaps it was the element of surprise which motivated Stilicho to attack.

As was normal with the late Roman armies, Stilicho's force was a mix of regular Roman troops and numerous so-called foederati, the Germanic and other mercenaries. These included many Alans under their commander, Saul. Stilicho entrusted the major assault to the Alans rather similarly to that in which Theodosius entrusted the Goths with the main assault on the western Roman army at the battle of the Frigidus River in 394. The Alans made good progress against the Gothic centre, pushing it back. However, Alaric's cavalry regrouped and counter-attacked, pushing the Alans back with heavy casualties and killing their leader. Stilicho took control of the Roman army and rushed the regular Roman legionaries forward. After hours of intense fighting, the legionaries defeated the Goths, who fled. Indeed, the Gothic panic was such that they surrendered their camp without a fight, including large numbers of Gothic women and children. Even Alaric's own wife was captured. Alaric withdrew north towards the Alps.

The battle of Pollentia was one of Stilicho's greatest triumphs. Many Romans had feared a repeat of the Battle of Adrianople. But it was the opposite. The Gothic army was routed, many Gothic women and children taken prisoner, and a huge amount of the plunder from their previous victories was recovered, including trophies taken at Adrianople and from their devastation of Greece. In addition, they released a multitude of Roman prisoners. The poet Claudian compared the victory to those achieved against Pyrrhus, Hannibal and Spartacus.[63]

Stilicho opened negotiations with Alaric and offered to let him return to Illyria. His priority was to remove him from

Italian soil. Alaric had by then retreated into the Apennines and, although the records are not clear on exactly what happened, he started to retreat east back towards Illyria. Stilicho pursued him. Alaric stopped at Verona. Perhaps he decided not to return to Illyria for fear of an attack by the eastern Roman army. Whatever the reason, and although we have almost no details about it, another battle took place outside Verona in the summer of 402. Again, Stilicho was victorious. According to the poet Claudian, Alaric was nearly captured, and it was only the failure of the Alan mercenaries to carry out their orders that allowed him to escape.

Alaric's power seemed to have been broken. Large numbers of Goths deserted to Stilicho, in particular the Gothic cavalry changed sides. Several senior Gothic commanders switched their allegiance to Stilicho, including Sarus, Sigeric and Ulfilas, all of whom became officers in the Roman army.

It looked as if Alaric was finished. But, to everyone's surprise, he survived. Stilicho let him return to Illyria, this time to the western half owned by the western empire, and to settle there with an official Roman title; we don't know exactly what it was but it was probably a title like *Dux Pannoniae* – the leader or Duke of Pannonia.

So, the key question has to be: why did Stilicho let him get away?

This has always been a mystery. Possible reasons could have been that Stilicho's army was not that strong, having taken heavy casualties in both the battles of Pollentia and Verona. In addition, an interesting argument put forward by one historian is that after the battle of Verona, Stilicho's army contained a fair number of Alaric's former followers who had switched sides, and these did not want to fight against their kinsmen, who remained loyal to Alaric.

My sense is that the real cause of Stilicho's failure to destroy Alaric was his ambition to control the eastern half of the empire. He wanted to keep Alaric in Illyria as a potential ally against the eastern empire. This was a colossal error of judgement. For by allowing Alaric to survive, Stilicho gave a license to the man who would eventually sack Rome.

23

Stilicho's Finest Hour

After Stilicho's defeat of Alaric, the senate in Rome rejoiced. The Gothic threat had been averted, or so they believed. A monument was built in the forum to commemorate his victories at Pollentia and Verona.

But just as the celebrations ended, a new Gothic invasion erupted. And this time it was not Alaric who was still minding his manners in Illyria, but a wholly new Gothic tribe led by their king, Radagaisus. Our sources on Radagaisus are limited, but it seems that he was the leader of a Gothic confederation that had remained north of the Danube next to the Huns. The first point that the sources make clear about the invasion is that it was not a raid. Similar to what happened in 376, this was a migration of an entire people, including women and children. The number of Goths cited is large, with Zosimus saying there were 400,000 and our other main Roman chronicler putting them at 200,000.

Why were they migrating and why did they choose this moment?

The consensus among historians is that the reason was the Huns. In the 390s, the main body of Huns was sited between the Don and Volga rivers, north of the Caucasus. The evidence for this is their large-scale raid into the Middle East made in 398, described in Chapter 17. Most historians think that after 398, the Huns continued to move west into the Carpathian Mountains in modern-day Romania, putting further pressure on the Germanic tribes to the west of them. It was this which resulted in a second Gothic migration much further west, into Italy itself.

Similar to Alaric's invasion in 401, there was panic in Rome and the whole of Italy. This time it was even worse, for two reasons: first, these Goths were not Christians, like Alaric's Visigoths. They were pagans who worshipped the same bloodthirsty gods that had dominated Germanic culture for centuries. Second, the numbers were large. As I mentioned, Zosimus said there were 400,000 of them, including women and children, and although this is almost certainly an exaggeration, the numbers were probably just as large as those of the first Gothic invasion across the Danube in 376 which had resulted in the Battle of Adrianople.

The invasion also caught Stilicho completely by surprise. At the time, he was at Ticinum (modern Pavia), in northern Italy, close to Milan, with most of the Italian army. But he did not want to offer battle, presumably because he thought he was outnumbered. His first concern was to stop Alaric's Goths from joining Radagaisus, which would have resulted in a truly enormous Gothic army in northern Italy, so he quickly sent deputations, no doubt laden with gifts and gold, to Alaric to persuade him to keep out of the situation. Fortunately for Stilicho, Alaric complied, probably because he felt threatened by Radagaisus as well.

Stilicho tried to mobilise as many troops as possible. He sent orders for the legions on the Rhine to make haste to Italy, as well as hiring Hunnic and Alan mercenaries and recruiting soldiers in Italy. Meanwhile, Radagaisus made a major strategic blunder by dividing his forces into three groups. This was probably because the Goths were finding it difficult to feed themselves and needed to forage over a wide area. As usual, they were incapable of capturing any of the large Roman towns in northern Italy and were forced to live off the land. Having three groups foraging was much more effective than one but it left them vulnerable to being picked off individually.

This was exactly what Stilicho did. According to the chronicler Zosimus, by August 406 he had mustered 30 *numeri*, meaning units or regiments. While some of these units would have been legions, others would have been regiments in the central field army. Historians think there were about 500 men per unit, making the Roman army at least 15,000 strong. In addition, Stilicho had hired considerable numbers of Alans and Huns, and it is even possible that the Hunnic king Uldin was leading these himself. So, in short, Stilicho had amassed a very considerable army, some 20–30,000 strong, and with a large contingent of the deadly Huns. Meanwhile, the Goths were divided into three groups, with the largest, led by Radagaisus himself, besieging Florentia, on the same site as modern Florence, whose walls, typical of the late Roman period, were strong enough to withstand the Gothic siege.

We have very few details of the battle, but when Stilicho approached, the Goths moved to the town of Fiesole, just outside Florentia as it is today, which was on a hill and more easily defended. There the besiegers became the besieged. Stilicho trapped the Goths by building earthworks all around the Gothic camp. The Goths failed to break through the Roman defences and then became critically short of food. The other two Gothic groups were unaware of what had happened to Radagaisus and so did not rush to help him.

What happened next is unclear, except that Radagaisus himself was captured, either trying to escape, or possibly after being tricked by Stilicho to enter negotiations. Stilicho promptly beheaded him and his Gothic warriors were offered the opportunity to enrol as mercenaries in the Roman army. This seemed like a pretty good deal in the circumstances, and 12,000 of them entered Roman service, and their wives and children were given food and shelter.

What happened to the other two Gothic groups remains unclear, but the Roman sources say that huge numbers of Goths were taken prisoner and sold into the slave markets, so much so that in Rome there was a complete collapse in the market price for slaves. This suggests the other two Gothic groups were also defeated, with one historian contending that Stilicho let the Huns loose on them.

Stilicho was the hero of the hour. Every Roman must have been comparing Stilicho's victory with the catastrophic defeat Valens suffered at Adrianople. The senate ordered the building of a triumphal arch in Rome to mark his victory, the first such celebration for many years.

But unfortunately for the Romans, history teaches us to expect the unexpected. This would prove to be the pinnacle of Stilicho's success, and within only two years he would be dead, and within four years Rome would be sacked.

24

All Gaul a Funeral Pyre

We have now reached what were perhaps the four most critical years in Rome's entire history.

These were from 407 to 410, when there was a sudden spiral towards disaster culminating in the sack of Rome. So, it might seem curious that at the end of the last chapter, Stilicho was at the very pinnacle of his success, having comprehensively defeated two Gothic invasions of Italy, the first by Alaric and the second by Radagaisus. But the Huns were about to exert their influence yet again, this time by causing a huge Germanic invasion of Gaul. In addition, Stilicho was about to make a catastrophic strategic blunder in pursuing his ambition to dominate the eastern empire.

Let us start with Stilicho. Ever since Theodosius I on his deathbed had whispered he should be guardian to both his sons, in east and west, Stilicho had harboured an ambition to achieve this dream. Yet it had only served to antagonise the eastern court who were convinced he had invented the story. Relations remained strained, especially as the east was effectively ruled by the indomitable empress Eudocia, who resisted any attempt by Stilicho to increase his influence.

But everything changed when Eudocia unexpectedly died on 6 October 404 from a miscarriage. With her death, there was a power vacuum in the east. Stilicho was convinced his time had come. He demanded the return of the eastern half of Illyria to the western empire as a prelude to what was probably a more ambitious power grab. But he overestimated his influence on Constantinople, since Arcadius' new first minister, Anthemius, rejected his demand. Stilicho then made a huge miscalculation. He declared war on the eastern empire and enlisted the help of Alaric.

Stilicho probably assumed that the eastern emperor Arcadius would simply cave in and give him Illyria. To begin with, things seemed to go well. Alaric was willing to play along with his game. In late 406, he marched south to Epirus, just opposite the Italian coastline, where he waited for Stilicho's army to cross the Adriatic, and then they planned to march together on Constantinople. But just as Stilicho was poised to achieve his dream, he was caught out by an event that quickly led to his downfall.

This event is reputed to have occurred on 31 December 406, when a huge Germanic invasion of Gaul was unleashed. Edward Gibbon famously said that vast numbers of Germans crossed the frozen Rhine on the night of 31 December, and so began the fall of the western Roman Empire. In fact, no Roman or any other source mentions the Rhine freezing that night, although it was correct that some Roman sources said the Rhine did occasionally freeze over. The truth is more likely that the German hordes crossed the Rhine over several days during December, using the various Roman bridges. However, Gibbon can be forgiven his poetic license, since it proved to be a genuinely pivotal turning point in the history of the Roman Empire.

The invaders were a diverse collection of tribes, including two groups of Vandals, the Asding and Siling, and a large group of Alans, an Indo-European nomadic tribe who had adopted many German customs. There was also a group called the Suevi by the Romans, which probably referred to a collection of Alemanni and Burgundians, although most of these peoples seem to have remained east of the Rhine.

Similar to the migrations of Fritigern's Goths in 376 and Radagaisus' Goths in 405/6, this Germanic onslaught was not a raid but a proper migration of men, women and children. This time the intention was to settle on Roman territory, in a repeat of what Alaric's Goths had achieved in Illyria. Why did this invasion happen and why then? Most historians believe that the Huns were yet again the prime culprits. Radagaisus' invasion of Italy in 405/6 was 800 miles further west than Thrace, which was the region invaded by Fritigern's Goths in 376, meaning the Huns had pushed the Germans all this way during the intervening 30 years. Yet again, the Huns were exerting a domino toppling effect on the Roman Empire by driving the Germanic tribes into it.

Why was the invasion so successful? The answer was that the Roman army was losing its grip on the west. The debilitating civil wars fought in Theodosius' reign weakened the Gallic army from being the pride of Julian's military machine to instead a shadow of its former self. Much of what was left of it was withdrawn by Stilicho to fight Alaric in 401/2, and then Radagaisus in 405/6. So, in 406 there were very few Roman troops left in Gaul to oppose the Germans.

In addition, and largely because of the failure of the Roman army to maintain a strong frontier defence, eastern Gaul had already started to become de-Romanised. This is not evidenced in written sources but it is discernible by digging into the past, for modern archaeology shows a significant decline in villa building in north-eastern Gaul in the late fourth century. This appears to have been a long-drawn-out process beginning in Constantius II's reign, when the usurper, Magnentius, took troops from the lower Rhine frontier to fight in the civil war of 350. This allowed the Franks to establish their first foothold across the Rhine, prompting Constantius to send his nephew, Julian, to restore order. Although Julian was remarkably successful, he seems to have allowed some of the Franks to remain west of the Rhine provided they defended the frontier against other German tribes. Julian may well have regarded this as a temporary expedient to free up sufficient forces to fight Constantius. But with Julian's defeat in Persia, the Franks stayed in the top north-eastern corner of the empire from the 350s onwards, and gradually extended their sphere of influence south and west.

A good example of the diminishing Roman presence in Gaul was the replacement of Trier by Arles as the Gallic capital in the early fifth century. Trier was a large fortified Roman city right on the German border. Indeed, today Trier boasts the best Roman remains north of the Alps as testimony to its size and grandeur during the late Roman period. It even became the de facto capital of the western empire during Valentinian I's reign from 364 to 375, when he campaigned frequently along the upper Rhine to keep the German tribes at bay. But by the end of the later fourth century, it was becoming marginalised as the Romans withdrew south. By the early fifth century, it was replaced by Arles as the Gallic capital. Arles was 400 miles to the south, close to the Mediterranean. This is a startling indication that the Romans were beginning to lose their grip on the Rhine frontier, well before the onslaught of 406.

The result of the weak Roman defences was an almost blitzkrieg-like invasion by the Germans as they streamed through Gaul. There is no surviving record of exactly what happened. The best that we have are fragments from the writings of some Christian Gallic poets who bewailed the unfolding disaster as marking the end of civilisation. Most famous of these is the often-quoted one-liner from Orientus, who said that, 'All Gaul was filled with the smoke of a single funeral pyre.'[64] Another poet believed that the end of civilisation was nigh and described the invasion as the collapse of 'the frame of the fragile world'.[65]

The most detail we have about the invasion is the long list of sacked Roman towns compiled by Saint Jerome. This includes almost all the main Gallic towns and cities except for those in Roman Provence. Mainz on the Rhine frontier was the first to go, followed by Rheims. The former Gallic capital of Trier might have held out, helped by its enormous walls. The invaders moved into central Gaul, sacking Tournai, Arras, Amiens and Paris (I am using the modern French names since they are easier to identify). Then they moved both west and south, sacking Orleans, Tours and Toulouse. By 409, after spending over two years devastating Gaul, this group of Vandals, Alans and Suevi reached the Pyrenees. Then they crossed into Spain.

Exhausted by their long journey of destruction, they settled down there. Again, there were no Roman defenders who could withstand them. They progressed through Spain to the straits of Gibraltar, where they stopped. If they had found boats to ferry them across to Africa, they would probably have done that, as the Vandals were to do two decades later. But instead, they partitioned Spain between them, with the Alans taking the centre, while the Asding Vandals and the Suevi occupied the north with the Siling Vandals in the south.

As if the devastation and loss of Gaul and Spain were not bad enough, there was also a rebellion in Britain. Britain was an unusual part of the late Roman Empire, since it had avoided the devastation of the crisis of the third century and, although it had always been an economic backwater, it emerged into the fourth century as one of the empire's more prosperous regions. However, it was prone to revolt because it was often left out of the inner circle of imperial decision-making and consequently rarely participated in the distribution of donatives and rewards by which emperors kept their generals and administrators loyal. Indeed, it seems likely that the British legions had not been paid for some time, which was probably the catalyst for a rebellion by the army in the autumn of 406, just before the Germanic onslaught on the Rhine.

The legions proclaimed two emperors in quick succession – Marcus followed by Gratian, both of whom were quickly rejected and executed – before choosing Flavius Claudius Constantinus, and naming him Constantine III. He quickly proved himself a capable leader, although very little is known about his early life other than he was an experienced soldier. His name Constantine was said to have been part of his attraction, since it reminded the legionaries of Constantine the Great, who the British legions had proclaimed emperor in York 101 years before in 306.

He crossed over to Gaul, where the battered remains of the Gallic legions immediately rallied to his standard. The few Roman soldiers in Spain also declared for him. This was very similar to what had happened in the third century AD when Britain, Gaul and Spain had broken away from Rome under the Roman general Postumus to create an independent Gallic Empire. Constantine III created another break-away Roman state consisting of the demoralised troops and landowners abandoned by Ravenna. To boost his standing, he led his soldiers to victory in some minor engagements with the Germans, as they left Gaul and moved into Spain. He also formed alliances with the Franks, Alemanni and Burgundian tribes who were generally hostile to the German invaders of Gaul. For example, the Franks defended their north-eastern corner against the marauding Germans with as much vigour as they had previously fought the Romans.

For Stilicho, these developments struck him like a bolt from the blue. Quite why he was unaware of the fragile condition of the Rhine frontier remains a mystery. After all he was the one who had withdrawn some of the Roman legions from Gaul to protect Italy. Maybe the answer is that the defence of Gaul was simply too low on his list of priorities. If so, he paid a full price for it. Not only had he lost half the western empire but he had also created a formidable rival in the form of Constantine III.

Stilicho immediately cancelled his planned invasion of the east and began transferring the Italian legions from the

Adriatic to the Alps to meet Constantine III. Honorius, guided by Stilicho, hastily wrote letters to his brother in Constantinople, apologising for Stilicho's aggressive demands and begging for a resumption of peace between the two halves of the empire. It was now a truly desperate situation. The fall of the west had begun.

25

Stilicho's Fall

Although the western empire had been shattered by the German invasion of Gaul, Stilicho's main concern was Constantine III's usurpation. This was a direct challenge to the emperor Honorius' rule and therefore to him. Constantine III's power base was also growing by the day. He was fortunate because he was not swept away by the invading Germans who were merely passing through Gaul rather than occupying it. His British and Gallic legions seem to have held out in some areas as the Germans made their way towards Spain, looting and pillaging as they went. Therefore, by the beginning of 408, he had recovered some of the central part of Gaul. Similar to other Gallic usurpers in the past, he was cautious about a civil war with the official Roman emperor, and proposed joint rule to Honorius, as evidenced by the coins he minted depicting both him and Honorius.

Despite this, Stilicho did not trust him and wanted to stamp out this rebellion as quickly as possible. So, in early 408, he sent an army from Italy across the Alps against Constantine. He also organised a small force led by Honorius' relatives to attack from Spain. The army from Italy was an elite force of cavalry, Gothic and Roman, under the command of Sarus, the Gothic general who had defected from Alaric's army to become one of Stilicho's most trusted lieutenants after the battle of Pollentia in 402. But it was still a small force, reflecting the depleted resources of the western Roman army. Even so, at first it looked as if it might beat Constantine, since in Sarus' first engagement near to Lyon, he defeated and killed one of Constantine's generals, Justinianus. Constantine took refuge in Valence, close to Lyon, and Sarus laid siege to the town. However, Constantine's son, Constans, brought a relief force down from northern Gaul and forced Sarus to flee back to Italy.

This was bad news for Stilicho. But far worse followed it. By the spring of 408, Alaric the Goth was getting impatient. It was over a year since he had dutifully followed Stilicho's orders to march to Epirus and await the western Roman army for their intended march on Constantinople. During that time, his followers had received no pay or provisions from Stilicho, and were almost certainly complaining that Alaric was not doing enough for them. Because of this, he now demanded 4,000 pounds of gold as compensation and threatened war if this was not forthcoming.

Yet again, Stilicho was caught out. Alaric marched north from Epirus to the Roman province of Noricum (modern Austria), ready to invade Italy. With Constantine III in Gaul, and Alaric in Noricum, Stilicho was surrounded by enemies. He appealed to the senate in Rome to pay the Goths. Initially, they resisted. Resentment was growing against Stilicho. Rumours circulated he was actually in league with Alaric. The senate was also dissatisfied with the growing use of German mercenaries in the army instead of Roman legionaries, although this was partly their fault since many of the wealthy senators were reluctant to allow able-bodied young men working on their estates to be recruited into the army. One senator criticised Stilicho by declaring in a speech that paying the Goths 'did not bring peace, but a pact of servitude'.

[66]Stilicho's growing unpopularity offered an opportunity to his rivals at court. In particular, a man called Olympius, who was *magister scrinii*, master of the imperial secretaries, and ironically Stilicho's own appointee, realised that he could use this to his advantage. His job meant he was almost always at the emperor Honorius' side, and he used this privileged position as a way to foment conspiracy theories against Stilicho in the weak-willed young (24 years old in 408) emperor's mind.

This was helped by news from Constantinople of the death of Honorius' brother, the eastern emperor Arcadius, in May 408, leaving his seven-year-old son, Theodosius II, as his heir. Honorius showed a rare moment of self-possession when he declared he wanted to go to Constantinople to arrange the governorship of the eastern empire. Stilicho objected, saying that it was best for him to go. He no doubt rightly feared that should Honorius go alone, he would fall under the influence of the ministers in the east, not least the highly capable Anthemius, who was no friend of Stilicho's.

Stilicho got his way, persuading Honorius that it was too dangerous for him to leave the west when the pretender Constantine III was at the gates of Italy. Interestingly, one argument he employed was that it would be too expensive for

Honorius to go. This provides an insight into how financially weak the western empire was, which is not surprising when you consider that the tax revenues from Britain, Gaul and Spain had all been lost, and that the wealthy senatorial class in Rome were excellent tax dodgers. Honorius was left frustrated that he could not go and resentful against Stilicho that he was going.

In the end, no-one went to Constantinople. Stilicho realised it would be political suicide for him to leave Italy. He then made another error of judgement by proposing that Alaric be sent to Gaul to confront Constantine III. Superficially, this made sense in view of the huge amount of money the Romans were paying Alaric. But it did not go down well with either the senate or the Italian legions. Both remembered the fear in Italy when Alaric had invaded in 401/2 and neither wanted him back on Italian soil. In particular, the legionaries and their officers had long disliked the use of Gothic and other German mercenaries in the army and particularly resented the payment of gold to Alaric's men. On hearing that Alaric's army could be transferred to the Gallic front, they feared they would be told to report to Alaric. This was too much for them. Rumours spread like wildfire that Stilicho was actually in league with Alaric against Rome.

It is worth pausing for a moment to consider this allegation, since it was popular with Romans at the time and has been much debated by historians. The suggestion was that because they were both barbarian generals, they shared a wish to destroy Rome. In my view, this is completely wrong. Stilicho was actually half Roman – his mother was Roman while his father had been a Vandal employed in the regular Roman army – and his entire career was spent working as a Roman general. This was very different from Alaric, who was a genuine outsider to the Roman world and who led a sort of twilight existence, on the one hand cultivating his identity as king of the Goths, but on the other hand attracted to the trappings of Roman power. In reality, there can have been little love lost between them.

But perception and reality can be very different. Stilicho's suggestion that Alaric should fight Romans in Gaul ignited the conspiracy bonfire. It was the scheming Olympius who added to this by alleging, according to the Roman chronicler Zosimus,[67] that Stilicho 'was planning the journey to the east in order to plot the overthrow of the young Theodosius and the transfer of the east to his own son, Eucherius'. This view spread faster than a video going viral. Not only did it shock Honorius, but it was also the last straw for the Roman army in Italy, which was headquartered at Ticinum (modern Pavia), ready to fight Constantine III. A mutiny erupted there in August 408. Officers who supported Stilicho were rounded up in a military coup d'état and executed. The emperor Honorius happened to be present at the time and was shocked by the insurrection. Indeed, one story said that when a pro-Stilicho officer, the *quaestor* Salvinus, fell at the emperor's feet begging for his life, the soldiers simply dragged him away from the speechless Honorius and butchered him. Honorius, who enjoyed a quiet life tending to his chickens, and who some historians think might have been mentally retarded, ran away scared for his own safety.

When Stilicho heard the news, he was in the town of Bononia, midway between Pavia and Ravenna. At first, he did not know what to do. Did the emperor want to punish the mutinous soldiers or to forgive them? If the latter, it meant he was finished. As usual, Honorius himself was unsure what to do. The real architect of the revolt was Olympius. He now told the emperor that the soldiers answered to him, not Stilicho. Honorius accepted this. Stilicho's death sentence had in effect been signed.

However, despite Olympius' betrayal, Stilicho was still in a strong position, since he had most of the barbarian mercenaries with him in Bononia. His supporters, including his trusted Gothic general, Sarus, told him to advance on Ticinum and confront the mutinous Roman regiments. But Stilicho refused to do this, knowing that it would mean a civil war with Honorius. Instead, he fled to Ravenna without a fight. This only infuriated his supporters. Indeed, Sarus was so angry that he even attacked and slaughtered Stilicho's personal Hunnic bodyguard, before abandoning the camp and leaving to roam Italy.

Shortly after Stilicho arrived in Ravenna, messengers from Honorius reached the city with orders to arrest him. Stilicho sought sanctuary in a nearby church. At daybreak on 22 August 408, soldiers led by an officer called Heraclianus entered the church and persuaded the bishop, who was protecting Stilicho, that they had orders to arrest but not to execute him. Stilicho agreed to leave the church, whereupon Heraclianus produced a second letter, condemning him to death for 'crimes against the state'. Stilicho still had some servants and bodyguards with him who wanted to put up a fight, but in an act universally admired by contemporaries and historians, Stilicho told them to put away their weapons and submitted his neck to the sword.

Historians have long been puzzled by Stilicho's willingness to concede victory to Olympius without a fight. Some have praised him for his integrity in wanting to avoid a damaging civil war. Others have seen him as foolishly loyal to the incompetent Honorius. I think the answer is that he wanted to save his family. In that he succeeded, because his son, Eucherius, who was with him in Ravenna, fled to Rome unharmed, although he would later be executed. His loyal wife, Serena, was also in Rome, where she was safe for the moment, although, as we will shortly discover, not for long.

With Stilicho's demise, the western empire lost its most trusted servant. The horror would now begin.

26

Alaric Triumphant

When Stilicho's head was severed from his body, government passed into the hands of the minister Olympius, who proved to be as incompetent as he was treacherous.

Almost the moment he took office, a tragic error of judgement sealed the fate of the western empire. This occurred when the Roman army based in Ticinum turned against the German mercenaries that were now so prominent in the western army. A German purge had of course already happened in the east with the effect that the eastern army was no longer so dependent on German mercenaries nor commanded so conspicuously by German generals. But whereas the eastern army had achieved this relatively efficiently, the western army botched its attempt to emulate its eastern cousin. The objects of the Romans' anger were the Gothic families who had been quartered in various Italian cities while their menfolk served in the Roman army. This arrangement had been Stilicho's idea following his defeat of Radagaisus' invasion in 404, and had worked well. These innocent women and children were now rounded up and massacred. This horrific act backfired on the Romans spectacularly, for it achieved nothing from a military standpoint other than to send the husbands of the slaughtered families – some 12,000 Gothic soldiers recruited from Radagaisus' defeated army – rushing to join Alaric, who in the meantime had advanced into northern Italy. That these Goths were not integrated into the Roman regiments meant they could easily move en masse.

At one stroke, the Romans had now achieved exactly what Stilicho had spent his career trying to prevent – the formation of a Gothic supergroup in Italy far more powerful than any of the Roman forces. For Alaric now commanded the largest Gothic army Rome had ever faced, probably with well over 30,000 warriors, if we add together his own army of some 20,000 and the 12,000 Goths who had been serving in the Roman army. In contrast, the Roman army in Italy, which was still headquartered at Ticinum in northern Italy, awaiting an attack over the Alps by Constantine III, was a shadow of its former self. It probably numbered only some 10–15,000 men. Italy was now effectively in the hands of Alaric and his Goths. The city of Rome was like a lamb waiting to be slaughtered.

However, Alaric was in no rush. Unlike Hannibal, who never felt he had the resources to take Rome, Alaric knew he had the city at his mercy. But he was not looking for its destruction so much as to use it as a bargaining tool to secure money and power for himself.

Over the next two years, he conducted three sieges of the city. The first resulted from his request to Honorius was for another payment of gold, similar to the one he had secured from Stilicho earlier that year. Olympius, the power behind the throne, refused. It is very doubtful whether Ravenna had the money to pay Alaric. Alaric led his troops south, taking Ariminum (modern Rimini) on the way. When they reached Rome, Alaric took Ostia, Rome's port and its supply base for the North African grain that fed its population. There was panic in the city. Serena, Stilicho's unfortunate widow, was arrested and strangled to death for fear that remorse for her husband might induce her to betray the city to the Goths. Honorius' sister, Galla Placidia, also resident in the city, raised no objection, although in her youth she had been brought up by Serena and Stilicho. Placidia's hard-heartedness was the first sign of the ruthless determination that would help her survive and prosper over the next few decades.

Alaric held the city in a tight grip. Aqueducts were cut and the Tiber River was blockaded. No supplies could reach it. Food quickly ran out. The population, which is estimated at around 800,000, began to starve. Unburied bodies filled the streets. Famine led to plague. 'The stench arising from the putrid corpses was sufficient to infect them with disease,'[68] according to Zosimus, our best source on the sack of Rome. The Romans were holding out, hoping a relief force would arrive from Ravenna or the army based at Ticinum would move south. But no help came. Honorius and Olympius were too worried about their own precarious position to save Rome. In desperation, a group of senators sought an audience with Alaric. When they said the people of Rome would fight just like their ancestors, Alaric laughed. They asked him what he wanted. He said all their gold and possessions, as well as the freedom of the slaves. When they asked him what he would give them, he said, 'Your lives.'

The senate resorted to invoking help from the ancient Roman gods. Even Pope Innocent I agreed to this. But when there was no divine intervention and there was no food left, the senate returned to Alaric to beg for terms. He demanded 5,000 pounds of gold, 30,000 of silver, 4,000 silk robes, 3,000 scarlet fleeces and 3,000 pounds of pepper. The terms were accepted and the senate levied the ransom from the city's inhabitants according to a means test. Zosimus recounts that the miserly senators, although many possessed enormous wealth, did their best to avoid contributing. All the gold and silver in the churches, and what remained in the pagan temples, was stripped to pay the Goths. Zosimus says that ancient statues made of gold and silver were melted down, including one of Virtus, the Roman god of Valour. 'With this being destroyed, all that remained of Roman valour was totally extinguished.'[69]

The less fortunate members of Radagaisus' Gothic followers, sold into slavery rather than coerced into the Roman army, also joined Alaric The exact numbers and locations of these slaves has always been a mystery, but our sources say a huge number of them joined Alaric when he was encamped outside Rome. They could easily have numbered 10,000 warriors, taking Alaric's total army to 40–50,000 and further strengthening his already dominant military position.

Despite this, in December 408 Alaric was as good as his word and, once he had been paid, he withdrew north to Tuscany. Food supplies flooded into the city, to the relief of its starving inhabitants. Rome had been saved. But for how long? In January 409, the senate sent an embassy to Honorius in Ravenna begging for a peace treaty with Alaric to prevent him from attacking Rome again.

However, Honorius, under Olympius' thumb, refused. Olympius wanted to restore Roman authority in Italy, yet he completely lacked the military strength to do this. In a pathetic show of force, Olympius sent a detachment of 6,000 Roman troops to Rome, taken from Illyria and supposedly of high quality, to provide it with a stronger garrison. But Alaric intercepted them and defeated them so comprehensively that only a hundred survivors reached the city.

Next, Olympius ordered the western army in northern Italy to confront Alaric's brother, Ataulf, close to Pisa. Although it remains unclear exactly what happened, some sort of minor engagement was fought which seems to have been inconclusive, although Olympius claimed 1,100 Goths were killed for the loss of only 17 Romans. This was almost certainly propaganda, and did not conceal Olympius' failure to defeat the Goths in battle. This resulted in a palace coup in Ravenna, in which he was ousted by the Praetorian Prefect for Italy, Jovius.

Honorius and Jovius knew time was running out and tried to secure an alliance with Constantine III, who had been sitting on the sidelines in Gaul waiting for events to unfold, by sending him a purple cloak to recognise his imperial aspirations. They also caved in to the Goths, offering Alaric an annual tribute of gold and corn, and allowing the Goths to settle in north-eastern Italy and Illyria. To everyone's surprise, Alaric accepted these terms provided he was also given a senior military position within the empire. The Roman historian, Olympiodorus, thought this was the best offer the Romans could hope for. Most modern historians agree with this.

But it was Honorius himself who blew it. He refused to give Alaric his coveted title. The reasons for this remain a mystery. Perhaps recognising both the usurper Constantine III and Alaric at the same time was just too much for his ego. Or perhaps his feeble mind simply failed to grasp what was going on.

Alaric was furious, and returned to Rome for a second time and put it under siege in the autumn of 409. But this time the senate had no faith in being rescued by Honorius. Nor did Alaric expect to extract a senior appointment from him. So, they joined forces. They agreed to circumvent Honorius and appointed their own emperor, a senator called Priscus Attalus.

Honorius realised his mistake in alienating both the senate and Alaric. He panicked and decided the best course of action was to flee to Constantinople. But there was yet another twist. As he was waiting to board ship to join his young nephew, Theodosius II, a fleet from Constantinople itself appeared, containing 4,000 elite troops from the eastern empire. The eastern empire had come to his rescue in the nick of time. He immediately rethought his plans and stayed in Ravenna. He also despatched a delegation to North Africa, laden with gold, to secure its support against Rome, which was of course critical since it provided the city with its grain supply. To counter this, Attalus sent a small Roman force to North Africa. Interestingly, he prevented a Gothic force from sailing, fearing this would lead to their occupation of Africa, suggesting he was at least trying to look after Roman interests even if he was a stooge of the Goths. But Attalus' mission failed, and the city was exposed to the prospect of another famine.

Alaric was now getting frustrated. Honorius would not recognise him. His puppet emperor, Priscus Attalus, was in fact only a puppet. And his vast army had not been paid since December 408, when the senate had ransomed the city. Therefore, in July 410, he deposed Attalus and reopened negotiations with Honorius to agree the sort of peace settlement that had nearly been signed the previous year. A meeting was arranged and Alaric moved to within 60 stadia (or about 12 kilometres) of Ravenna.

However, Honorius could not even control his own Gothic mercenaries. His senior general was the Goth, Sarus, who had a vendetta with Alaric stretching back to the 390s, when the two had been rivals for leadership of the Goths in Illyria. Now he wanted his revenge. He prepared an ambush and attacked Alaric as he was coming to negotiate with Honorius. Alaric's men beat their fellow Goths off, and the attack was a failure. But it was enough to enrage Alaric. Exasperated with both Honorius in Ravenna and the senate in Rome, he left Ravenna and headed to Rome for his third siege of the city. But this time, he was not looking for gold or to promote another pretender like Priscus Attalus.

This time he was going to sack the eternal city.

27

The Death of the Roman Army

In the tale of events leading to the sack of Rome in AD 410, one thing stands out like a sore thumb. The Roman army completely failed not only to defend the western frontiers but also to defend the city of Rome itself. The sack of Rome was first and foremost due to Roman military failure. The army that had formed the basis of the empire's strength for centuries had melted away, leaving Alaric's Goths as the masters of Italy. So, the question has to be how and why did this happen?

The answer lies with a marked decline in both quantity and quality in the 50 years after Julian's defeat in Persia. To start with quantity, there is no doubt the western army received a mortal blow when Gaul was overrun by invading Germans in 406–8. Not only was the Gallic army lost to Ravenna but Britain broke away from central control at the same time, and Spain was subsequently lost to the Germans when they crossed the Pyrenees. What survived of the legions in these areas then gathered to support the usurper Constantine III.

This meant the western army commanded by Ravenna was reduced to just the legions in Italy, Africa and Illyria.

In one fell swoop, the western empire had lost about half its army. Although we have no information on the size of Roman losses defending Gaul nor on the numbers in Constantine III's rebel legions, we do have the *Notitia Dignitatum*, which is a list of late Roman army units that has survived to this day. Despite the many gaps in the information it presents, historians believe that it does suggest around half of the field army in the western empire disappeared in the years between 406–10.

This explains the decline in quantity. But what of quality?

My sense is that there was also a marked decline in quality. A valuable source is Flavius Vegetius Renatus, a Roman writer on military matters, who is most famous for his maxim, 'He who desires peace, should prepare for war.'[70] We know little about him other than he seems to have been a military adviser to either Theodosius I or Valentinian III. In his major work, the *De Re Militari*, he begged the emperor to improve the poor condition of the Roman army. What is striking in the passage below is his almost vitriolic criticism of the Roman infantry, who he regarded as next to useless (although he noted the cavalry were still good).

> *For though after the example of the Goths, the Alans and the Huns, we have made some improvements in the arms of the cavalry, yet it is plain the infantry are entirely defenceless. From the foundation of the city [of Rome] until the reign of the emperor Gratian, the foot wore cuirasses and helmets. But negligence and sloth having by degrees introduced a total relaxation of discipline, the soldiers began to think their armour too*

heavy, as they seldom put it on. They first requested leave from the emperor to lay aside the cuirass and afterwards the helmet. In consequence of this, our troops in their engagements with the Goths were often overwhelmed with their showers of arrows. Nor was the necessity of obliging the infantry to resume their cuirasses and helmets discovered, notwithstanding such repeated defeats, which brought on the destruction of so many great cities.[71]

His criticism of the Roman infantry stands in stark contrast to what the Greek historian, Polybius, writing in the second century BC, said about how impressive *all* the soldiers of the republican Roman army were about 600 years before. So, what had gone wrong with the Roman army? The answer lies with a major structural decline in the late Roman army which explains why it ceased to be a premier fighting force.

This was a very gradual process spanning a century, so let us start with the 'crisis of the third century' in the years 250–70. At this time, the Roman army was nearly annihilated. It suffered perhaps a quarter of a million casualties[72] and two emperors were killed or captured in battle (Decius in 251 and Valerian in 260). Yet despite this, it rose from the ashes. A succession of soldier-emperors from the militarised province of Illyria seized power and restored the army. It still had large numbers of heavily armoured legionaries and it also had a strengthened cavalry arm which became its primary strike force. This 'new model army' reached its apogee under Diocletian, probably the most visionary emperor in the entire history of Rome other than Augustus.

But then the problems began.

For evidence of this we need to turn to another Roman chronicler, this time Zosimus. He was a fierce critic of Constantine and there is no doubt that he was prejudiced against him because he was a pagan and resented Constantine's conversion to Christianity, but nevertheless his writings reveal an important structural change in the fourth-century army. He claimed Constantine weakened the empire's defences by taking troops away from the frontiers to join his field army, which he suggested became privileged and indulged very similar to what the old Praetorian Guard had been (he disbanded the traditional Praetorian Guard after he defeated them at the battle of the Milvian Bridge in 312).

> *Constantine abolished this [Diocletian's frontier] security by removing the greater part of the soldiery from the frontiers to cities that needed no auxiliary forces. He thus deprived of help the people who were harassed by the barbarians and burdened tranquil cities with the pest of the military, so that several straightaway were deserted. Moreover, he softened the soldiers, who treated themselves to shows and luxuries. Indeed (to speak plainly), he personally planted the first seeds of our present devastated state of affairs.*[73]

Zosimus suggests that because Constantine lacked Diocletian's political skills, he had to rely on a central field army to crush internal opposition. Constantine's field army became the centre of the entire Roman army. It rapidly developed its own structure, which displaced the old focus on having legions dispersed around the empire. Instead, it contained large numbers of new elite regiments like the *Scholae Palatinae*, each around 500 strong. Constantine did not abolish the legions as military units, and we still hear about old legions even from the days of Augustus; however, these had been reduced from about 5,000 to 1,000 men probably in the third century when legions had been split up to make them more flexible. He appointed two commanders of the field army, the magister peditum and the magister equitum, literally the commander of infantry and the commander of cavalry. These became the effective commanders-in-chief of the entire army.

By dividing the Roman army between border troops and a central field force, Constantine created a two-tier system. This is shown in the change of army nomenclature in the fourth century. The army was no longer referred to as one unit – the legions – as had been the practice for centuries. Instead, two types of soldiers emerged. One was stationed along the frontiers called the *limitanei* or *ripenses* (literally meaning border and river guards). The other was the field army called the *comitatenses* (best translated as the emperor's companions).

The problem with Constantine's new system was that over time, the limitanei were neglected and became a second-rate border police. It was only the comitatenses who kept the professionalism of the old legions. This explains why the late Roman army seemed to get smaller and smaller, something that has long baffled historians since the entire late Roman army might have been larger than Augustus' on paper at least. Augustus probably had some 300,000 legionaries and auxiliary troops, organised into 30 legions (each with 5,000 legionaries and 5,000 auxiliaries). In comparison, Constantine's army may have been larger, with some 400,000 soldiers in total, but over half of these were border guards (limitanei) and not used for campaigns. Therefore, the real comparison was between the field army (comitatenses) and the old legions. Here, there was a sharp drop in numbers. Compared with Augustus' 300,000, Constantine had maybe 150,000 comitatenses, so half the number of truly professional soldiers.

By dividing the Roman army into two types of soldiers, Constantine had effectively devalued it. Roman armies on campaign got smaller and smaller in the fourth and fifth centuries because they comprised just the field army without the border troops. The emperor Julian's reign is instructive in this respect. The sources say there were only about 15,000 soldiers at the Battle of Strasbourg in 357, which is strikingly small for such an important battle with the hordes of Alemanni. These 15,000 were clearly top-quality troops as evidenced by their performance in the battle. Yet there must have been many border troops stationed across Gaul who Julian chose not to use in the battle. In previous centuries, they would have been used on campaign to create a much larger and more effective Roman army.

Continuing with Julian's reign, when he led his great expedition against Persia in 363, the army was allegedly around 100,000 strong, containing the field armies from both halves of the empire. He left behind the limitanei to defend the borders. But in previous centuries, legions defending the borders were sent on such expeditions. This enabled emperors like Trajan and Septimius Severus to field even larger armies than Julian's. The old Roman Empire could mobilise huge numbers of high-quality troops. By the fourth century, it could still mobilise a powerful field army, but it was smaller than its classical equivalent. The result was that Julian's campaign was a failure.

The next step in the army's downfall was the replacement of its professional soldiers with barbarian mercenaries. This began with its defeat by the Goths at Adrianople in 378. The professional core of the eastern field army was destroyed, comprising some 30,000 elite Roman soldiers. Instead of reconstituting these elite regiments, the Romans began a process which some historians call the 'barbarisation' of the army. But this term is sometimes misunderstood. It was not a question of barbarians being recruited as legionaries, although admittedly this may have happened with some of the low-quality Roman border troops (limitanei). It was about barbarians being used *instead of* legionaries. This proved catastrophic for the late Roman army because it replaced its professional core with mercenaries.

I suggest Theodosius I was mainly responsible for this development. We have already discussed the damage he did to the empire in Chapter 19. After the treaty of 382, Theodosius used the Goths as his elite troops. He disguised this by calling them foederati, meaning allies, but in reality, they were nothing more than mercenaries. This was a catastrophic blunder.

Theodosius' mistakes continued when he used the Goths in his civil wars with the western empire. He defeated the two usurpers in the west, Maximus and then Arbogast, using

Goths not Romans as his crack troops. The truly tragic result for the Romans was that Theodosius won these battles by destroying the western field army. By 394, when the Frigidus River battle was over, both halves of the empire had lost most of their best native troops – the eastern army at Adrianople, and the western army at the Frigidus River. Theodosius had effectively destroyed the professional core of the Roman army.

After Theodosius' reign, the Romans became increasingly reliant on mercenaries – the so-called foederati – instead of Roman troops. By Stilicho's reign, he was using Goths, Germans and Huns backed up by what remained of the legions. This proved fatal since, as Alaric proved, the Goths fought not for Rome but for the highest bidder.

In summary, the architects of the Roman army's decline, so vividly described by Vegetius, were first Constantine when he consigned half the army to becoming second-rate border troops, and second Theodosius I when he used barbarian mercenaries instead of Roman troops. Luck also played a significant part on this road to damnation. For example, without Valens' disastrous defeat at Adrianople, the process of barbarisation would probably not have taken place. The Romans had often enjoyed good fortune on their path to greatness (such as with the unexpected collapse of the Greek states in the second century BC). In the fourth century AD, their luck ran out.

The principal victim of this would now be the city of Rome itself.

28

The Sack of Rome

To understand why Alaric sacked Rome, we need to see things through his eyes.

We need to understand that he was conflicted. On the one hand, he had been a senior Roman military commander – a magister militum – first appointed by the eastern empire and then by the western, but on the other hand he was also king of the Goths. One historian[74] has argued that Alaric was like an illegal immigrant, admitted into the Roman Empire but still reviled by the Romans. Stilicho, and before him Theodosius, wanted to incorporate the Goths into the empire without their being Roman citizens. This flawed strategy could only lead to disaster.

This is exactly what happened in August 410, when Alaric decided to sack Rome. He was exasperated with the emperor Honorius' refusal to recognise him, and then outraged by the unexpected attack on him by Sarus, his Gothic rival in Honorius' pay. In addition, his attempt to set up his own rival emperor, Priscus Attalus, had failed to win any support other than from the powerless Roman senate. Most pressing of all was his need to keep his followers happy. They had received no gold from the Romans since the first siege of Rome ended in late 408. Now they needed a pay-off and the sack of Rome was the best way of giving that to them.

We have no first-hand accounts of the sack of Rome, and historians divide between those who believe it was a relatively mild affair and those who think the Goths wrought destruction on a massive scale. Certainly, what archaeological evidence we have suggests the city was not burned to the ground or its inhabitants entirely slaughtered. But it would be surprising if the Goths did not rape and kill many of its inhabitants. The few sources that remain to us suggest the story went like this.

On 24 August 410, someone, perhaps vengeful slaves, opened the Salarian Gate,[75] one of the main gates in the Aurelian walls to the north of the city. The Goths flooded into the city. Nevertheless, Alaric did his best to ensure moderation. He ordered the Goths to plunder but not to kill. In particular, the two main Christian churches, the basilicas of St Peter and St Paul, were nominated places of sanctuary where Roman citizens would be safe, if they could get to them. The Goths were Arian Christians and, although many of the Romans were Nicene Christians, as well as pagans, there was at least some sort of religious kindred spirit between the invaders and the invaded. Certainly, the sack was mild compared with the later sack of the city by the Vandals in 455, or the utterly brutal sacking of northern Italian Roman cities 40 years later by Attila the Hun.

In particular, two stories illustrative of Gothic clemency have become well known. One, recounted by Saint Jerome, is of Marcella, a nun who protested to the Goths ransacking her house that she had no wealth, for she had no need for material possessions, which so impressed them that they took her to the safety of St Peter's.

Another, recorded by the Christian writer Sozomen, says that when a Gothic soldier saw a pretty young Roman woman, he 'was conquered by her loveliness', and felt compelled to escort her to the safety of St Peter's, where he paid the guards to protect her until the danger was over.[76]

Nevertheless, the pillage of the city would *not* have been a pretty sight. The historian Edward Gibbon provides us with a more plausible description,[77] highlighting that the large slave population in the city must have used the Gothic invasion as an opportunity to get their own back on their masters.

> *The writers, the best disposed to exaggerate their clemency, have freely confessed, that a cruel slaughter was made of the Romans; and that the streets of the city were filled with dead bodies, which remained without burial during the general consternation. The despair of the citizens was sometimes converted into fury; and whenever the barbarians were provoked by opposition, they extended the promiscuous massacre to the feeble, the innocent, and the helpless. The private revenge of forty thousand slaves was exercised without pity or remorse; and the ignominious lashes, which they had formerly received, were washed away in the blood of the guilty, or obnoxious, families.*

It is almost certain that the Goths seized a huge amount of gold and silver and other precious possessions from the city's inhabitants. Although they seem to have respected most of the churches, they could not resist taking a 2,000-pound silver ciborium (a canopy covering an altar) which had been a gift from Constantine the Great. They burned several large Roman administrative buildings, including the senate house itself and the basilicas of Aemilia and Julia.

No-one came to Rome's rescue. The Italian legions based in northern Italy at Ticinum did nothing. Still guarding the frontier against Constantine III, they did not try to move south to confront the Goths. In Ravenna, the story goes, according to the sixth-century Roman writer, Procopius, that the feeble-minded emperor Honorius was feeding his chickens when a eunuch rushed in to tell him that Rome had perished. The emperor looked up in horror and said, 'And yet it has just eaten from my hands!' The eunuch had to explain he was referring to the city of Rome and not the chicken which Honorius had nicknamed *Roma*. Apparently, Honorius breathed a sigh of relief and said, 'But I thought my chicken had perished.'

After three days of looting, Alaric called a halt, and the Goths left the city. Together with their plunder, they took Galla Placidia, Honorius' sister, who they treated with respect as befitted an imperial princess. She would later marry Alaric's brother-in-law, Ataulf, in 414. But that story, and the story of the battle for control of the western empire that would be fought over the next half century, lies with the next volume in this series.

So, where could the Goths go now? Alaric had destroyed any chances of a peaceful settlement with Honorius. There was apparently dissatisfaction within the Gothic ranks.

Although Alaric had delivered the riches of Rome to his followers, they were frustrated with their itinerant lifestyle and wanted to settle down. So, he promised them a land of plenty, a land where corn grew in abundance, a land of sunny warmth beside the Mediterranean Sea, a land with civilised Roman cities which they could occupy. He promised them North Africa.

The Goths marched into southern Italy, which was untouched by war. Our records are thin but the Goths may well have sacked the cities of Nola and Capua. However, their plans came to nothing. When they reached the straits of Messina, the ships they gathered for the crossing to Sicily were wrecked by a storm. The Visigoths were not skilled sailors, and they turned back, unable even to reach Sicily let alone North Africa. Then, another misfortune hit them. Alaric died in the winter of 410/11 of unknown causes. According to the Romano-Gothic historian, Jordanes, his death was 'untimely', so it seems to have been a surprise. Historians have speculated that it might have been malaria. Whatever the truth, his death just months after the sack of Rome was a blow to the Goths, who lacked a powerful leader to replace him. His brother-in-law, Ataulf, was crowned king. Lacking Alaric's vision, Ataulf led the Goths back north towards Gaul, which they considered the best location to settle within Roman territory.

Alaric was buried with a hoard of treasure in the bed of a river which had been diverted temporarily. Once he was placed in his grave, the river was redirected to flow back over it. To prevent any discovery of his resting place and the treasure, all the slaves who had dug it were killed. Thus, in a rather grisly fashion, ended the story of Alaric the Goth.

As for the Roman Empire, while Honorius might have been relieved that his chicken survived, most of the inhabitants of the empire regarded the sack of Rome as a turning point. Not for 800 years had Rome fallen to a foreign invader. The last time was in 390 BC, when the Gauls sacked it, and even then, the Capitol had still held out, according to Livy, with the help of its geese, who warned the defenders of Gallic attacks. In Constantinople, the first minister Anthemius told the nine-year-old Theodosius II to proclaim three days of mourning. Saint Jerome, one of our principal sources for this period, wrote, 'If Rome can perish, what can be safe?'[78] Christians blamed the pagans in the empire, and the pagans blamed the Christians. Orosius, a leading Christian theologian, blamed the impious pagans for the sack of Rome. But the pagan chronicler Zosimus blamed the Christians for causing the pagan gods to be rejected. Everywhere, divine vengeance was cited as the reason for the worst disaster to afflict the empire in 800 years.

Amidst this confused and vengeful anger surrounding Rome's demise, there rose to prominence one of the Christian Church's most influential thinkers – Saint Augustine. He was the bishop of Hippo in North Africa in 410 when Rome was sacked, and he wrote *The City of God*, a treatise that became foundational for the Christian Church because it established a new way of evaluating Rome's relationship with Christianity. This great work would run to 22 volumes and was not completed until 425, but by 413 he had written the first three books, which put forward the view that the sack of Rome was not a defeat for Christianity, since the Roman Empire was not the same as the Christian Church. This went against much of the thinking of the time, in particular Constantine the Great's linking of Christianity with the office of the emperor.

Saint Augustine wrote that the sack of Rome in 410 was no disaster for Christianity because it was not in fact dependent upon Rome. This was a revolutionary idea when most early Christians argued it was no coincidence that Augustus, the first Roman emperor, and Christ had lived at the same time. Augustine now suggested that this was *truly* just a coincidence, and that the city of Rome and the heavenly city of God existed independently of each other, with the latter far more important, as he described: 'The Heavenly City outshines Rome beyond comparison. There, instead of victory, is truth; instead of high rank, holiness; instead of peace, felicity; instead of life, eternity.'[79]

But for most people, the sack of Rome was a shattering blow. It certainly marked the beginning of the city's rapid decline to becoming little more than a village in the Middle Ages. Refugees fled the city and flooded into Africa, Egypt and Constantinople. One historian[80] has estimated that Rome's population fell from around 800,000 in 410 to some 500,000 in 419. By 600, there were less than 20,000 people left, barely enough to fill a corner of the Colosseum.

The western empire had passed a point of no return. The future of the Roman Empire now lay in the east.

29

The Survival of the East

While the western empire was reduced to chaos, the eastern empire was doing well. In May 408, the eastern emperor, Arcadius, had died and was succeeded by his seven-year-old son, Theodosius II. Another child emperor was at least not a surprise. To manage affairs on his behalf, a first minister called Flavius Anthemius took the reins of government. He was exemplary in every way. Praetorian Prefect for the East since 404, prior to which he had occupied several senior positions in Arcadius' court, including that of consul, he came from a distinguished family and was free of the back-stabbing jealousies that dominated the actions of so many of the senior bureaucrats in both the eastern and western courts. As such, he implemented several initiatives that strengthened the eastern empire.

To start with, he negotiated a peace treaty with the Persian king of kings, Yazdegerd, who was a fairly enlightened ruler, tolerant of Christians and reasonably well disposed towards the Romans. One reason for his willingness to make peace was that a tribe of Huns, the Kidarites, were threatening his eastern border. This was probably caused by the same drought on the Asiatic steppes which drove the European Huns west. While the western Roman Empire suffered from the movement of the Germanic tribes west because of the Huns, the eastern Roman Empire benefited from the pressure which the Kidarites put on the Persians.

Despite this, the eastern empire still felt threatened by the Huns, and it was Anthemius who responded by building one of the most important defensive constructions in the history of the world – the Theodosian walls of Constantinople. These replaced the existing walls built by Constantine, none of which survive today. But the Theodosian walls were far larger and built nearly two kilometres further west, almost doubling the size of the enclosed city. The story of exactly when and why they were built is still debated by historians. The Theodosian Code suggests Anthemius completed them in 413, but no-one knows quite when construction began, although one inscription uncovered in 1993 suggests it was as early as 404. They were later damaged in 447 and hastily rebuilt to fend off Attila the Hun.

What were the Huns doing at this time? In 408, there was a well-documented invasion of Thrace by a Hunnic leader, Uldin. Uldin had been an ally of Rome's and had defeated and killed the renegade Gothic general, Gainas, in 400, sending his head to the emperor Arcadius. However, by 408, Uldin sensed an opportunity to attack the empire when eastern Roman troops were despatched east to intimidate the Persians as part of Anthemius' negotiating tactics. Our source is the chronicler, Sozomen, who described a large invasion of Thrace by Uldin, capturing the Roman town of Castra Martis, whereupon he made an intimidating claim to the

Roman ambassadors: 'He pointed to the sun and declared that it would be easy for him, if he so desired, to subjugate every region of the earth that is enlightened by that luminary.'[81]

Historians have assumed, based on Sozomen's description, that this was a major invasion of the eastern empire which prompted the building of the walls. However, more recent research suggests a different explanation. Uldin was probably only a minor Hunnic warlord, and one of many. His army was defeated by the Romans, suggesting it was only a small force. Uldin then disappears from history. The conclusion is that the Theodosian walls were not built because of Uldin, but because the Romans were worried about the much greater force of Huns living to the north of the Danube. These Huns were probably the ones who forced Radagaisus' Goths to flee to Italy, and then caused the Germanic invasion of Gaul in 406-7.

The Theodosian walls of Constantinople would go on to play a pivotal role in global history. They were impregnable for nearly 800 years until 1204, when the Fourth Crusade broke through a section of the sea walls. The land walls themselves were only breached by the Ottoman Turks in 1453, when they used cannons to destroy them. Their strength lay in a double circuit of walls with a moat and a third small wall behind that, and anyone who has visited them in modern Istanbul can see why they were so effective. For the attacker had first to cross the moat and overcome the small wall protecting that. They then had to batter or scale their way through the outer wall before making it to the gigantic inner wall. Both the inner and outer walls had towers armed with powerful Roman artillery. Should an attacker get through the moat and the outer wall (which virtually nobody did until 1453), they would be trapped in a gully between the outer and inner walls, and subjected to a murderous barrage of missiles from the towers. It is little wonder the walls became the best defensive system ever built in the ancient world.

In conclusion, in 410, the eastern and western empires were in very different places. Barbarians had overrun most of the west and a massive army of Visigoths was wandering around Italy. Compared with this, the eastern empire was thriving, with its most prosperous provinces safe, including Egypt, Syria, Cappadocia and Anatolia. The eastern half of the empire was becoming stronger and would soon inaugurate a Roman revival. The western empire might be dying but the history of the Roman Empire was far from over.

30

The End of Civilisation?

So far, this book has focused almost entirely on political, military, economic and climate history. I have said little about life for the 'ordinary' person. But for them, the fall of the Roman Empire meant perhaps the most of all.

For being Roman was to lead a life of civilised comfort, certainly in comparison with what happened after Rome fell. One of the best ways we have of assessing how ordinary people lived is to compare the archaeological record before and after the fall of the Roman Empire. One distinguished archaeologist[82] has done just this by comparing the four main surviving artefacts of Roman civilisation: pottery, roof tiles, coinage and graffiti. His analysis is revealing. In many archaeological digs from Britain to Africa, he sees a fundamental change in living conditions that took place in the west in the fifth century and in the east in the seventh century.

In the west, the Romans led a life of relative comfort and even of luxury until the early fifth century. The sheer volume of finds of Roman pottery, roof tiles and coins evidences this. But this archaeological treasure trove comes to an abrupt end in the fifth century in the west. It was not until the beginning of the modern era, in the fifteenth and sixteenth centuries, that a similar quantity of archaeological finds comparable with those from ancient Rome began again. We are not just talking about quantity, but also quality. For example, Roman pottery was consistently high quality. Light and smooth to the touch, and very tough, it was amazingly 'modern' and was mass-produced in centres across the empire, which exported their products to its remotest corners. Archaeological discoveries show it was humble villages and isolated farmsteads which enjoyed the use of this superb pottery just as much as the great urban centres.

Remains of roof tiles are equally impressive. Almost all Roman buildings had sturdy and high-quality roof tiles, from agricultural sheds and barns, to temples and basilicas. They protected Roman livestock from the wind and rain just as much as their human owners. Yet starting in the fifth century in the west, roof tiles almost disappeared from more humble dwellings for over a thousand years. Thatched roofs replaced tiled ones, a regression only favoured as a fashion statement today, since a thatched roof is far inferior to a tiled one, requiring remaking every 30 years compared to hundreds of years for well-made tiled roofs, and even then, it is normally less successful at keeping out wind and rain.

Coinage was another victim of the fall of Rome in the fifth century. Until then, Roman coins were abundant and available in three metals: gold, silver and copper. But in the west, during the fifth and sixth centuries, coins disappeared. Some of the new Germanic kingdoms in the west minted them for a short time, more for prestige than for economic purposes, but by the seventh century coinage had all but disappeared.

Surviving remains of graffiti also provide us with an insight into the scale of change for ordinary people. Graffiti was written to be read and the abundance of graffiti found in Pompeii (destroyed by the fatal eruption of Vesuvius in AD 79) suggests ordinary Romans were highly literate. Pompeii's walls were covered in graffiti, some of it vulgar, in the style of the often quoted 'Here Phoebus the perfume-seller had a really good fuck' on the wall of a brothel, but the majority is less crude and can be nuanced and amusing, such as with the following famous inscription found four times in Pompeii, each time in different handwriting:

Wall, I admire you for not collapsing in ruins
When you have to support so much tedious writing on
you!

Although Pompeii remains our only source of Roman graffiti, we can assume that it was widespread in Roman towns and cities until the fifth century, after which the Germanic invasions resulted in a staggering loss of literacy, so much so that during most of the Middle Ages, literacy was confined to a few monks.

We should also acknowledge that not all the empire's inhabitants lived a life of comfort before its fall. Roman society comprised haves and have nots. There was a substantial slave population in both halves of the empire, whose lives are poorly documented and about whom we know little. Common sense would suggest that while some slaves led lives of unimaginable suffering, such as those labouring until they dropped dead in mines, quarries and on the vast agricultural estates of the wealthy, others lived in relative comfort, such as domestic servants, many of whom were cooks, hairdressers and even teachers. We also know that there was an under-class of peasants happy to rise in rebellion when the central authority of the empire collapsed. These are well documented in Gaul, where they were called the *bagaudae* (meaning warriors in Gallic) and comprised lawless peasantry and slaves who turned to pillage and plunder just as violently and destructively as the barbarians. Nevertheless, the bagaudae were a minority and for the great majority of the empire's inhabitants in the west, the fall of Rome was a decidedly bad thing.

One conspicuous example of this was fifth-century Britain. When Constantine III rebelled against the emperor Honorius in late 406, he crossed over to Gaul with the British legions never to return. Abandoned, Britain declared its independence from Rome in 409, and thereafter we have no idea what happened on the island. About the only thing mentioned in Roman sources is that some of the wealthier Britons fled across the channel to Amorica, which became known as Brittany, the land occupied by the Britons, the name it still keeps in modern France.

Apart from that, there is almost no surviving source material[83] covering the period from 410 to 600, although by 600, the sources start again and show that the Anglo-Saxons dominated most of central and eastern England. What happened to the Romano-Britons is a mystery. The absence of almost any archaeological record suggests Britain reverted to a prehistoric level of society, less advanced than before the Romans arrived, when there had been a flourishing pottery industry, trade with Gaul, and even the minting of native silver coins. What little has survived shows the art of making pottery on a wheel completely vanished in the early fifth century and was not reintroduced for almost 300 years. Building in mortared stone or brick also disappeared. No coinage was minted. There is no evidence of any trade.

This dystopian post-Roman future is the stuff of horror stories, and a grim reminder of what can happen when a sophisticated economy, reliant on specialisation, is suddenly cast adrift to survive on its own. We, in the twenty-first century, with our hugely complex and specialised global economy, would do well to heed the warning of what happened in fifth-century Britain.

But the example of Britain was extreme, even by fifth-century Roman standards, and it is important to emphasise that the experiences of the two halves of the Roman Empire were quite different – a subject to which we will return in the later books in this series. Although the western economy collapsed in the fifth century, its eastern cousin prospered until the Arab invasions of the seventh century reduced it to a state similar to that of the west. In short, when Britain was reverting to a prehistoric lifestyle, Roman civilisation in the eastern Mediterranean was booming.

In conclusion, the archaeological record after the sack of Rome suggests that in the west a life of relative luxury continued only for a small minority such as wealthy landowners, clerics, aristocrats and the ruling elites. For the majority of people, the fall of the western empire plunged them back into a primitive lifestyle not experienced for centuries, an uncertain life of insanitary dwellings, undernourishment and the absence of quality manufactured goods.

One historian[84] has summed this up well.

> *In my opinion, the fifth century witnessed a profound military and political crisis, caused by the violent seizure of power and much wealth by the barbarian invaders. The native population was able, to some extent, to adapt to these new conditions, but what is interesting about this adjustment is that it was achieved in very difficult circumstances. I also believe that the post-Roman centuries saw a dramatic decline in economic sophistication and prosperity, with an impact on the whole of society, from agricultural production to high culture, and from peasants to kings. It is very likely that the population fell dramatically, and certain that the widespread diffusion of well-made goods ceased. Sophisticated cultural tools, like the use of writing, disappeared altogether in some regions, and became very restricted in all others.*

In short, for most people in the west, the fall of the Roman Empire was the end of civilisation.

Conclusion

Was Climate Change Rome's Real Killer?

The sack of Rome in 410 marked the effective end of the western empire, if not its official end. Some historians consider this to be 476, when the last emperor of the west, Romulus Augustulus, was deposed by the Germanic ruler of Italy, Odoacer. However, in my view, the western empire received a mortal blow in the years 406–10. After 410, it never had a serious hope of returning to where it had been even in the days of Stilicho, let alone to the glorious majesty it had enjoyed for most of the past 500 years. After 410, the narrative changed. It was no longer about the restoration of the western empire; it was about the battle for political supremacy between several barbarian powers which supplanted Rome within the former territory of the western empire.

The sack of Rome was the culmination of a remarkably rapid story of Roman decline, unthinkable only a few years before. Historians have long debated the reasons for it. Almost every argument has been proposed. Indeed, one German scholar[85] listed 210 reasons! For a long time, it was popular to see Roman decline as an internal problem, in particular some sort of moral decay which caused them to lose their military prowess and become corrupt and degenerate. Edward Gibbon was the main proponent of this view and blamed the Christians for depriving the Romans of their militaristic zeal, dividing society with obscure doctrinal disputes, and diverting resources into the vast Church organisation, especially the recruitment of men and women into monasteries and nunneries which were, in his view, socially and economically unproductive. This partly reflected the anti-Christian views fashionable in his own time, when the radical 'enlightenment' thinking of Voltaire and Montesquieu condemned the eighteenth-century Catholic Church.

This view was not confined to Gibbon. Indeed, he echoed views expressed by many Romans. Pagans like the emperor Julian the Apostate, and the chronicler Zosimus, were fiercely critical of Christianity as the enemy of the empire's traditional values, including its bellicose ethos. But ultimately, Christianity cannot be blamed for Rome's fall, since it was the eastern Roman Empire which survived the fall of the west, where Christianity was if anything stronger.

For a time in the mid-twentieth century, scholarly consensus settled on Roman economic decline as the principal culprit. A leading scholar at Oxford called A.H.M. Jones developed this argument based on a careful study of the Roman literary sources which frequently criticised overtaxation for increasing poverty and destroying the economic vitality of the empire. But recent archaeological evidence disproved this by uncovering evidence of a strong economic revival in the empire in the fourth century.

This has caused modern historians to move away from internal causes to external ones. There is now a consensus that it was the Germanic invasions of the late fourth and fifth centuries – the Völkerwanderung (wandering of the peoples) as it is known – which caused Rome's fall in the west. Geography helps to explain why the eastern empire survived. The narrow straits of the Bosphorus and Dardanelles protected the Middle Eastern provinces from barbarian attack. Constantinople was strategically better placed than Rome to defend itself, helped by its mighty Theodosian walls.

It is also widely agreed that it was the Huns who drove the Germans west into the Roman Empire. And this made the crisis of the fourth century different from the crisis of the third. As the Huns moved west, they found their method of fighting was superior to that of their new neighbours. Their hit-and-run tactics, the ferocious power of their bows, and their ability to mobilise large numbers of horsemen ensured their success over Alans, Goths and Germans.

Pushed by the Huns, the Germans were not raiders, as they had been in the third century, but migrants desperately seeking survival. In a sort of domino-toppling effect, the Huns drove the great age of Germanic migration which burst upon the Roman Empire like the waters of a dam bursting through its wall. This meant that the military pressure exerted on Rome in the fifth century was far greater than it had been in the third.

This has become the consensus view of the fall of Rome. It is one that I think is correct. But we can add some important new perspectives. First, Rome's fall was not inevitable. In my view, the potential significance of Julian the Apostate's reign has been underestimated. His all too short life represents the biggest 'what if?' in the history of the fourth century, and perhaps in the entire history of Rome. He was the most far-sighted emperor since Diocletian and embarked on a policy of radical reform to restore Rome to greatness. What would have happened had he lived? Aside from the question mark over the future of Christianity, he came close to averting the army's decline and could have restored Roman military dominance had he defeated Persia. I doubt the Goths would have won the Battle of Adrianople if Julian had been emperor instead of Valens. He held the key to unlocking the fourth century for Rome, but unfortunately for Rome, that key was lost in the sands of Persia.

Second, I think some historians have underestimated the importance of the decline of the Roman army. Rome was sacked in 410 because the Roman army could not defend it. Unlike in the third century, when the Roman army was reinvented by Aurelian and Diocletian, by the fifth it was a shadow of its former self. Its decline began with Constantine's downgrading of the border legions in favour of an elite field army with which to crush opponents. The next downwards step was the failure of Julian the Apostate's Persian campaign. The defeat of what proved to be the last great Roman military initiative seems to have led to a serious loss of self-belief and morale. Then the professional core of the eastern army was destroyed at the Battle of Adrianople. Finally, Theodosius' catastrophic civil wars destroyed the professional core of the western army. He also started the disastrous policy of using mercenaries like the Goths instead of Roman legionaries. By the time Stilicho took charge of the western army, it relied on hiring the services of Goths, Alans and Huns, and it had no professional core worth speaking of. This proved catastrophic.

Another point is the failure of Roman political leadership after Julian the Apostate's death. Both Valentinian I and Theodosius I lacked vision. After Theodosius' death, his sons, Honorius and Arcadius, were merely puppets manipulated by self-serving ministers. This political weakness paralysed the Roman Empire and caused a damaging division between east and west which facilitated its military breakdown and allowed Alaric to survive and thrive.

Luck also played an important part. As I have mentioned several times during the course of this book, the Romans suffered from a good deal of bad luck such as Julian's death, Valens' incompetence at Adrianople and the almost comic inability of the Theodosian dynasty to rule.

This brings me to my final point which is to highlight another example of Roman bad luck, this time on a truly apocalyptic scale. Historians have never adequately explained why the Huns appeared on the eastern edge of Europe in the 360s. Until now. Palaeoclimatology has only just unearthed evidence of a catastrophic megadrought in the Asiatic steppe-lands which drove hundreds of thousands, maybe millions, of nomads to find new pastures.

So, is climate change the final missing link in explaining the fall of Rome? The answer appears to be yes. Without a megadrought on the Asian steppes in the fourth century, it is hard to see why the Huns should suddenly have migrated all the way to Europe. Without the Hunnic migration, there would have been no domino effect that pushed the Germans west. Without that, there is no obvious reason why Rome should have fallen.

Drought is also something that historians are becoming more familiar with as a catalyst that changed the course of history in other parts of the world and at other times. Examples are the end of Mayan civilisation in Central America and the fall of the Khmer Empire in Cambodia.

This revelation is timely. Drought is one of the most significant results of modern, human-made climate change. In 2022, Europe endured its worst drought for over 500 years.[86] Perhaps we can now see the awe-inspiring ruins of the Colosseum in a different light. Not just as a relic of Rome's lost grandeur but as a grim warning from the past.

Find Out More About the Fall of the Roman Empire

The fall of the Roman Empire was one of the greatest events in world history.

Debate about why, when and how it happened has been as wide-ranging as the opinions on its significance. One historian has written that it was the greatest setback to humanity *in all of human history*.[87] Others have argued that it was a positive catalyst for Europe, releasing forces of creativity and mercantilism.[88] But whatever your view, no-one can deny that we live today in the shadow of that great empire. For example, the letters I am now writing on this page are those of the Roman alphabet. Romance languages – such as French, Spanish and Italian – are derived from Latin and are still spoken not only in former Roman territories but in much of the Americas as well. Roman law underpins many of the world's legal systems. Christianity was the religion of the late Roman Empire. Need I say more?

So, if you are interested in finding out about it, look no further!

This book is the second in a series covering the full story of the fall of the Roman Empire. The first covered the 'crisis of the third century', Rome's adoption of Christianity and the move of the capital to Constantinople. The third and future books will continue the story of the fall of the western empire after AD 410, the eastern Roman Empire's revival and reconquest of the west under the emperor Justinian, the rise of Islam and the loss of most of the eastern Roman Empire's territories to the armies of the Umayyad Caliphate, culminating in the great siege of Constantinople in 717–18, in which the eastern Roman state survived but in a diminished and greatly changed form. In my view, it was the rise of Islam that marked the true fall of the Roman Empire, and not the fall of the western half of the Roman Empire in the fifth century. The Arabs, not the Germans, destroyed Rome.

In this way, my series will follow much of the same course taken by that eminent historian, Edward Gibbon, in his masterpiece *The History of the Decline and Fall of the Roman Empire*. While I would not even dream of suggesting that my work in any way rivals or replaces his, I would very humbly propose that it to some extent updates the story in terms of modern research and archaeology. But my most important aim, inspired by the genius of Gibbon's timeless classic, is simply to tell the reader a captivating story. For the fall of the Roman Empire is not just any old story. It is, in my view, as Gibbon himself described it, the greatest story ever told.

Podcast
My podcast *The Fall of the Roman Empire* accompanies my books and is available on all the main podcast apps.

Website

If you want to find out more about the fall of the Roman Empire, check out my website www.nickholmesauthor.com where you will find my books, podcasts and special offers. Please sign up for my newsletter for news and views on Roman history.

Book One of
The Fall of the Roman Empire

The Roman Revolution

'An enlightening and lively interpretation of an
important but neglected historical period.'
Kirkus Reviews

The Roman Revolution is the first book in my series on the
Fall of the Roman Empire. It describes the little-known 'crisis
of the third century'. Long before the collapse of the Roman
Empire in the fifth century, in the years between AD 235–75,
barbarian invasions, civil war and plague devastated ancient
Rome. Out of this ordeal, there arose a revolutionary new
Christian Roman state, ruled from Constantinople.

It was the first step in the history of Rome's fall and the
beginning of the modern world.

Acknowledgements

I would like to thank all those people who have kindly helped me with this book, in particular my editor, Scott Pack, who has given me so much valuable input. Nick Castle, for his striking front cover. Bek Cruddace, for making the clear and elegant maps. Helen Peters, for making such a thorough and intelligent index. Mark Swift for his tireless and thorough copy-editing. I would like to thank the London Library and its staff for providing an excellent haven of study and creativity in the middle of central London. I have written most of this book in its elegant reading rooms and at the desks among its endless bookshelves.

Finally, I would like to thank my family. My now young adult children, William and Anna, you are a constant source of admiration and pride for me as I see you establish yourselves in your exciting lives, and this book is for you. My wonderful wife, Sarah – all roads lead to Rome, and all my roads lead to you – you are my true love and companion in all I do. Thank you for your patience, support and understanding, and for putting up with both me and the Romans! *Amor vincit omnia.*

Roman Emperors

(Augustus to Theodosius II)

Augustus	27 BC – AD 14
Tiberius	AD 14 – 37
Caligula	37 – 41
Claudius	41 – 54
Nero	54 – 68
Galba	68 – 69
Otho	69
Vitellius	69
Vespasian	69 – 79
Titus	79 – 81
Domitian	81 – 96
Nerva	96 – 98
Trajan	98 – 117
Hadrian	117 – 38
Antoninus Pius	138 – 61
Marcus Aurelius	161 – 80
Commodus	180 – 92

Pertinax	193
Didius Iulianus	193
Septimius Severus	193 – 211
Caracalla	211 – 17
Macrinus	217 – 18
Elagabalus	218 – 22
Severus Alexander	222 – 35
Maximinus Thrax	235 – 38
Gordian III	238 – 44
Philip the Arab	244 – 49
Decius	249 – 51
Trebonianus	251 – 53
Aemilianus	253
Valerian	253 – 60
Gallienus	260 – 68
Claudius Gothicus	268 – 70
Vetranio (Rebel in West)	350 – 50
Julian 'The Apostate' (Sole)	361 – 63
Jovian (Sole)	363 – 64
Valentinian I (Sole then West)	364 – 75
Valens (East)	364 – 78
Procopius (Rebel in East)	365 – 66

Gratian (West)	375 – 83
Magnus Maximus (Rebel in West)	383 – 88
Valentinian II (West)	388 – 92
Eugenius (Rebel in West)	392 – 94
Theodosius I (East then Sole)	379 – 95
Arcadius (East)	395 – 408
Honorius (West)	395 – 423
Constantine III (Rebel in West)	407 – 11
Theodosius II (East)	408 – 50
Priscus Attalus (Rebel in West)	409 – 10

Chronology of the
Later Roman Empire

(AD 211–411)

211	Death of Septimius Severus
	Accession of Caracalla
216–17	Caracalla campaigns successfully against Parthia
226	Sasanian Persian dynasty founded by Ardashir, who overthrows the Parthians
235	Murder of Alexander Severus by his own troops and succeeded by Maximinus Thrax
238	Revolts against Maximinus result in Gordian III becoming sole emperor
	Sasanians attack Roman east
241	Death of Ardashir
	Shapur I becomes Shah of Persia
243–4	Philip the Arab concludes humiliating treaty with Shapur in order to go to Rome to be proclaimed emperor
248	Philip celebrates Rome's millennium
249–50	Goths cross Danube and invade Balkans
251	Battle of Abrittus – Gothic victory and Emperor Decius killed
252–3	Shapur's second great invasion of Roman east
	Antioch sacked
253	Valerian becomes emperor and makes his son Gallienus co-ruler in the west
260	*Annus horribilis* for Roman Empire

Valerian defeated and captured by Shapur at Battle of Edessa

Franks invade Gaul

Postumus creates breakaway Gallic Empire

Alemanni invade Italy and are defeated by Gallienus at Mediolanum

261   Odenathus seizes power in Palmyra

262–7   Odenathus defeats Sasanians

Goths invade Balkans

Heruli sail into Aegean

267–8   Goths and Heruli sack Athens

Odenathus murdered and succeeded by Zenobia

268   Murder of Gallienus

Claudius II becomes the first of the Illyrian soldier-emperors

269   Claudius defeats Alemanni at Lake Garda and Goths at the Battle of Naissus

270   Claudius dies of plague

Aurelian becomes emperor after brief reign of Quintillus

Palmyra invades Arabia and Egypt

271   Aurelian defeats Juthungi invasion of Italy

Riots at Rome

Postumus killed by his own troops and succeeded by Tetricus

Aurelian defeats Goths and initiates the evacuation of Dacia

272   Aurelian campaigns against Palmyra

Egypt recaptured by Probus

Aurelian defeats Palmyrene army at Immae and Emesa, and captures Palmyra

273   Revolt in Palmyra suppressed and city sacked

274   Aurelian defeats Tetricus and reintegrates west into empire

Triumph held in Rome

275   Aurelian murdered at Caenophrurium

Tacitus made emperor

276   Tacitus defeats Gothic invasion

Tacitus murdered

Probus made emperor after brief reign of Florian (June–July)

279   Probus defeats Vandals in Pannonia

282   Probus assassinated and succeeded by Carus

283   Carus defeats Quadi and Sarmatians on Danube and defeats
Sasanians, possibly capturing Ctesiphon

Carus dies in mysterious circumstances

284   Diocletian proclaimed emperor by army of east

286   Diocletian makes Maximian co-emperor in west

Carausius sets up breakaway state in Britain and northern
Gaul

293   Diocletian establishes tetrarchy, appointing Constantius and
Galerius junior emperors (Caesars) while he and Maximian
remain senior emperors (Augusti)

296   Constantius subjugates breakaway British state

297–8   War with Persia won by Rome

301   Diocletian issues the Edict on Maximum Prices

303–4   Great Persecution of Christians

305   Diocletian and Maximian abdicate

Tetrarchy continues with Galerius and Constantius as senior
emperors and Severus and Daia as junior emperors

305–10 Tetrarchy breaks down

306   Constantine proclaimed western emperor by Roman army in
York following his father's death (Constantius)

311   Edict of Toleration by Galerius grants Christians freedom of
worship in the eastern empire

312   Battle of Milvian Bridge – Constantine defeats Maxentius and secures western empire; Licinius rules the east with Daia

313   Licinius defeats Daia

324   Constantine defeats Licinius and becomes sole Roman emperor

Constantinople founded

325   Council of Nicaea

330   Constantinople dedicated and becomes the imperial residence

337   Death of Constantine

His sons, Constantine II, Constans and Constantius II become co-emperors

340   Civil war between Constantine II and Constans in the West. Constantine II dies.

350   Magnentius rebels in West and kills Constans

351   Constantius II defeats Magnentius at Battle of Mursa and becomes sole ruler of the empire

355   Julian made Caesar

357   Battle of Strasbourg: Julian defeats Alemanni

c.360   Hunnic attacks on Alans and Goths begin

361   Civil war between Julian and Constantius II; Constantius dies and Julian becomes sole emperor

363   Julian invades Persia and is killed in battle

363-4   Jovian succeeds Julian and makes humiliating peace with Persia

364   Death of Jovian; Valentinian becomes emperor and takes the West while his brother, Valens, takes the East

367-8   War with Persia and Germans; Britain invaded by Saxons, Picts and Irish

371-2   Peace with Persia and revolt by Firmus in North Africa

375   Death of Valentinian I in a rage with Quadi

376-7	Migration of Goths across the Danube, fleeing the Huns, results in war
378	Battle of Adrianople: catastrophic defeat of the eastern Roman army and death of eastern emperor, Valens
379	Theodosius made emperor of east by Gratian
382	Treaty with Goths after several years of warfare; they are given land south of the Danube in unprecedented Roman capitulation to barbarians
383	Rebellion of Magnus Maximus in Britain, Gaul and Spain
388	Theodosius defeats Maximus at battles of Siscia and Poetovio
392	Valentinian II found hanged; rebellion of Arbogast and Eugenius
394	Theodosius defeats Arbogast and Eugenius at the Battle of the Frigidus River
395	Death of Theodosius; succeeded by his sons Arcadius in the east and Honorius in the west; Stilicho guardian of the west; Huns raid middle east from Caucasus
395-7	Rebellion of Goths led by Alaric; Alaric made *magister militum* for Illyria
401-2	Stilicho defeats Alaric's first invasion of Italy at the battles of Pollentia and Verona
405-6	Treaty between Stilicho and Alaric; Radagaisus invades Italy and is defeated by Stilicho
406-7	Germans cross Rhine and devastate Gaul; Constantine III leads rebellion in the West
408	Stilicho executed; Alaric invades Italy and lays siege to Rome; minor Hunnic leader Uldin invades eastern empire
409	Alaric's second siege of Rome; Germans cross into Spain
410	Third siege and sack of Rome by Alaric
411	Alaric dies

Further Reading

Given that probably over a thousand books have been written about the Roman Empire, I thought a relatively concise selection that I have found essential reading would be more useful for the reader than a general bibliography. I have divided these into relevant sections. The main primary sources are listed at the end.

My Top Five

These are all landmark academic works which are also very readable. Two outstanding examples are Peter Heather's *The Fall of the Roman Empire* (Oxford UP, 2006), and Bryan Ward-Perkins' *The Fall of Rome and the End of Civilisation* (Oxford UP, 2005). They are both updates on Peter Brown's classic, *The World of Late Antiquity* (Thames & Hudson, 1971), which has had an enduring influence on academic scholarship. Arther Ferrill's *The Fall of the Roman Empire: The Military Explanation* (Thames and Hudson, 1988) is a somewhat forgotten classic on Rome's military decline, in my view. More recently, a compelling work which provides new and thought-provoking research, especially about the effects of climate change and pandemics on the Roman Empire, is Kyle Harper's *The Fate of Rome: Climate, Disease, and the End of an Empire* (Princeton UP, 2017).

General Overview of the Later Roman Empire

For many decades, the most famous scholarly work on the late Roman Empire was by A.H.M. Jones, *The Later Roman Empire 284–602*, Volumes I and II (Blackwell, 1964), although archaeological discoveries since it was written have made much of Jones' economic analysis redundant. J.B. Bury's two volumes on the *History of the Later Roman Empire: From the Death of Theodosius I to the Death of Justinian* (Dover Publications, 1958) still make compelling if somewhat outdated reading. Essential reading for the Roman economy is Richard Duncan-Jones, *Money and Government in the Roman Empire* (Cambridge UP, 1994). The difficult subject of the impact of the Huns on Rome and Europe is presented, somewhat controversially, by Hyun Jin Kim, *The Huns* (Routledge, 2016). Walter Scheidel provides an entertaining new view of Rome's legacy in his *Escape from Rome: The Failure of Empire and the Road to Prosperity* (Princeton UP, 2019). Going further back in time, the classic work remains Edward Gibbon's *The History of the Decline and Fall of the Roman Empire* (first published in 1776 and more recently by Penguin, 2005). Hugely influential are two older works published in French with English translations – Ferdinand Lot's *The End of the Ancient World* (first published in 1931 and more recently by Routledge, 1996) and Henri Pirenne's *Mohammed and Charlemagne* (first published in 1939 and more recently by Martino, 2017).

The Crisis of the Third Century

The crisis of the third century was of huge significance not just for Rome but also for world history, and yet remains sadly under-researched because of the lack of surviving source material. Probably the most insightful works are Alaric Watson's *Aurelian and the Third Century* (Routledge, 1999) and John F. White's *The Roman Emperor Aurelian: Restorer of the World* (Pen and Sword, 2015). Edward Luttwak's *The Grand Strategy of the Roman Empire: From the First Century A.D. to the Third* (John Hopkins, 1976) is interesting. More recent and thought-provoking are Ilkka Syvanne's *The Reign of Emperor Gallienus: The Apogee of Roman Cavalry* (Pen and Sword, 2019) and, by the same author, *Aurelian and Probus: The Soldier Emperors Who Saved Rome* (Pen and Sword, 2020).

Diocletian and Constantine

Diocletian and Constantine have received more attention than the crisis of the third century. Strongly recommended on Diocletian are Stephen Williams' *Diocletian and the Roman Recovery* (Routledge, 1985) and Roger Rees' *Diocletian and the Tetrarchy* (Edinburgh UP, 2004). On Constantine: A.H.M. Jones' *Constantine and the Conversion of Europe* (first published in 1948 and more recently by Medieval Academy of America, 1994); Timothy Barnes' *Constantine: Dynasty, Religion and Power in the Later Roman Empire* (Wiley-Blackwell, 2014) and David Potter's *Constantine: The Emperor* (Oxford UP, 2013). Extremely valuable on Christianity is Rodney Stark's *The Rise of Christianity* (Princeton UP, 1996).

Julian the Apostate

Of the many books written about Julian, three stand out: G.W. Bowersock's *Julian the Apostate* (Harvard UP, 1978); Robert Browning's *The Emperor Julian* (Weidenfeld and Nicolson, 1975); and Adrian Murdoch's *The Last Pagan: Julian the Apostate and the Death of the Ancient World* (Inner Traditions, 2008).

From Valentinian to the Sack of Rome in AD 410

The Valentinian and Theodosian dynasties are relatively under-researched. A good overview is provided in David Potter's *The Roman Empire at Bay: AD 180–395* (Routledge, 2004). The reign of Theodosius is well covered by Stephen Williams and Gerard Friell in *Theodosius: The Empire at Bay* (Routledge, 1998). Books on other main fourth-century figures are Neil McLynn's *Ambrose of Milan: Church and Court in a Christian Capital* (University of California Press, 1994); Ian Hughes' *Stilicho: The Vandal Who Saved Rome* (Pen and Sword, 2010); and Douglas Boin's *Alaric the Goth: An Outsider's History of the Fall of Rome* (Norton, 2020).

Roman Army

The most interesting works on the late Roman army are Pat Southern and Karen Dixon's *The Late Roman Army* (Yale UP, 1996) and Hugh Elton's *Warfare in Roman Europe AD 350–425* (Oxford UP, 1996). For an understanding of the development of the Roman army, Lawrence Keppie's *The Making of the Roman Army: From Republic to Empire* (Routledge, 1998) and Adrian Goldsworthy's *The Roman Army at War 100 BC–AD 200* (Oxford UP, 1996) are strongly recommended. For the Praetorian Guard, see Sandra Bingham's *The Praetorian Guard: A History of Rome's Elite Special Forces* (Baylor UP, 2013).

Persia
Sasanian Persia remains somewhat under-researched. Three useful books are Beate Dignas and Engelbert Winter's *Rome and Persia in Late Antiquity* (Cambridge UP, 2007); Eberhard Sauer's *Sasanian Persia* (Edinburgh UP, 2017); and Touraj Daryaee's *Sasanian Persia: The Rise and Fall of an Empire* (I.B. Tauris, 2013).

Climate Change
Paleoclimatology is rapidly becoming a major focus for historians. Kyle Harper's *The Fate of Rome* (Princeton UP, 2017) is the most comprehensive scholarly analysis yet published of how the climate (and pandemics) affected Roman history. I also strongly recommend Brian Fagan's *The Great Warming: Climate Change and the Rise and Fall of Civilisations* (Bloomsbury, 2008) for a fascinating account of the medieval warm period. The view put forward in this book that it was probably a mega drought that prompted the Huns to migrate west is informed by the research paper called 'Megadroughts, ENSO, and the Invasion of Late Roman Europe by the Huns and Avars' presented by Edward R. Cook to the Dumbarton Oaks Workshop for Climate Change Under the Late Roman Empire in April 2009. Another relevant research paper is 'Climate and the Decline and Fall of the Western Roman Empire: A Bibliometric View on an Interdisciplinary Approach to Answer a Most Classic

Historical Question' by Werner Marx, Robin Haunschild and Lutz Bornmann, published on 15 November 2018 in the Multidisciplinary Digital Publishing Institute (MDPI).

Primary Sources

For ease of accessibility, the sources listed below are only those referenced in this book that can currently be purchased in paperback/hardback. Other versions and more material are accessible online and in academic libraries. It should be noted that the history of the republic and early empire is so rich in sources that my list is very concise. In contrast, the third, fourth and fifth centuries have relatively few sources, the most significant of which are listed.

Republic/Early Empire

Cicero, *Selected Works* (Penguin, 1971)

Livy, *The Rise of Rome* (Oxford UP, 1998)

Marcus Aurelius, *Meditations* (Oxford UP, 2011)

Polybius, *The Histories* (Digireads, 2019)

Suetonius, *The Twelve Caesars* (Penguin, 1957)

Tacitus, *Annals and Histories* (Everyman, 2009)

Virgil, *The Aeneid* (Oxford UP, 1986)

Later Empire (emphasis on AD 180–410)

Ambrose (Saint), *On the Mysteries and on Repentance* (Veritatis Splendor Publications, 2014)

Ammianus Marcellinus, *The Later Roman Empire* (Penguin, 1986)

Augustan History (Historia Augusta) – first half published as *Lives of the Later Caesars*, translated by Antony Birley

(Penguin, 1976); full work published by Loeb Classical Library in three volumes as *Scriptores Historiae Augustae*, translated by D. Magie (Loeb, 1932)

Cassius Dio – the first and last sections of his incomplete *Roman History* have been published i) by Penguin (1987) covering Books 50–6 from 32 BC to AD 14, and ii) by Echo Library (2007) covering Books 77–80 from AD 211 to 229

Claudian, *Volumes I and II* (Loeb Classical Library, 1922)

Eusebius, *Life of Constantine* (Oxford UP, 1999)

Eusebius, *Ecclesiastical History* (Baker Book House, 1989)

Jerome, *Chronicle* (Akademie Verlag, 1956)

Jerome, *Letters* (Aeterna Press, 2016)

Jordanes, *The Gothic History* (Sophron Editor, 2018)

Julian, *Volumes I to III* (Loeb Classical Library, 1923)

Lactantius, *On the Deaths of the Persecutors* (Oxford UP, 1984)

Notitia Dignitatum – the original version in Latin compiled by Otto Seeck in 1876 has been reproduced by Forgotten Books (2018); a summarised English translation compiled by William Fairley in 1899 has been reproduced by BiblioLife

'Res Gestae Divi Saporis' ('The Great Inscription of Shapur I') are rock carvings located in modern Iran containing essential information on the Roman/Sasanian wars in the third century (see online for best accessibility)

Vegetius, *The Military Institutions of the Romans (De Re Militari)*, (Ancient World Books, 2018).

Victor (Aurelius), *De Caesaribus* (Liverpool UP, 1994)

Zosimus, *The New History* (Byzantina Australiensia, 1984)

Notes

Introduction

1   Bryan Ward-Perkins, *The Fall of Rome and the End of Civilisation* (Oxford UP, 2005), p. 1.

2   Cullen Murphy, Are we Rome? (Houghton Mifflin, 2007), p. 6.

Part I Between Two Worlds

3   For a detailed discussion of just how democratic the republic was, see my first book in this series – *The Roman Revolution*, Chapter 4.

4   Boris Johnson, *The Dream of Rome* (Harper Perennial, 2007).

5   A more detailed account of the 'Crisis of the Third Century' is contained in the first book in this series called *The Roman Revolution* (Puttenham Press, 2022), p. 91.

6   Kyle Harper, T*he Fate of Rome* (Princeton UP, 2019), p. 179.

7   Spectacular remains of both the baths of Caracalla and Diocletian still stand in modern Rome.

8   Theodor Mommsen, *A History of Rome Under the Emperors* (Routledge 1996), p. 455.

9   A more detailed discussion of Palmyra is contained in the first book in this series called *The Roman Revolution* (Puttenham Press, 2022), p. 122.

10   The plentiful supply of surviving Kushan coins today provides one of the best historical records of this forgotten state.

11   Ammianus Marcellinus, *The Later Roman Empire*, translated by Walter Hamilton (Oxford, 1986), Book 14, p. 41.

Part II The Empire of Julian the Apostate

12 Julian, Epistle 23, *The Works of the Emperor Julian*, Vol. III, (Loeb Classical Library, 1913).

13 Ammianus Marcellinus, *The Later Roman Empire*, translated by Walter Hamilton (Penguin, 1986), Book 16, section 12.21, p. 109.

14 Ibid., p. 111.

15 Ibid., p. 106.

16 Ibid., p. 113.

17 Ibid., p. 238.

18 A.H.M. Jones, *Constantine and the Conversion of Europe to Christianity* (Toronto UP, 1978), p. 49.

19 Hermias Sozomen, *The Ecclesiastical History* (Jazzybee Publishing, 2019), p. 157.

20 Arianism was a doctrine established by Arius, an Egyptian priest, that Christ was subordinate to God the Father. This conflicts with the concept of the Holy Trinity, where Christ is equal to God, as taught by the Catholic Church.

21 Ammianus Marcellinus, *The Later Roman Empire*, translated by Walter Hamilton (Penguin, 1986), p. 263.

22 Ibid., p. 283.

23 Ibid., p. 282.

24 Ibid., p. 283.

25 Ibid., p. 285.

26 Ibid., p. 288.

Part III The Road to Disaster

27 Hyun Jin Kim, *The Huns* (Routledge, 2016), p. 28.

28 Ammianus Marcellinus, *The Later Roman Empire*, translated by Walter Hamilton (Penguin, 1986), p. 411.

29 Ambrose of Milan, *Commentary on the Gospel According to Luke* (Maenchen-Helfen, 1973), p. 20.

30 Ammianus Marcellinus, *The Later Roman Empire*, translated by Walter Hamilton (Penguin, 1986), p. 411.

31 Ambrose of Milan, *Commentary on the Gospel According to Luke*

(Maenchen-Helfen, 1973), p. 20.

32 Ammianus Marcellinus, *The Later Roman Empire*, translated by Walter Hamilton (Penguin, 1986), p. 412.

33 Peter Heather, *The Fall of the Roman Empire* (Oxford UP, 2006), p. 155.

34 Ibid., p. 154.

35 Hyun Jin Kim, *The Huns* (Routledge, 2016), p. 38.

36 According to the United Nations, this was reached on 15 November 2022.

37 Kyle Harper, *The Fate of Rome* (Princeton UP, 2019), p. 15.

38 Edward R. Cook, 'Megadroughts, ENSO, and the Invasion of Late Roman Europe by the Huns and Avars', 2009, Dumbarton Oaks Workshop for Climate Change Under the Late Roman Empire.

39 Brian Fagan, *The Great Warming* (Bloomsbury, 2008).

40 Ammianus Marcellinus, *The Later Roman Empire*, translated by Walter Hamilton (Penguin, 1986), p. 303.

41 Ibid., p. 305.

42 Ibid., p. 320.

43 Ibid., p. 416.

44 Ibid., p. 417.

45 Eutropius, *Breviarium Historiae Romanae* (The Perfect Library, 2014), p. 39.

46 Ammianus Marcellinus, *The Later Roman Empire*, translated by Walter Hamilton (Penguin, 1986), p. 329.

47 Ibid., p. 419.

48 Ibid., p. 426.

49 Ibid., p. 426.

50 Ibid., p. 432.

51 Ibid., p. 433.

52 Ibid., p. 434.

53 Ibid., p. 435.

54 Ibid., p. 435.

55 Ibid., p. 435.

56 Ibid., p. 436.

57 Ibid., p. 436.

58 Ibid., p. 439.

59 Zosimus, *The New History* (Odin's Library Classics, 2018), p. 76.

60 A more detailed discussion of the Council of Nicaea is contained in the first book in this series called *The Roman Revolution* (Puttenham Press, 2022), p. 214.

61 Saint Ambrose, Gutenberg Ebook of the Letters of Saint Ambrose, 2019 (Richard Hulse, 2019), Epistle 57.

Part IV The Fall of the West

62 Constantine ruled alone for the last 13 years of his reign, Julian for less than two years in his reign and Theodosius for barely five months.

63 Claudian, *The Gothic War* (Loeb Classical Library, Claudian Volume II), p. 173.

64 Peter Heather, *The Fall of the Roman Empire* (Oxford UP, 2006), p. 207.

65 Ibid., p. 207.

66 Ibid., p. 221.

67 Ibid., p. 222.

68 Zosimus, *The New History* (Odin's Library Classics, 2018), p. 108.

69 Ibid., p. 109.

70 Flavius Vegetius, *De Re Militari* or *The Military Institutions of the Romans* (Ancient World Books, 2018), p. 50.

71 Ibid., p. 21.

72 More detail is contained in the first book in this series called *The Roman Revolution* (Puttenham Press, 2022), p. 122.

73 Zosimus, *The New History* (Odin's Library Classics, 2018), p. 34.

74 Douglas Boin, *Alaric the Goth* (W. W. Norton & Company, 2020).

75 The Salarian Gate was demolished in 1871 after it was damaged in the battle for Rome of 1870. It was subsequently rebuilt and then demolished a final time in 1921 to make way for the modern Piazza Fiume.

76 Sozomen, *The Ecclesiastical History*, Book IX, Chapter 10. Hermias Sozomen, *The Ecclesiastical History* (Jazzybee Publishing, 2019), p. 273.

77   Edward Gibbon, *The History of the Decline and Fall of the Roman Empire*, Vol. III (first published 1781 and republished by Penguin 1994), p. 202.

78   Peter Brown, *Augustine of Hippo: A Biography* (University of California Press, 2000), p. 288.

79   Peter Heather, *The Fall of the Roman Empire* (Oxford UP, 2006), p. 231.

80   Bertrand Lançon, *Rome in Late Antiquity*, Trans. Antonia Nevill (Routledge, 2001), p. 119.

81   Peter Heather, *The Fall of the Roman Empire* (Oxford UP, 2006), p. 196.

82   Bryan Ward-Perkins, *The Fall of Rome and the End of Civilisation* (Oxford UP, 2005), p. 87.

83   The only two sources for this period are the *Anglo-Saxon Chronicle* and *The Ecclesiastical History of the English People* by the Venerable Bede, neither of which provides any detail whatsoever about the fate of the Romano-British population.

84   Bryan Ward-Perkins, *The Fall of Rome and the End of Civilisation* (Oxford UP, 2005), p. 183.

85   Alexander Demandt, *Der Fall Roms* (C.H. Beck, 2014).

86   Conclusion of European Commission's Global Drought Observatory.

Find Out More About the Fall of the Roman Empire

87   Ian Morris, *Why the West Rules – For Now* (Profile Books, 2010).

88   Walter Scheidel, *Escape from Rome* (Princeton UP, 2019).

Index

absolute power 7
Abundantius, General 178
Achaemenid Empire 11, 76
Actium, Battle of 8, 161
Ad Salices, Battle of 134
Adrianople 132, 135, 137, 142
Adrianople, Battle of xxv–xxvii,
    117, 138–47, 165–6, 176, 183,
    193, 197, 199, 228, 229, 250,
    251
agriculture 107–8
Alans 202, 223, 249
    annual tribute of gold and corn
    219
    and the Goths 134, 136, 139
    and Gratian 150
    and the Huns 97–8, 100, 124
    invade Gaul 202, 204
    invade Raetia and Noricum 189
    invade Spain 205
    as mercenaries in Roman army
    162, 193, 194, 198, 251
    rivalry with Sarus 221
Alaric, King of the Goths xxix,
    175–80, 185, 187, 197, 222
    besieges Rome 216–19, 220–1

    death of 234
    first invasion of Italy 189,
    190–5, 196, 200, 211
    Gothic mercenaries join after
    massacre 216
    and Honorius 216, 217,
    218–21, 230, 233
    needs to keep Goths happy
    230–1, 233–4
    sack of Rome 195, 221, 230–4
    and Stilicho 188, 193–5, 201,
    209, 211–12, 216
Alemanni 13–15, 65, 68, 118,
    120, 135
    Battle of Strasbourg 56–64, 139,
    227
    Constantine III allies with 206
    cross Rhine 53
    invade Gaul 202
    as mercenaries in Roman army
    162
Alesia, Battle of 47
Alexander the Great 4, 6, 11, 76,
    79, 99, 147
Alexandria 41, 42
Altar of Victory (Rome) 161

Ambrose, Bishop of Milan 100,
  149, 154, 155, 156–7, 160, 161
Amida, Siege of 67, 80
Amiens 204
Ammianus Marcellinus
  on Alans 124
  on Battle of Adrianople xxvii,
    139, 140–1, 142
  on Constantine 33–4
  end of writings 150
  on Gallus 41–2
  on Goths 124, 125, 129–31,
    132, 134, 142
  on Huns 100–2, 124
  on Jovian 114, 115, 116
  on Julian 52, 53, 57, 58–9, 60,
    61, 62, 63, 67, 74, 77, 81–2, 84,
    86, 87, 88–9, 90, 91, 92, 93, 94
  on Valens and Valentinian 118,
    122, 136
Amorica (Brittany) 244
Anatha 83
Anatolia 25, 143, 147, 185, 240
Anglo-Saxons 244
Anthemius, Flavius 210, 235, 237,
  238
Anthropogene period 107
Antigonids 4, 6
Antioch 11, 12, 20, 41, 77, 78,
  115, 116, 181
Antony, Mark 8
aqueducts, cutting of 217
Aquileia 69, 155, 190
Arab invasions 245
Arab tribes 31–2
Arazdat 127
Arbogast (Flavius Arbogastes)

158–64, 175, 228
Arcadius, Emperor 164, 170–1,
  188, 200, 207, 251
  death of 210, 237
  declares Stilchio public enemy 179
  and Eutropius 185, 186
  and Gainas 186–7, 238
  and Galla Placidia 175
  halts Stilicho's advance on Alaric
    177
  Stilicho as guardian of 173–4,
    187, 200
archaeological remains 241–2
Ardashir of Persia 12
Arianism 74, 149, 152–4, 156,
  165, 192, 231
Ariminum (Rimini) 217
Arius 153
Arles 203, 204
Armenia 30, 34, 35, 80, 115, 126,
  127, 133, 155, 181
Arminius 13
army, Roman
  barbarian mercenaries 162, 165,
    166, 175, 187, 193, 210, 211,
    213, 215, 221, 228, 229, 250–1
  cavalry 57, 58–9, 61, 62, 63, 91,
    223, 224
  and choice of emperors 15–16,
    35, 36–9, 51, 113, 116–17, 205,
    224
  decline in quality 223–9, 250
  Diocletian's reforms 17–18, 224–5
  discipline 60, 62, 63
  Eutropius and 185
  factions in 113
  failure to defend western frontier

and Rome 222
hierarchy 60
Illyrian legions 34, 38, 39
infantry 223–4
lose grip on west 203
mutinies 67, 77
pay 66, 85
plunder 85, 86
reduction in professional soldiers 227–8
slaves invited to volunteer 190
strength of 6
two-tier system 226
under Constantine 225–7, 229
under Julian 55, 59, 227–8
under Theodosius 144, 162, 165–6, 228–9
see also eastern army; western army
Arras 204
Arshak II of Armenia 91, 115, 126
art 21–2
Asding Vandals 202, 205
asylum, requests for 125, 127, 128, 133
Ataulf 219, 233, 234
Athanaric 128
Athanasius, Bishop of Alexandria 74
Athens 4, 50, 51, 52, 79
Attalus 220
Attila the Hun 100, 231, 238
Augustine, Bishop of Hippo (St Augustine) xxix, 235–6
Augustus, Emperor 8–9, 71, 161, 171, 192, 224, 236
army under 226–7
senate under 72

Aurelian, Emperor 15–16, 34, 37, 124, 250
Aurelian (Praetorian Prefect) 186, 187
Aurelian Walls (Rome) 191, 231
autocracy 7, 9

bagaudae 244
Bagavan, Battle of 126
banking 20
baptism 24
Bar Sabbae, Shemon 33
Barbatio 56
Barnabus 78
Baths of Diocletian (Rome) 21
baths, too many xxvii
Belisarius 141
Berber tribesmen 120
bows, composite recurve 102–3, 249
Bracchiati 58, 62
Britain
after fall of Rome 244–5
collapse of Roman rule 118, 119, 122, 222, 244
grain supply from 65
pre-Roman 245
rebellion of 406 205
rebellion of Magnus Maximus 151–2
revolt of Magnentius 37
British legions 151, 205–6, 208
Brutus, Marcus Junius 8
Burgundians 58, 202, 206
Bury, J.B. 111
Butheric 155–6
Byzantium 2, 19

Caesar, Julius 8, 9, 47, 48, 55, 59, 62, 63, 142, 190

Caesarea 126

Caligula, Emperor 10

Cannae, Battle of xxvii, 5, 141

Cappadocia 49, 67, 240

Caracalla, Emperor 10

Carthage 4–6, 27, 82, 84, 109

Carus, Emperor 16

Cassius Longinus, Gaius 8

Castra Martis 238

Catholic Church *see* Christianity/ Christian Church

cavalry, Roman 57, 58–9, 61, 62, 63, 91, 223, 224

Chamavi 65

Charietto, General 119

chariot racing 22

China 99–100, 103–4, 111

Chnodomar 57, 59–60, 63

Christianity/Christian Church
  in Antioch 78
  Arian debate 149, 152–4
  authority over Roman state 156–7
  Constantine adopts 18, 19, 73, 157
  and decline of Roman Empire 248
  divisions in early Church 74
  Gothic conversions 128
  Jovian and 116
  Julian's hostility to xxviii, 43, 47, 49, 70, 72–5, 78, 94
  militancy 74, 75
  pagan threat to 162–3
  persecution in Persia 33
  persecution under Diocletian 33, 73
  rise of xxvii, xxviii, 19, 20
  and sack of Rome 231–2, 233, 235–6
  Theodosius and 165

Chrysostom, John 20

Cimbri 58

Circesium 81, 83

citizenship 4
  Goths denied 146, 175, 230
  universal Roman 10, 21

city administration 71

City of God, The (Augustine of Hippo) 235–6

city states, Greek 4

civil service 71

civil wars
  32-30 BC 8
  340 AD 27, 28, 34
  under Constantius 40–1
  under Theodosius 149–52, 155, 157, 159, 161–4, 165, 166, 202

civilisation, Roman 241–6

Claudian (poet) 193, 194

Claudius, Emperor 50

Claudius Gothicus, Emperor 15

Cleopatra 8

climate change
  current xxx, 107, 112, 252
  and fall of Rome 251–2
  historical 105–7, 112, 252
  and mass migration 104, 110, 111–12, 182
  and Roman history 107–12

co-emperors 17

coinage 20, 241, 242–3, 245

Colias 132
Cologne 51, 53, 55, 65
comitatenses 131, 226, 227
commonwealth, Roman 3, 4
concrete 21
Constans I, Emperor 24, 27–8,
    34, 35
  killing of 36–7
Constans II (son of Constantine
    III) 209
Constantina (daughter of
    Constantine I) 38–9, 41–3
Constantine I the Great, Emperor
    xxviii, 16, 18–20, 42, 71, 79,
    172, 236
  adopts Christianity 18, 19,
    23–4, 32–3, 73, 74, 157, 225
  and Arianism 153
  death of 23, 25, 26, 34
  foundation/relocation of capital
    to Constantinople 1–2, 18, 19
  and Persia 33–5
  succession 24–8, 172
  weakens empire's defences
    225–7, 229, 250
Constantine II, Emperor 24, 26–7,
    34
Constantine III (usurper) 205–6,
    208, 209, 210, 212, 216, 219,
    220, 222, 233, 244
Constantinople
  Alaric threatens 176
  building projects 21
  foundation of 1–2
  Goths and 134, 135, 143
  growth and strength of 192
  Procopius in 117–18

relocation of capital to 18
  rises against Gainas' Gothic
    troops 187
  rivalry with Milan 171
  Roman refugees in 236
  strengthened fortifications in
    238, 239–40, 249
Constantius II, Emperor 24, 25–8,
    118
  and Christianity 74, 154, 161
  civil wars under 40–1
  death 69
  extravagant court of 70–1
  and Julian 48, 49, 50–2, 55,
    65–9, 113
  Julian's revolt against 67–9,
    76–7, 83
  rebellion in the west 35, 36–40,
    151, 203
  and Rhine frontier 54
  war with Persia 28, 34–5, 76, 77
Constantius, Julius 48
consuls 7, 185
Cornuti 58, 62
corruption 6–7, 41–2, 51, 248
courier system, imperial 72
credit 20
crisis of the third century xxviii,
    11–16, 20, 70, 71, 171, 205,
    224
crop failures 109
Crusades, Fourth 239
Ctesiphon 79, 80, 87, 88, 89, 92,
    93, 181
Cyprian, Bishop of Carthage 109
Cyrus the Great of Persia 11

Dacia 124
Dagalaifus 86
Dalmatius (brother of
  Constantine) 24
Dalmatius, Flavius Julius, Caesar
  25, 26, 41
Danube river/frontier 13, 40,
  120–1, 122, 171, 192
  Goths arrive on 125–6, 127
  Goths cross 197
  Huns north of 239
Decius, Emperor 11, 224
democracy 7
Diocletian, Emperor 16, 17–19,
  23, 34, 37, 41, 71, 114, 131, 159
  army under 17–18, 224, 225, 250
  Great Persecution 33, 73
  tetrarchy 17, 18, 171–2
divine vengeance 26, 235
Dnieper river 124
Don river 124, 197
drought 97, 109, 110, 112, 182,
  252

Easter 153, 192
eastern army xxvii, 76, 118, 134,
  139–40, 141, 144, 166, 176,
  183, 250
  Gainas as commander-in-chief
    of 186–7
  German purge in 215
  resists barbarisation 187
eastern empire
  anti-German course 187
  breakdown of 109
  Christianity in 248
  Eutropius and 185

Huns invade (395) 181–3
  peace with Persia 237
  prosperity until Arab invasions
    245
  sends help to Honorius 220
  survival of 236, 237–40, 245
  threat from Huns 238
economy
  4th century recovery 20, 248
  decline of Roman 248
  global 245
  reliant on specialisation 245
Edessa 126
Edessa, Battle of 12, 29
edict of universal religious
  toleration 73–4
Egypt 5, 9, 107, 109, 236, 240
El Niño 110
elephants 88, 91, 92, 108
Eleusian Mysteries 50
environmental disasters xxix–xxx,
  97
Ermanaric 124
Etruscans 3
Eucherius (son of Stilicho) 212, 214
Eudocia (wife of Arcadius) 174,
  177, 185–6, 188, 200–1
Eugenius, Emperor 160, 161, 162,
  163, 164
eunuchs 185
Euphrates river 79, 80, 81, 83–4,
  85, 87, 92
Eusebia (wife of Constantius II)
  51–2
Eusebius, Bishop of Nicomedia
  48, 153
Eutropius (historian) 127

Eutropius (Praetorian Prefect) 174,
  177–8, 179–80, 181–2, 183,
  185–6, 187, 188

famine 109, 112, 217, 220
Fiesole 198–9
Firmus, Prince 120
Flavianus (Praetorian Prefect) 161,
  162–3
fleet, Roman 5
Florentia, siege of 198
Florentius 67
foederati 193, 228, 229
food shortages 217, 218
fort building
  Diocletian's programme of 131
  Valentinian's programme of 121
Franks 14, 58, 65, 68
  Constantine III allies with 106
  cross the Rhine 53, 203
  invade Gaul 13
  as mercenaries in Roman army
  162
Fravitta, General 187, 188
Frigidus River, Battle of the
  163–4, 166, 173, 175, 176, 178,
  193, 229
Fritigern 128, 130, 132, 135, 138,
  139, 142, 146, 165, 202

Gabinus, King of the Quadi 121
Gainas, General 185, 186, 238
Galatia 147
Galla 154–5, 160
Galla Placidia 174–5, 217, 233
Gallic Empire 206
Gallic legions 67, 77, 139, 162,

  178, 206, 208, 222
Gallienus, Emperor 14
Gallus, Constantius, Caesar 26,
  41, 41–3, 48, 51
Gaul/Gauls
  Alemanni invade/raid 14, 118–19
  Battle of Strasbourg 56–64
  Caesar's conquest 47, 48, 55, 62
  Constantine III crosses into 206
  de-Romanised on eastern
  frontier 203
  Franks invade 13
  Germanic invasion 200, 201,
  204, 207, 222, 239
  grain supplies from 184
  invasion of Greece 147
  Julian in 51–3, 54–64
  rebellion of Magnus Maximus
  151–2
  revolt in 36–40
  sack of Rome (390 BC) 235
Genghis Khan 112
Georgia 30, 133
Germania 11, 13–15
Germanic tribes
  consolidation of 14–15
  cross Danube and Rhine 11
  and fall of western empire xxvii,
  249
  increased threat from 14
  invasion of Gaul 200, 201–2,
  204, 222, 239
  militarisation of 14, 58
  pushed west by Huns 100, 238,
  249, 251–2
Gibbon, Edward xxvii, xxix, 94,
  150, 156, 201, 232, 248

Gibraltar 205
Gildo (governor of North Africa) 162, 183, 184
gladiators xxix, 22, 108
global warming, human-made 107
gold standard 20
Goths 100, 124–37, 157
    allowed to settle in north-eastern Italy and Illyria 219
    Arianism 192, 231
    arrive on Danube 125–6, 127
    Battle of Adrianople xxv–xxvii, 138–47, 228
    battles with Huns 124–5, 199
    cavalry 139
    as crack Roman troops 228, 229
    desertions to Stilicho 194–5
    designs on North Africa 234
    Eutropius makes alliance with 180
    first invasion of Italy 189, 190–5
    forced west by Huns 125, 181, 196–7, 239, 249
    formation of a Gothic supergroup in Italy 216
    and homosexuality 156
    inexperienced in siege craft 142, 190, 191
    kill Decius 11
    massacred in Italian cities 215–16
    as masters of Italy 222
    as mercenaries in Roman army 162, 163, 166, 175, 193, 210, 211, 229, 251
    paganism 197
    pillaging and plunder 132, 143, 231, 232–3
    prisoners sold as slaves 199, 218
    resent Romans for lack of concessions 175–6
    revolt of 395 175–6
    sack of Rome (410) xxvii, 94, 166, 169–70, 175, 230–6
    second invasion of Italy 196–9
    in southern Italy 234
    Stilicho's campaign against 179
    Theodosius and 144–6, 147
    treaty of 382 145, 145–6, 146, 149, 162, 175, 228
    Valens and 126, 127–8, 131, 132–7
graffiti 241, 243
Gratian, Emperor xxv, 131, 133, 134, 135, 136, 141, 143, 144, 161
    demise of 150, 151
    dissatisfaction with 149, 150–1
Gratian (usurper) 205
grazing land, summer and winter 111
Great Conspiracy 119
Great Wall of China 99
Greece/Greeks
    Alaric plunders 178–9, 193
    city states 5, 229
    hostilities with Persia 76, 79
    olive cultivation 108
    Roman victory over 5, 6
Gregory of Nazianzus 50
Greuthungi 125, 128, 129, 135–6, 139, 142

Hadrian, Emperor 10, 192
Hadrian's Wall 119

Han dynasty/empire 99, 103, 111

Hannibal 5, 141, 193, 216

Hannibalianus, Caesar 25, 26, 41

harvest failures 109

Helena (mother of Constantine I) 23

Helena (wife of Julian) 52

Helenopolis 23

Hellenisation 12

Heraclianus 213

Herculians 37, 58

Hibernia 119

Hierapolis 81

Holocene period 105, 106

Homer 49

homosexuality 156

Honorius, Emperor xxix, 161, 164, 170–1, 191, 207, 212, 251
  and Alaric 216, 217, 218–21, 230, 233
  alienates senate 220
  Constantine III challenges rule of 208
  and sack of Rome 233, 235
  and Stilicho 173, 184, 200, 210–11, 212, 213, 214

Hormizd (brother of Shapur II) 32, 79, 84, 85, 93

Hormizd II of Persia 30

human migration
  climate change and 109–12
  out of Africa 106

Huns 22, 94, 97–104, 113, 177, 192
  battles with Goths 124–5
  bows 102–3
  cause huge Germanic invasion of

Gaul 200, 202
  climate change and 109–12, 182
  conquests of 99
  fighting methods 101–2
  focus on western empire 183
  grazing land 111
  invade eastern empire 181–3
  invasion of Thrace 238
  as mercenaries in Roman army 162, 198, 229, 251
  push Germanic tribes west 125, 181, 196–7, 238, 249, 251–2
  reinforce Goths in Thrace 134, 136
  subjugate Alans 124
  threat to eastern empire 238–9

Iberia 133

ice ages 105, 108

Illyria 38, 120, 131, 143, 155, 163, 176, 178, 190, 193, 194, 195, 200, 202, 219, 221, 224

Illyrian legions 34, 38, 39

Imperial Guard 173

Innocent I, Pope 218

Intertropical Convergence Zone 106

Ireland 119

Isis 47

Italy
  Alaric invades 160–5, 189, 196, 200, 211
  formation of a Gothic supergroup in 216
  Radagaisus invades 196–9

Jerome, Saint 204, 231, 235

Jin dynasty 99

Jones, A.H.M. 248
Jordanes (historian) 234
Jovian, Emperor 113–16, 126
Jovians 37, 58
Jovinus, General 119
Jovius (Praetorian Prefect) 219
Julian the Apostate, Emperor xxv,
    26, 40, 142, 202, 203
    army under 227–8, 250
    Battle of Strasbourg 56–64, 139,
    227
    becomes emperor 69
    Constantius undermines 66
    cuts court expenditure 71
    death xxviii, 70, 92, 93–4, 113,
    116, 249–50, 251
    decentralisation policy 71–2
    and eastern army 76, 118
    education and philosophy 48–50
    fascination with siege warfare 84
    in Gaul 54–64, 65
    hostility to Christianity xxviii, 43,
    47, 49, 70, 72–5, 78, 94, 248
    jealousy of 55, 56
    as last pagan emperor 64, 70–5,
    94
    leaves no successor 93–4, 113
    made Caesar and sent to Gaul
    51–3
    and pagan religions 73, 77–8,
    90, 94, 116, 161
    Persian expedition xxviii, 76–94,
    113, 114, 203, 222, 227, 250
    as philosopher emperor 70–5
    reforms of 71–2, 250
    and religious toleration 73–4
    restructures imperial

    administration 71
    revolt against Constantius 67–9,
    83
    risk-taking 83
    and senate 72
    significance of early death for
    Rome 249–50
Jupiter 47
Justina, Empress 37, 152, 154,
    155, 159
Justinian I, Emperor 109, 141
Justinianus, General 209

Khmer Empire 112, 252
Kidarites 237–8
Kushano-Sasanian Kingdom 29, 31
Kushans 126, 127

La Niña 110
Lake Trasimene, Battle of 5
Lampadius (centurion) xxv–xxvii
Lancearii 140
Late Antique Little Ace Age 108–9
Late Holocene 106
Latin League 3–4
lead poisoning xxvii
legions, reduction in size 226
Lentienses 135
Leo, General 185
Lepidus 8
Licinius, Emperor 35
limitanei 131, 226, 227
literacy levels 243, 246
living conditions 241, 243–4,
    245–6
Livy 3, 235
Londinium 119

Lucillianus 116
Lugdunum (Lyons) 56, 209
Luoyang 99
Lupicinus (governor of Thrace) 129–31, 132
Lyad tribe 31

Macedonia 4, 6, 145, 147
Magnentius (usurper) 35, 36–8, 39–40, 51, 53, 65, 68, 151, 203
Magnus Maximus (rebel emperor) 151–2, 154, 155, 178, 228
Mainz 204
Maiozamalcha, Siege of 85–6
manpower, Roman 5
Marcella (nun) 231–2
Marcellianus (governor of Pannonia) 121
Marcellinus 36
Marcellus, General 54, 55
Marcianople 129, 132, 134
Marcomanni 13, 125
Marcus Aurelius, Emperor 10, 13, 70, 72, 127
Marcus (usurper) 205
Mardonius 49
Maris, Bishop of Chalcedon 73
Marius, Gaius 7
Martiarii 140
Mascezel 183, 184
massacre of the princes 25–6, 41, 48
Massagetae 35
Mauretania 120
Maxentius, Emperor 21
Maximian, Emperor 83, 159
Maximinus 144
Maximus, Emperor *see* Magnus Maximus

Maximus, General 129, 228
Mayan civilisation 112, 252
Medieval Warm Period 112
Mediolanum, Battle of 14
megadrought 110, 182
Middle Holocene 106
migration, mass xxx, 97, 104, 128, 196–7, 202, 249, 251
Milan 14, 42, 51, 54, 152, 154, 155, 171, 190
  Goths besiege 191
Milankovitch, Milutin 105
military service 4
Milvian Bridge, Battle of 58, 225
Mithras 47
Modu 99
Moesia 120, 144, 145, 175
Mongol Empire 112
Mongolia 99
Mons Seleucus, Battle of 40
Montesquieu 248
moral decay 248
mosaics 21–2
Mursa Magna, Battle of 39–40, 51

Naqsh-e Rostam 29
navy, Roman 5, 79, 81, 87, 88, 89, 90
Nepotianus, Julius 38
Nero, Emperor 10
Nicaea, Council of 153
Nicene Christians 231
Nicene Creed 153, 155, 165
Nicomedia 23, 50
Nile floods 109
Nisibis 114, 115, 116

Nisibis, Peace of 29–30, 114
Nisibis, Second Peace of 115, 126
Nola Capua 234
nomads 111
  from Asian steppes 35, 37, 80,
  102–3, 111, 124, 251
Noricum 189, 209
North Africa
  Alaric promises to Goths 234
  collapse of Roman rule 118,
  120, 122
  fertility of 107–8, 109
  grain shipments 162, 183, 184,
  217, 220
  Roman refugees in 236
  Vandals cross into 205
Notitia Dignitatum 223

ocean cycles, Pacific 110
Octavian *see* Augustus
Odoacer 247
oligarchy 7
Olt river 124
Olympiadorus (historian) 219
Olympius (*magister scrinii*) 210,
  212, 213, 214, 215, 216, 217,
  219
Orientus (poet) 204
Orleans 204
Ostia 217
Ottoman Turks 239

pagan religions xxviii, 2, 50, 116
  Altar of Victory 161
  Arbogast attempts to restore
  162–3
  blame Christianity for decline of

Rome 248
  Christians blame for sack of
  Rome 235
  gods 47, 49
  Julian and 73, 77–8, 94
  Theodosius and 165
Palatine Hill (Rome) 3, 9
paleoclimatology 109, 110, 112,
  251
Palmyra 29
Pannonia 13, 120, 121
Pap (Papas) 126–7
Paris 204
Pars 31
Parthians 12, 79
Paul, the Apostle 78
Pax Romana 9, 21, 71, 127
peasantry 244
pentarchy 24
Persia
  eastern empire negotiates peace
  with 237–8
  First Roman-Persian War 28,
  34–5
  Huns and 181, 182
  Jovian's humiliating peace with
  114–16, 126
  Julian's war with 76–94, 113,
  222, 227, 250
  Roman retreat from 114–15
  takes Antioch 11, 12
  Theodosius' war with 151, 155,
  157
  and third century crisis 11–12
  Valens and 126–7, 131
  wars with xxvi, xxviii, 11–12, 23,
  29, 66, 76–82

Picts 119
plague 109, 217
Plato 70
Pliny the Elder 108
Poetovio, Battle of 155
political leadership, quality of 251
Pollentia, Battle of 192–3, 194, 196, 209
Polybius 224
Pompeii xxix, 243
Pompey 7–8
Porisabora, Siege of 84–5
Postumus, General 206
pottery 241, 242, 245
poverty 248
Praetorian Guard 225
Primani 58, 62
Priscus (writer) 182
Priscus Attalus (puppet emperor) 220, 221, 230
Probus, Emperor 16
Procopius (rebel emperor) 80, 81, 86, 91, 93
  bid for power 117–18, 126, 128
Procopius (writer) 233
Profuturus, General 133
Ptolemaic Empire 5, 6
Punic Wars 5–6
Pyrrhus of Epirus 161, 193
Quadi 13, 120–2, 125, 131

Radagaisus (Gothic king) 196–9, 200, 202, 215–16, 218, 239
Raetia 189, 190
rainfall 108, 110
Ravenna 191–2, 206, 213, 214, 216, 217, 219, 220, 221, 233

refugees
  from climate change 110, 111
  from Rome 236
Rhine river/frontier 13, 54, 120–1, 122, 157, 171, 203
  Alemanni assault 135
  Franks and Alemanni cross 53
  German hordes cross 201–2
  Julian's operations on 54–64
  legions on 198, 206
  rebellion on 36–43, 53
  Romans start to lose grip on 204, 206
  Valentinian fights Alemanni on 118
Rhône Valley 13–14
Richomer, General 133, 136, 139
road maintenance 71
Roman Empire
  4th century recovery 17–22
  breakdown of eastern 109
  civilisation following sack of Rome 241–6
  and climate change 107–12
  crisis of the third century 11–16
  division following Theodosius 171
  east/west disputes 171–80, 183, 200, 207
  origins of 8–10
  reasons for decline 247–52
  under Constantine 18–20
  under Diocletian 17–19
  vulnerability from Gothic supergroup 216
  see also eastern empire; western empire

Roman Gothic Wars
  376-382 131
  First 126, 128
Roman Persian War, First 34–5
Roman Warm Period 108, 109
Romanness, concept of 10
Romanus (governor) 120
Rome
  besieged by Alaric 216–18,
    220–1
  building projects 21
  city walls 15
  foundation of 3
  no-one comes to rescue from
    Goths 233
  population 19, 236
  rise from city state to superpower
    2–10
  sack of (410) xxvii, 22, 94, 166,
    169–70, 175, 221, 230–6, 247
  Vandals sack (455) 231
Romulus Augustulus, Emperor 247
Romulus and Remus 3
roof tiles 241, 242
Rufinus (Praetorian Prefect) 174,
    176–7, 187

Salutius Secundus 55, 66, 113,
    116–17
Salvina (daughter of Mascezel) 183
Salvinus (quaestor) 212
Samarra, Battle of 91–2
Samnites 3
Sarmatians 40, 120, 121
Sarus, General 188, 194, 209, 213,
    221, 230
Sasanian dynasty 12, 23, 28,

    29–31, 35, 84, 88, 89, 131, 133,
    155
Saul (Alan commander) 193
Saxons 14, 118, 119
Scipio Africanus 84
scorched earth policy 90
Scotland 119
Sebastian, General 135, 136
Second Triumvirate 8
Seleucid Empire 4–5, 6, 11–12
senate
  under Honorius 220, 221
  under Julian 72
  under Stilicho 183–4, 209–10
Septimius Severus, Emperor 171,
    228
Serapion, King 60
Serdica 39
Serena (wife of Stilicho) xxix,
    172–3, 175, 177, 214, 217
Severianus, General 119
Severus, General 56, 59–60, 61,
    62, 65
Shapur I of Persia 12, 29, 30
Shapur II of Persia 28, 30, 31–5,
    37, 66, 77, 79, 80, 83–4, 86, 87,
    88, 89, 91, 114, 115, 116, 126,
    127, 133
Shapur III of Persia 151, 155
Sicily 234
siege warfare 84–5, 142–3, 190,
    191
Sigeric, General 194
Siling Vandals 202, 205
silk roads 29
Silvanus, General 39, 51
Singara 114

Singara, Battle of 35
Siscia, Battle of 155
slaves
  and Alaric's grave 234
  Goths enslaved 129, 132, 199,
  217, 218
  living conditions 243–4
  military service 190
  vengeful 169, 170, 231, 232
socii 4
Socrates 47, 92
Sol 47
soldier emperors 15–16, 35, 36–9,
  51, 113, 116–17, 205, 224
Solicinium, Battle of 119
Sozomen, Hermias 232, 238–9
Spain
  Germanic invasion of 204–5,
  206, 222
  and revolt of Magnentius 37
Spartacus 193
St Paul, Basilica of (Rome) 231
St Peter, Basilica of (Rome) 231,
  232
steppes. Asian xxix–xxx
  droughts/climate change 110,
  238
  nomads from 35, 37, 80, 102–3,
  111, 124, 251
Stilicho xxix, 162, 172–80, 183–4,
  186, 187, 188, 217, 229, 247,
  250–1
  and Alaric 188–9, 193–5, 201,
  202, 209, 211–12, 216
  ambitions of 200, 201
  and Arcadius 173–4, 177, 187,
  200

conspiracy against 211–14
and Constantine III 206–7, 208
death of 214
and Germanic invasions of Gaul
  206
and Gothic invasions of Italy
  190–5, 196–9, 200
and Honorius 210–11, 212,
  213, 214
stirrups 103
Strasbourg, Battle of 54, 56–64,
  65, 66, 118, 139, 166, 227
Sueridas 132
Suetonius 9, 50
Suevi 202, 204, 205
Sulla 7
Surena 84, 85, 88, 89
Symmachus (senator) 178, 183
Syria 131, 181, 240

Tacitus 58
taxation 10, 18, 21, 71, 211, 248
technological change 105
Tertiaci 91
testudo xxvi, 60–1, 140
tetrarchy 17, 18, 171–2
Teutoburg Forest, Battle of 13
Teutones 58
thatched roofs 242
Themistius (senator) 146–7
Theodoret, Bishop of Cyrus 156
Theodosian Code 238
Theodosian Walls
  (Constantinople) 135, 143, 238,
  239–40, 249
Theodosius, Count Flavius
  119–20, 143, 144

Theodosius I the Great, Emperor
119, 143–4, 158–66, 192, 251
and the army 144, 162, 165–6,
228–9
and Bishop Ambrose of Milan
156–7
and Catholic Church 165
civil wars 149–52, 155, 157,
159, 161–4, 165, 166, 193, 202
death 164, 170, 171, 172
division of Empire after 171
and Goths 144–6, 147
legacy of 164–6
and Magnus Maximus 151–2,
155, 158, 178, 228
marriage to Galla 155
Persian war 151, 155
as sole emperor 164
and Stilicho 173, 200
succession 170–1, 173–4
Theodosius II, Emperor 210, 212,
220, 235, 237
Thervingi 125, 127–8, 132, 135,
165, 176
Thessalonika 154, 155–6
Thessalonika, Edict of 165
Thrace 128–9, 131, 133, 134, 135,
143, 144, 187, 238
Tiber
blockaded by Alaric 217
floods 108
Tiberius, Emperor 127
Ticinum (Pavia) 197, 212, 213,
215, 216, 217, 233
Tigris river/frontier 30, 79, 80, 87,
88, 89, 91, 92, 114, 115, 171
Timasius, General 178

Tolkien, J.R.R. 101
Toulouse 204
Tournai 204
Tours 204
Traianus, General 127, 133, 141
Trajan, Emperor 10, 79, 81, 87,
108, 228
tribal federations 14
Tribigild 186
Trier 203–4

Uldin (Hunnic king) 187, 198,
238–9
Ulfilas, General 194
United States, similarities with
Rome xxix

Vadomarius (Alemannic king) 68
Valens, Emperor xxv–xxvi, 117,
118, 122, 125–8, 154
Battle of Adrianople 138, 140,
141–2, 199, 229, 250, 251
death 141, 144
and the Goths 126, 127–8, 131,
132–7
and Persia 126–7, 131, 133
Valentinian I, Emperor 117,
118–22, 133, 151, 203, 251
Valentinian II, Emperor 142, 152,
154, 158, 159, 192
Valerian, Emperor 11, 12, 29, 224
Valerianus, General 141
Vandals
cross into North Africa 205
invade Gaul 202, 204
invade Raetia and Noricum 189
sack Rome (455) 231

Varus 13

Vegetius Renatus, Flavius 223–4, 229

Verona, Battle of 194, 196

Vesuvius, Mount xxix, 243

Vetranio (rebel emperor) 38–9

vexillations 58

Victor, Count 88, 89, 133, 136

Victor (son of Magnus Maximus) 158

Vidal, Gore 94

Virgil 3

Visigoths
  Christianity 197
  in Italy 240
  as mercenaries in Roman army 163, 175
  poor sailors 234
  revolt of 395 175
  see also Goths

volcanic eruptions 108–9

Volga river 124, 197

Völkerwanderung 148, 249

Voltaire xxix, 94, 248

western army 166, 176, 178, 192
  decline in quality 223, 250
  depleted resources 209, 216
  failure of 222
  losing its grip 202–3
  loss of manpower 222–3
  mutiny (408) 212–13
  turns against German mercenaries 215

western empire
  capital moves to Ravenna 191–2
  economic collapse 245

fall of xxvii, xxviii, 22, 207, 247–52

impact of fall on civilisation 241–6

loss of Stilicho 214

point of no return 236

population 246

Stilicho as commander-in-chief 173

swallowed up by barbarians 148, 240, 249

Xenophon 79

Xiongnu Empire 99, 103–4

Yazdegerd of Persia 237

Zonaras 40

Zoroastrianism 12, 33

Zosimus
  on Arbogast 159
  on Battle of Mursa Magna 40
  on Christianity 235, 248
  on Constantine 225
  on Eugenius 160
  on Goths 196, 197, 217, 218
  on Gratian 150
  on the Huns 102
  on Julian 57, 61
  on Maximus 151, 154–5
  on Rufinus 174, 176
  on sack of Rome 235
  on Stilicho 184, 198, 212
  on Theodosius 154–5

NICK HOLMES is a British author, podcaster and historian. His passion is Roman history. He is currently writing a multi-volume series on the Fall of the Roman Empire. His podcast *The Fall of the Roman Empire* accompanies his books. In 2021, he gave up a career in investment banking to write full time.

Check out his website at nickholmesauthor.com for more on his books, podcasts, newsletter and special offers.

Made in the USA
Monee, IL
04 January 2024